i

GARDENING
INDOORS

INTERPORT USA INC.
Portland, OR 97202

Published and distributed by Interport U.S.A. Inc.
P.O. Box 02009
Portland Oregon 97202
Art work: D. Turner
Art work: Connie Cohen
Book Design: Susan Applegate/Publishers Book Works
Cover Design: Susan Applegate/Publishers Book Works
Cover Photo: Buko
The cover photo was taken in a Seattle basement in the dead of winter. Photo courtesy of Wonderwool, Seattle Washington.

Typesetting: Nickel Ads
                 M. Monnie
                 G. Cervantes
Photos: George Cervantes
Other photos are given individual credit.

Paste-up: Michael Tran

Published in the United States by Interport U.S.A. Inc., Portland Oregon 97202
Editors: John Bushwell
         Jim Estes
         Roger Thayer

This book is dedicated to my precious wife.

CONTENTS

Back Cover Photographs, left to right.

The cover photo was taken in a Seattle basement in the dead of winter. Photo courtesy of Wonderwool, Seattle, Washington, Seattle Washington.

Peter's Honey Fig on the back cover was courtesy of Northwoods Nursery, Mollala Oregon.

Photos were taken at many garden stores and of numerous products. Below, credit is given to each store by page number. I give my sincere thanks to all of the garden centers listed below. They are an excellent source to answer all of your gardening questions.

Introduction

This book provides a simple, complete, *how to* description of basic gardening techniques used to grow foliage and pot plants, flowers and vegetables indoors today. Horticulture is the art and science of growing plants. High Intensity Discharge (HID) lamps have made indoor gardening grow by leaps and bounds. Today it is possible to grow large quantities of fresh tomatoes, cucumbers, succulents and all kinds of flowers in your own home all year round.

Many factors should be considered when gardening indoors. To have the best garden possible, you will need to monitor and control all environmental factors and understand the needs of your plants. Which environmental factors have indoor horticulturists found to be most important for a productive and healthy garden? What are the most common obstacles faced by indoor gardeners?

 RULES OF THUMB are given for a quick, easy reference. They are an easy-to-remember guide that is somewhere between an educated guess and a scientific formula. The RULES OF THUMB give everyone a *feel* for the task or subject.

This book deals mainly with annual flowers and vegetables. We refer to these plants as annuals throughout the text. If the plants you are growing do not fit in this category, look up the specific growing conditions (temperature, humidity, light etc.) requirements in the chart on page 276 in the back of the book.

Publications such as *Organic Gardening, Sunset, Mother Earth News* and *Harrowsmith* and the gardening section of the local newspaper offer valuable background information on gardening. Reading such publications regularly will help round out your gardening knowledge.

SECTION I

The Indoor Environment

CHAPTER ONE

Indoor Gardening

The key to successful gardening is to understand how a plant produces food and grows. Plants may be cultivated indoors or out, but still have the same requirements for growth. All plants needs light, air, water, nutrients, a growing medium, and heat to manufacture food and to grow. Without any one of these essentials, growth will stop and death will result. Of course, the light must be of the proper spectrum and intensity; air must be warm, arid, and rich in carbon dioxide; water must be abundant, and the growing medium must be warm and contain the proper levels of nutrients. When all these needs are met consistently, at levels, optimum growth results.

Most flowers and vegetables are normally grown as annual plants, completing their life cycle in one year. A seed or bulb that is planted in the spring will grow strong and tall through the summer and flower in the fall, producing more seeds. The annual cycle starts all over again, with the new seeds. Marigolds, zinnias, tomatoes and lettuce are just a few examples of annual plants.

Biennials are plants that normally complete their life cycle in two years. They bloom the year after seeds are planted, and die after flowering and producing seed. Examples of biennials are pansies, hollyhocks, foxglove and parsley.

Perennial plants live for two years or more. Foliage perennials are valued for their lush and interesting foliage. These plants may also bloom but it is secondary to their foliage. Plants in this category include the Benjamin fig, pothos and elephant ear philodendrons.

Flowering perennials generally have shorter blooming seasons and may or may not remain green all year round. Examples of this group are wisteria, clematis, azaleas and vinca.

The *seed* has an outside coating, to protect the embryo plant, and a supply of stored food within. Given favorable conditions, including moisture, heat and air, a healthy seed will usually germinate. The seed's coating splits, a rootlet grows downward, and a sprout with seed leaves pushes upward in search of light. A seedling is born!

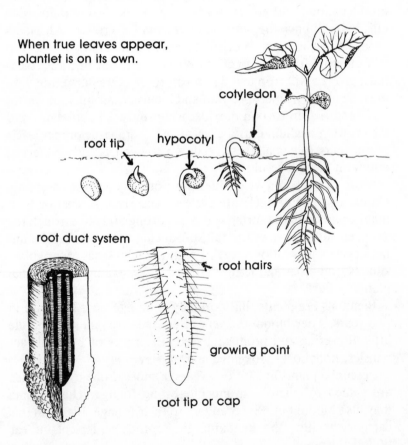

When true leaves appear, plantlet is on its own.

cotyledon

root tip

hypocotyl

root duct system

root hairs

growing point

root tip or cap

The single *root* from the seed grows down and branches out, similar to the way the stem branches out above ground. Tiny rootlets draw in water and nutrients (chemical substances needed for life). Roots also serve to anchor a plant in the ground. As the plant matures, the roots take on specialized functions. The center and old, mature portions contain a water transport system and may also store food. The tips of the roots produce elongating cells that continue to push farther and farther into the soil in quest of more water and food. The single-celled root hairs are the parts of the root that actually absorb water and nutrients, but must be in the presence of oxygen. Without water and air these frail root hairs will dry up and die. They are very delicate and may easily be damaged by light, air or careless hands if moved or exposed. Extreme care must be exercised during transplanting to ensure success.

Like the roots, the *stem* grows through elongation, also producing new buds along the stem. The central or terminal bud carries growth upward; side or lateral buds turn into branches or leaves. The stem functions by transmitting water and nutrients from the delicate root hairs to the growing buds leaves, and flowers. Sugars and starches, manufactured in the leaves, are distributed through the plant via the stem. This fluid flow takes place near the surface of the stem. If the stem is bound too tightly by string or other tie-downs, it will cut the flow of life-giving fluids, thereby strangling and killing the plant. The stem also supports the plant with stiff cellulose, located in the inner walls. Outdoors, rain and wind push a plant around, causing production of much stiff cellulose to keep the plant supported upright. Indoors, with no natural wind or rain present, stiff cellulose is minimal and plants may need to be staked up, especially during flowering.

Once the *leaves* expand, they start to manufacture food (carbohydrates). *Chlorophyll*, the substance that gives plants their green color, converts carbon dioxide (CO_2) from the air, water (containing nutrients) and light energy into carbohydrates and oxygen. This process is called *photosynthesis*. It requires water drawn up from the roots, through the stem, into the leaves where it encounters CO_2. Tiny pores located on the underside of the leaf, called *stomata* (Stomata can be spelled several ways - stomatae, stoma or stomata - in this book we will spell it stomata) funnel CO_2 into contact with the water. In order for photosynthesis to occur, the leaf's interior tissue ·must be kept moist. The stomata open and close to regulate the flow of moisture, preventing dehydration. Plant leaves are also protected from drying out by an outer skin. The stomata also permit the outflow of water vapor and waste oxygen. The stomata are very important to the plant's well-being and must be kept clean at all times to promote vigorous growth. Dirty, clogged stomata breathe about as well as you would with a sack over your head!

Most flowers and vegetables will *flower* if conditions are right; for short-day plants, the main variable is the photoperiod. In the fall, the days become shorter and plants are signaled that the annual life cycle is coming to an end. The plant's functions change. Leafy growth slows and flowers start to form.

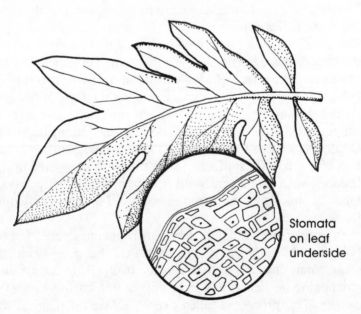

Stomata
on leaf
underside

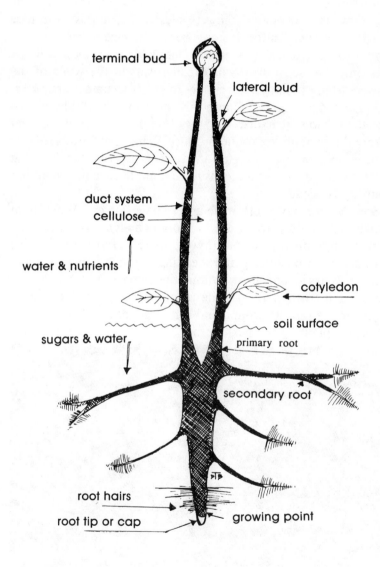

terminal bud

lateral bud

duct system

cellulose

water & nutrients

cotyledon

soil surface

sugars & water

primary root

secondary root

root hairs

root tip or cap

growing point

The majority of long-day plants bloom according to chronological age. That is, when they are two or three months old, they start to bloom. Flowers such as marigolds, petunias, pansies, cosmos, California poppies, zinnias etc. will continue to bloom once flowering starts. Long-day vegetables will set blossoms that soon drop when fruit forms in the wake of the flower. Many common vegetables such as tomatoes, peppers, egg plants, squash etc. fall into this category. Vegetables grown for their roots (carrots, potatoes, onions) generally bloom before the final underground produce is ripe. Leaf crops such as lettuce, spinach, parsley etc. are very productive indoors. All parts of these crops are consumed and little concern about maturity is needed.

Some plants have both male and female flowers. When both female and male flowers are in bloom, pollen from the male flower lands on the female flower, thereby fertilizing it. The male dies after producing and shedding as much pollen as possible. Seeds form and grow within the female flowers. As the seeds are maturing, the female plant slowly dies. The mature seeds then fall to the ground and germinate naturally or are collected for planting the next spring.

This lush long-day indoor garden produces both tomatoes and flowers.

Indoor vs. Outdoor Gardening

Gardening indoors is very different from outdoor cultivation, even though all plants have standard requirements for growth. The critical factors of the outdoor environment must be totally recreated indoors if a plant is to grow well. Outdoors, a gardener can expend a minimum of effort and Mother Nature will control many of the growth-influencing factors. *Indoors, the horticulturist assumes the cherished role of Mother Nature.* The horticulturist is able to wield control over many factors influencing growth. Since few people have ever played *Mother Nature* before, they usually do not fathom the scope of the job. We must realize that *Mother Nature* constantly provides the many things plants require to grow. The indoor gardener must manufacture the most important elements of the outdoor environment. This requires a general knowledge of the environment about to be created, as well as specific guidelines to follow.

Outdoor cultivation is limited to one season (two in the tropics). Light can be inadequate, especially if it is midwinter and you live in a city or an apartment or both. Outdoor air is usually fresh, but can become uncontrollably humid, arid, cold or windy. Water and nutrients are usually easy to supply, but acid salts could keep the nutrients unavailable to the plants.

With indoor horticulture, light, air, temperature, humidity, ventilation, CO_2, soil, water and nutrients may be precisely controlled to yield a perfect environment for plant growth.

Not long ago, with fluorescent tubes, this was not true. An inexpensive, easy-to-manage artificial light source, providing adequate *intensity*, was the main factor that limited growing many varieties of plants indoors.

Technological breakthroughs and scientific research have shed bright light on indoor horticulture, by producing the *metal halide and High Pressure (HP) sodium, High Intensity Discharge (HID) lamps.* Now a reasonably priced artificial light source, providing the color spectrum and intensity necessary to grow any plant imaginable, is on the market. With the HID lamp, a gardener may totally control the indoor environment. The high pressure sodium lamp can be used in conjunction with a halide or in a greenhouse to augment the sun. It emits a light spectrum similar to the autumn or *harvest* sun, providing the intense yellows, oranges and reds most flowers need to grow flower buds 20 to 100 percent larger than if only a single metal halide were used. The HID lamp is essentially a small sun in your basement, spare room or attic. By using a timer, a regular day-night schedule (photoperiod) may be set up. The HID, with a timer, may be even better than the sun! Exact control may be exercised over the hours of light per day, letting the horticulturist create his or her own seasons. Spring and summer and fall are recreated over and over, winter is forgotten and virtually non-existent to the indoor horticulturist!

In climates where the season is "long" (eight or nine months)

Healthy cauliflower is just forming under a super metal halide.

a much larger selection of flowers and vegetables can be cultivated. Gardeners living in northern climates can grow tomatoes in containers outdoors until the weather cools, then move them under the basement halide for a complete winter crop. Halides are also used very effectively to get an early start on annuals and vegetables. Since HID's are so bright, the little plantlets get a very strong start in life. This strong, early start is carried on throughout life.

Flowers and vegetables can also be grown in a greenhouse. The HP sodium lamp works extremely well providing supplemental light to natural sunlight. Young seedlings get an early start with more hours of light per day and fruit or flowers that are normally late can be forced to produce faster. All of the extra hours of intense light will make them think it is midsummer!

Outdoors, seeds are normally sown in the spring, mature and bear fruit and flowers in the summer.

Indoors, all growth factors may be individually controlled to give the plant exactly what it needs to promote any stage of growth.

The air outdoors is usually fresh and contains .03 to .04% CO_2. Ventilation is usually adequate, but the wind sometimes howls, burning leaves or even blowing plants over. Humidity and temperature are almost impossible to control.

Indoors, air may easily be controlled to promote growth and create an unfriendly environment for bugs and fungus. The CO_2 content may be enriched to double or triple plant growth. An open door and/or forced-air ventilation system will provide circulation and ventilation necessary to keep air *fresh*. Humidity is raised by misting the air with water or evaporating water from a bucket. Humidity is lowered by drying the air with heat from the HID system, heater, furnace or dehumidifier. Circulation, ventilation, humidity and temperature regulation are also fundamental to bug and fungus control. Clones root much faster in a warm, humid indoor environment. Temperature is easy to keep constant. Usually heat from the HID system provides ample heat for the grow room. An indoor garden will flourish between 70 and 75° F, but clones root best at 80 to 85° F. Air temperature may be raised with extra heat and lowered by means of an exhaust fan attached to a thermostat, if outside air is cooler.

Outdoor soil may vary greatly. It could be too acidic or alkaline, have toxic qualities, drain poorly, be full of harmful bugs, fungus and bad micro-organisms.

Indoor growing mediums may be purchased from a nursery in the form of potting soil or soilless mix. They will contain a minimum of fungus, insects or weeds. These growing mediums usually have the proper acid-to-alkaline or pH balance. Potting soils usually contain complete, balanced nutrients, while soilless mixes may or may not be *fortified* with nutrients. Nutrient levels may easily be checked in these growing mediums. Nutrients may then be added or leached (washed) out of containers, providing total soil control. The moisture content of the growing medium may be precisely monitored with a moisture meter and controlled. Potting soil and soilless mixes are blended to retain water evenly and provide good aeration and consistent root growth.

Outdoors, insects and fungi are usually kept in check by *Mother Nature* and are easy. Indoors, the gardener must take over in *Mother Nature's* absence. Keep the insects out of the grow room by simple sanitary precautions. It is easy to wash your hands, use clean tools and sweep the floor regularly. If insects and fungus do get started, they are easy to control in an enclosed room, since the gardener may control the factors that inhibit their well-being. Organic or chemical sprays may be used in conjunction with humidity, ventilation and temperature regulation to control the pests.

 Indoors you must assume the role of *Mother Nature.*

In summary, indoor gardening is far superior to outdoor cultivation for many gardeners, especially in northern climates. It provides exacting control of all growth-inducing factors and the indoor garden yields vine ripened produce, flowers and exotic plants the year round!

About Grow Rooms

The best location for a grow room is an unused corner of the basement. The basement is probably the best room in most homes for indoor gardens, since the temperature is easy to keep constant the year round. Humidity that would destroy the rest of the house can be easily managed in the plant room. Insecticides may be used without endangering the entire family. The unsightly pots, soil and flats do not have to be shared with the public. The room is well insulated by concrete walls and soil. Basements also remain cool, which helps prevent heat build up.

The size of the grow room and the light intensity required by plants grown determine the wattage of lamp used. A 400-watt lamp are just fine for smaller rooms spaces from 10 to 40 square feet of floor space. A 1000-watt bulb should be employed for a grow room of 50 to 100 square feet.

The drawings on page 20 show several common grow room floor plans. As the rooms demonstrate, there are several basic approaches to grow room production. A good deal of what the grow room is like depends on what plants are to be grown.

A second method is very similar to the first, but utilizes two rooms. The first room is for vegetative growth and rooting clones. Since plants are small, the room is about a third to half the size of the flowering room. The flowering room is harvested and the vegetative crop is moved into flower. A clone crop is transplanted into large pots to start the vegetative cycle.

A third method provides a perpetual crop. Several clones are taken each day or week. The same amount of plants are moved from the vegetative room to the flowering room. Of course the harvest is almost perpetual!

About Greenhouses

Greenhouses or growing environments using natural and artificial lighting are very productive. The same principles can be applied to both the indoor grow room and the greenhouse. However the heat and light intensity variables might be substantially different.

When combined with natural sunlight, artificial light is most optimally used during non-daylight hours. Greenhouse growers turn the HID lights on when sunlight diminishes, off when sunlight strengthens.

 Turn the light "on" in a greenhouse at sunset and "off" at sunrise.

This large greenhouse in Seattle is illuminated by two HP sodium lamps.

Turn the HID on when the daylight intensity is less than two times the intensity of the HID. Simply measure this point with a light meter. Many greenhouse owners simply calibrate a light photo cell to turn the HID on and off when daylight intensity is less than two times the intensity of the HID.

Supplementary lighting has greatest effect when applied to the youngest plants. It is least expensive to light plants when they are small, and this should be considered when budgets are concerned.

Setting Up The Grow Room

Before any plants are introduced, the grow room should be set up. Construction requires space and planning. There are a few things that need to be accomplished before the room is ready for plants.

STEP ONE: Choose an out-of-the-way space with little or no traffic. A dark corner in the basement would be perfect. Make sure the room is the right size. A 1000-watt HID, properly set up, will efficiently illuminate *up to* a 10-by-10-foot room if a "light balancer" is used. The ceiling should be at least 5 feet high or higher. Remember, plants are set up about one foot off the ground in containers and the lamp needs about a foot of space to hang from the ceiling. This leaves only three feet of space for plants to grow. However, if forced to grow in an attic or basement with a low 4-foot ceiling, much can be done to compensate for the loss of height, including cloning, bending and pruning.

STEP TWO: Enclose the room, if it's not already enclosed. Remove everything not having to do with the garden. Furniture and especially drapes or curtains harbor many a fine fungus. Having it totally enclosed will permit easy, precise control of everything and everyone that enters and exits and who and what goes on inside. For most gardeners, enclosing the grow room is simply a matter of tacking up some sheet rock in the basement or attic and painting it flat white.

STEP THREE: See: "Setting Up the Vent Fan" page 206 constant circulation and a supply of "fresh" air are essential. There should be at least one fresh-air vent in a 10-by-10-foot room, preferably two. Vent may be an open door, window or heat vent. Most gardeners have found that a small *exhaust* fan, vented outdoors, pulling new "fresh" air through an open door will create an ideal air flow. A small oscillating fan works well for circulation. When installing such a fan, make sure it is not set in a fixed position and blowing too hard on tender plants. It could cause windburn, or in the case if young seedlings and clones, dry them out. If the room contains a heat vent, it may be opened to supply extra heat or air circulation.

A vent fan and a circulation fan are necessary for adequate ventilation in a grow room.

STEP FOUR: The larger your garden gets, the more water it will need. A 10-by-10-foot garden may need as much as 30 gallons a week. You may carry water in, one container at a time (1 gallon of water weighs 8 pounds). It is much easier to run in a hose with an on/off valve or install a hose bib in the room. A 3 to 4-foot watering wand may be attached to the hose on/off valve. The wand will save many broken branches when watering in dense foliage. It is best to hook the hose up to a hot and cold water source, so the water temperature may be regulated easily.

STEP FIVE: Cover walls, ceiling, floor, everything, with a highly reflective material such as *flat white paint* see page 77. The more reflection, the more light energy that is available to plants. Good reflective light will allow effective coverage of a 1000-watt HID lamp to increase from 36 square feet, with no reflective material, to a maximum of 100 square feet, just by putting $10 to $20 worth of paint on the walls.

STEP SIX: Ideally, the floor should be concrete or a smooth surface that can be swept and/or washed down. A floor drain is very handy. In grow rooms with carpet or wood floors, a large, white, painter's dropcloth or thick white Visqueen plastic, will save floors from moisture. A tray may also be placed beneath each container for added protection and convenience.

STEP SEVEN: Mount a hook, strong enough to support 30 pounds, in the center of the growing area to be serviced by the lamp. Attach an adjustable chain or cord and pulley between the ceiling hook and the lamp fixture. This will make it easy to keep the lamp at the proper distance from the growing plants and up out of the way when maintaining them.

CAUTION: A hot HID may break if touched by a cold water. Be very careful and make sure to move the HID out of the way when servicing the garden.

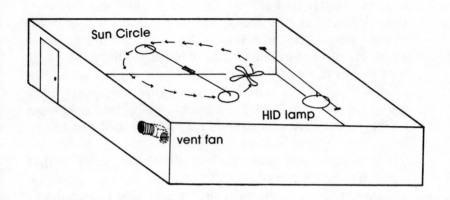

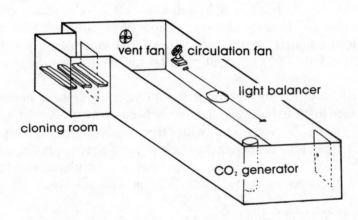

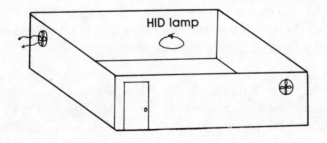

STEP EIGHT: There are some tools an indoor gardener must have and a few *extra* tools that make indoor horticulture much more precise and Cost-effective. The extra tools help the horticulturist play Mother Nature and make the garden so efficient that they pay for themselves within a few weeks. It is best to purchase all the tools or hunt them up around the house before the plants are brought into the room. If the tools are there when needed, chances are they will be put to use. A good example is a hygrometer. If plants show signs of slow, sickly growth due to high humidity, most gardeners will not notice the exact cause right away. They will wait and guess, wait and guess, and maybe figure it out before a fungus attacks and the plant dies. When a hygrometer is installed before plants are in the grow room, the horticulturist will know, from the start, when the humidity is too high and causing sickly growth. See page 22: tool closet and list of tools)

STEP NINE: Read and complete: "Setting Up the HID Lamp" at the end of Chapter Two.

STEP TEN: Move in the seedlings or rooted clones. Huddle them closely together under the lamp. Make sure the HID is not so close to small plants that it burns their leaves. Usually seedlings require the lamp to be at least 24 inches away.

flowering room

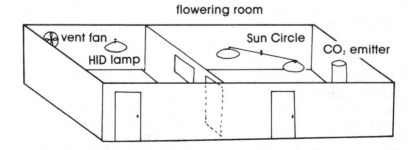

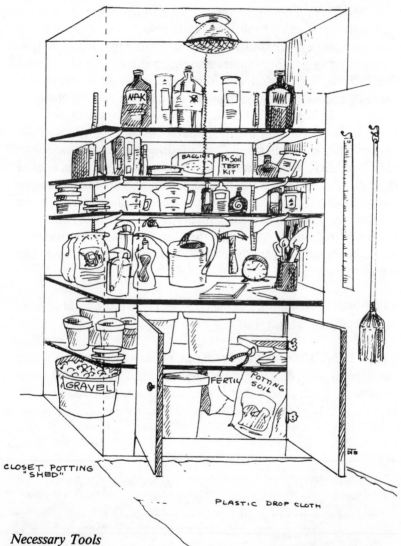

CLOSET POTTING
"SHED"

PLASTIC DROP CLOTH

Necessary Tools
Thermometer
Spray Bottle
Pruner or scissors
Hammer and nails
Notebook
Yardstick (to measure growth)

Extra Tools
pH & soil test kit
Hygrometer
Wire (bread sack) ties
Measuring cup
Measuring spoons
Moisture meter

CHAPTER TWO

Light, Lamps and Electricity

Light and Plants

Light is one of the major factors that contribute to plant growth. Indoors, light has been, until recent years, the main limiting factor to growing more than a small indoor garden of limited variety. By understanding how a plant uses light, the indoor horticulturist can use the technology provided by the High Intensity Discharge (HID) lamps to fulfill light requirements and grow spectacular gardens. The subject of light as used by plants can become very complex. This book will look at the *basic* ways light affects plant growth.

A plant combines light energy with carbon dioxide (CO_2), water and nutrients to form green *chlorophyll* and carbohydrates, releasing oxygen as a by-product. Without light, a plant will not be able to produce green chlorophyll, leaves soon turn yellow, and eventually death results. With the proper spectrum and intensity of light, chlorophyll is rapidly produced and rapid growth occurs.

Outdoors, the sun usually supplies enough light for rapid growth. The sun also supplies much light that plants do not use. Scientists have found that plants need and use only certain portions of the light spectrum. The most important colors in the spectrum for maximum *chlorophyll production* and *photosynthetic response* are in the blue (445 nm)[1] and red (650 nm) range.

Phototropism is the movement of a plant part (foliage) toward illumination. Positive tropism means the foliage moves toward the light. Negative tropism means the plant part moves

---

[1] nm = nanometers, one nm = .000001 meter. Light is measured in wavelengths, the wavelengths are divided into nm.

away from the light. Positive tropism is greatest in the blue end
of the spectrum at about 450 nm. At this optimum level, plants
lean toward the light, spreading their leaves out horizontally to
absorb the most light possible.

The **photoperiod** is the relationship between the length of the
light period and dark period. The photoperiod affects the life
cycle of all plants. Short-day plants will stay in the vegetative
growth stage as long as a photoperiod of 18 to 24 hours light is
maintained. Sixteen to 24 hours of light per day will give short
day plants all the light they need to sustain optimum seedling
and vegetative growth. The plants will think it is the longest and
sunniest day (June 22) every day of the year. Many plants can
use 16 to 18 hours of light in a 24-hour period before a point of
diminishing returns is reached. The light has a minimal effect on
growth after 16 to 18 hours.

Greatest efficiency is obtained by adding supplemental light
to a greenhouse crop after the sun goes down. The HID lights

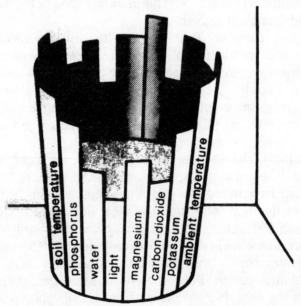

*A plant will only grow as fast as the least available factor will
allow.*

are not as bright as the sun and should not compete with the sun. Plants can also reach a maximum saturation point, where the extra light they receive does not increase growth in relation to the amount of light shed. After this point of diminishing returns is reached, additional light has only a minimal effect. If this supplemental light is added during dark periods or very cloudy days, plants get the entire benefit of the supplemental lighting. many experiments have proven that adding supplemental light during the dark hours is 50 to 100% more productive than adding more light during sunlight hours.

Flowering is induced most efficiently in short-day plants with 12 to 14 hours of *uninterrupted darkness* in a 24-hour photoperiod. It is possible to gradually decrease the daylight hours while increasing dark hours to simulate the natural photoperiod. This practice follows the natural photoperiod but it prolongs flowering for several weeks.

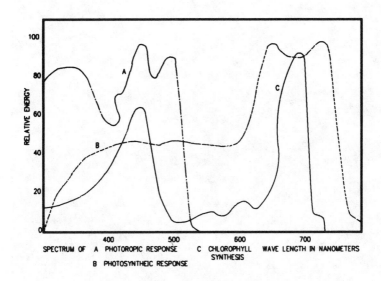

SPECTRUM OF   A PHOTOROPIC RESPONSE   C CHLOROPHYLL   WAVE LENGTH IN NANOMETERS
              B PHOTOSYNTHEIC RESPONSE   SYNTHESIS

Optimum flowering potential is reached when the 12-hour photoperiod is coupled with high levels of *intense* light from the red end of the spectrum. After short-day plants are two to 12 months old, altering the photoperiod to an even 12 hours, day and night, will induce flowering in two to four weeks. The 12-hour photoperiod represents the classic equinox and is the optimum daylight-to-dark relationship for flowering. For most of the plants that fall in this category, less than 12 hours of light will not induce flowering any faster and may substantially reduce flower formation and yield. More than 12 hours of light

Young Cyclamen are flourishing under this horizontal 400 watt HP sodium lamp.

will prolong flowering; visible signs of flower formation take much longer.

The photoperiod can also be the signal to stay in (or revert to) vegetative growth. Short-day plants must have 12 hours of *uninterrupted, total darkness* to flower properly. Tests have shown that even dim light during the dark period in the pre-flowering and flowering stages will prevent the plants from blooming. Chrysanthemums are forced to bloom at various times of the year by interrupting their nighttime with a few 10-to-30 minute bursts of bright light.

When the 12-hour dark period is interrupted by light, the plant gets confused by the light's signal saying, "It's daytime, start vegetative growth." The plant will try to revert to vegetative growth and flowering will take forever. Make sure to keep flowering short-day plants in *total* darkness; no midnight visits or lit-up open doorways!

Gardeners growing tropical plants (orchids, bromeliads etc.) from equatorial regions give their gardens 12 hours of light throughout the life cycle. They want to replicate the less dynamic photoperiod of the tropics. (On the equator, days and nights are almost exactly the same length the year round.) When this method is used, plants tend to bloom when they are chronologically ready, after thoroughly completing the vegetative growth stage.

The average house plant is "night neutral" since it will grow and bloom well with six to eight hours of darkness. These plants require 14 to 16 hours. Examples of these "night neutral" plants are most gesneraids, oxalis, exacum affine and many begonias.

Chrysanthemums, poinsettias, species columnea, orchids and some Begonias, Christmas cactus and related forms will bloom only if given a long night of 14 to 16 hours and less than eight to 10 hours of light per day.

Summer-blooming plants and vegetables need 18 hours of light per day and a short night of six hours. Geraniums, annuals, tuberous begonias and seedlings of almost all plants are in this category. In fact, African violets will double their blossom production if they are given 18 hours of light rather than 12 hours.

Foliage plants are raised for green foliage, and flowering is not important. These plants can have varying amounts of light and dark and not be affected. Examples are rex Begonias, aroids, palms, marantas and ferns.

Intensity

HID's are incredibly bright! In fact, it is this brightness that makes them so useful. However, this intense light must be properly managed to get a bumper crop. Intensity is the magnitude of light energy per unit of area. It is greatest near the source of the light and diminishes with distance from the source. The drawing below demonstrates how rapidly light intensity diminishes. Plants that are 4 feet away from the lamp get a fourth as much light as plants one foot away! The closer plants are to the light source, the better they grow. Six inches to 12 inches is a safe distance for plants to be from the lamp (tender seedlings require 24 inches to 36 inches). Any closer and plants run the risk of growing so fast they run into the hot bulb, burning tender growing tips.

A 1000-watt *standard* metal halide emits 100,000 initial lumens and 88,000 mean (average) lumens[2]. Super halides emit 125,000 initial lumens and 100,000 mean lumens. The HP sodium emits a whopping 140,000 initial lumens! The indoor horticulturist is interested in how much light is emitted by the HID, as well as how much light is *received* by the plants. Light received is measured by the light and distance chart or in watts-per-square-foot or in foot-candles (f.c.)[3].

Watts per square feet is easy to calculate, but not very accurate. It measures how many watts are available from a light source in a given area. A 1000-watt HID will emit an average of 10 watts per square foot in a 10-by10-foot room. Mounting height is not considered in watts per square foot; the lamp could

---

[2] One lumen is equal to the amount of light emitted by one candle that falls on one square foot of surface one foot away.

[3] One foot-candle equals the amount of light that falls on one square foot of surface located one foot away from one candle.

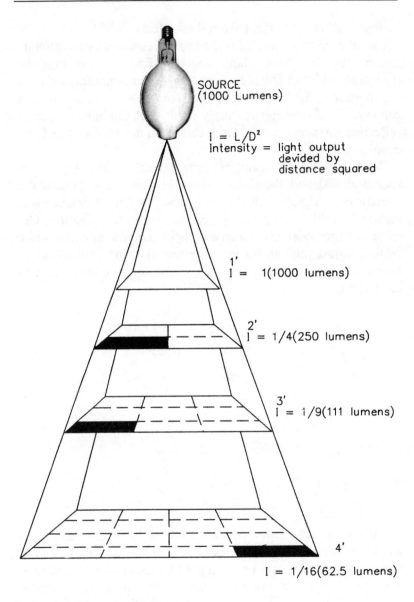

SOURCE
(1000 Lumens)

$I = L/D^2$
Intensity = light output
devided by
distance squared

1'
I = 1(1000 lumens)

2'
I = 1/4(250 lumens)

3'
I = 1/9(111 lumens)

4'
I = 1/16(62.5 lumens)

Light and Distance Chart

be mounted at any height from 4 to 8 feet.

Calculating foot-candles is the most accurate way to estimate the amount of light plants receive. Foot-candles may be measured with a light meter reading in foot-candles, or by a photographic light meter, either hand-held or built into a camera. The f.c. meter is simply pointed at the light source or reflective surface at any given location, and a read-out in foot-candles is given.

When using a photographic light meter, set the ASA (film speed) at 200 and the shutter speed at $\frac{1}{125}$ second. Focus the camera on a rigid white sheet of paper in the proposed plant location. Hold the paper so it gets maximum illumination. Get close enough so all the camera or light meter sees is the white paper. Adjust the camera lens aperture (f stop) until a correct exposure registers on the light meter. Use the following chart to calculate f.c.

f4″	" 64 f.c.
f5.6″	"125 f.c.
f8″	" 250 f.c.
f11″	" 500 f.c.
f16″	" 1000 f.c.
f22″	" 2000 f.c.

Now we get to the facts: Almost all the light research that is available was done by Europeans or scientists and expressed in watts per square meter. You will need to convert foot-candles to watts per square meter to get the most out of this chapter. Please notice that each lamp and the natural sunlight have different conversion factors. The conversion factors are found in the chart on page 32 and the conversion chart follows this paragraph.

CONVERSION CHART

Formula:
1. Multiply footcandle reading by conversion factor for the light source (See page 32) to obtain the number of watts per square meter.

2. For mixed lighting (using multiple sources) determine the watts per square meter level for each light source and add the readings for the total.

Examples:
1. A site has 100 foot-candles of daylight and 100 footcandles of HP sodium light.
Daylight: 100 × 0.055 = 5.5 watts per square meter
HP sodium light: 100 × 0.034 = 3.4 watts per square meter
Total: 5.5 + 3.4 = 8.9 watts per square meter

2. A site has 100 foot-candles of HP sodium light and 100 foot-candles of metal halide light.
HP sodium light: 100 × 0.034 = 3.4 watts per square meter
Metal halide light: 100 × 0.34 = 3.4 watts per square meter
Total: 3.4 + 3.4 = 6.8 watts per square meter

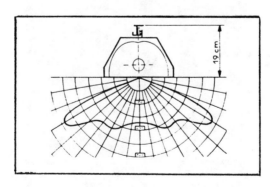

This drawing shows the light distribution curve for the PL-780, a Dutch 400 watt horizontal HP sodium lamp.

CONVERSION FACTORS FOR DETERMINING WATTS
PER SQUARE METER FOR VARIOUS LIGHT SOURCES

Light Source	Conversion factor
Daylight	0.055
HP sodium lamp	0.034
LP sodium lamp	0.022
Metal halide lamp	0.034
Cool white fluorescent	0.030
Warm white fluorescent	0.30
Fluorescent grow lamps	0.044
Incandescent lamps	0.090

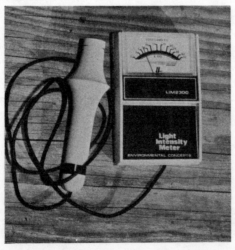

An inexpensive light meter will help you get the most out of your lamp.

Milliwatts per square meter ((mW/m2) is the irradiance produced by one-thousandth of a watt of light energy beamed into a surface of one square meter.

Plants are too close to the lights when they are (sun) bleaching, or have curled or stunted leaves. Move plants demonstrating these symptoms farther away from the lamp. Plants that require more light should be set up on a stand or overturned container.

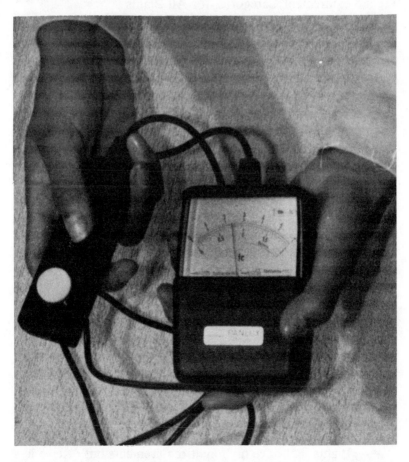

More expensive light meters are very exacting and only necessary for the most serious of growers.

One of the best ways to demonstrate how light intensity can retard a harvest is found in the outdoor vegetable garden. Have you ever planted 65-day broccoli that took 100 days to mature? Think about it. Did the plants get full sun all day long? It is assumed that the seeds were planted at the peak of the season and perfect temperatures prevailed. Plants that got less light matured slowly and produced less than ones getting full sun all day long.

Light Requirement Categories for All Plants

3,000 mW/m2: Lighting after flower induction (forcing) during the latter part of cultivation; growing long-day plants, giving a little growth stimulation as well.

4,500 mW/m2: Cultivation of vegetables, flowers (for produce and flowers) through harvest; young spaced vegetative plants.

6,000 mW/m2: For rooting and young plants while still packed under the HID; high light vegetables, flowers (for produce and flowers) plants.

7,500 mW/m2: Rooting some nursery stock and some high-light plants.

9,000 mW/m2: Expensive plants; fast and programmed crops; special cases. Producing this much supplemental light in a room is very expensive.

For more information about specific light requirements for plants check the Plant Selection Guide, pages 277-283. The U.S. Department of Agriculture also provides information about light requirements of many plants at different stages of life.

 Plants that have high light requirements but receive less *intense* or filtered light will yield less and take longer to mature.

When combined with natural sunlight, artificial light is optimally used during non-daylight hours. Greenhouse growers turn the HID lights on when the point of diminishing returns is reached. The time to turn on or off the HID is when daylight reaches twice the intensity of the HID.

For Example: Turn the HID on when the daylight intensity is less than twice the intensity of the HID. Simply measure this point with a light meter. A photo cell can also be used to turn one or several HID's on and off when this point is reached.

Turn the HID off when the daylight intensity is greater than twice the intensity of the HID.

Overhead 400 watt HP sodium lamps provide a blanket of even lighting.

Spacing

Ideally plants should be spaced out under lamps so that they do not touch one another. This will provide for more air movement and allow enough growing space for each plant. It also allows more even saturation of light.

Bedding plants are given a level of 6,000 mW/m2 for 16 to 18 hours a day. This will give the little guys a big jump on the season outdoors or keep many of them blooming all year long indoors.

When light intensity is too low, plants s-t-r-e-t-c-h for it. Low intensity is often caused by the lamp being too far away. When the plant is too far away, branches usually form farther apart on the stem than if the lamp were close. Simply by keeping the lamp as close as possible, leggy plants are kept to a minimum.

When light shines on a garden, the leaves near the top of plants get more intense light than the leaves at the bottom. The top leaves shade the bottom leaves, absorbing light energy, making less light energy available to lower leaves. If the lower leaves do not receive enough light, they yellow and die. Do not pick off perfectly good leaves so lower foliage gets more light! Tall 6-to-8 foot plants take longer to grow and yield more overall then shorter 4-foot plants, but the yield of flowers and foliage will be about the same. The taller plants have large flowers on the top 3 to 4 feet and spindly buds nearer the bottom, due to lack of light. Tall plants tend to develop flower tops so heavy that the stem cannot support the weight, and they need to be tied up. Short plants support the weight of the tops better and have much more flower weight than leaf weight.

Annual flowers and vegetables should not be over waist-high before fruit and flowers are set. Due to their high light requirements, these plants do not respond very well to weak light.

Several hundred two-week-old seedlings or clones may be huddled directly under a single HID. The young plants will need more space as they grow. Plants that are packed too close together sense the shortage of space and do not grow to their maximum potential. Leaves from one plant that shade another plant's leaves slow its development. It is very important to space young plants just far enough apart that their leaves do not touch. This will keep shading to a minimum and growth to a maximum. Check and alter the spacing every few days.. Eight to 16 mature tomato plants will completely fill the space under one 1000-watt HID.

The *stadium* method is a very good way to get the most from an uneven garden profile. Tall plants go on the perimeter, while shorter plants crowd toward the center of the garden. The intensity of light all the plants receive is about the same. See drawing below.

 Keep HID 6 to 12 above garden. Tender clones, seedlings and transplants require 24 to 36 inches. For other than fast-growing annuals, consult the plant selection guide in the back of the book, page 276

The stadium method places the tallest plants on the perimeter of the garden.

The HID Lamp Family

Incandescent lamps create light by passing electricity through a very fine wire or filament. HID lamps make light by passing electricity through vaporized gas under *high* pressure. Fluorescent and low-pressure (LP) sodium lamps create light by passing electricity through gaseous vapor under *low* pressure. All of these principles are relatively simple.

The chart (page 39) shows various lamps with their *lumen-per-watt* conversion. This formula is used to measure the lamp's efficiency: the amount of lumens produced for the amount of watts (electricity) consumed. Note the high lumen-per-watt conversion of the halides and sodiums.

All the HID lamps work on the same principle, passing or do arcing electricity through gas or vapor, rather than using a tungsten filament, as household incandescent bulbs. The gas is inside a heat-resistant glass or ceramic *arc tube*, sealed under high pressure. The materials contained in the arc tube dictate the colors or spectrum the lamp will produce, except for the effect of the phosphor coating. Passing electricity through vaporized elements is an easy enough principle, but putting it into action requires a little technology.

Below is a diagram of an HID lamp. They may all work on the same principle; however, their starting requirements, line voltage, operating characteristics and physical shape are unique to each lamp. Remember this: DO NOT TRY TO MIX AND MATCH BALLASTS WITH LAMPS! The fact that a lamp fits a socket attached to a ballast does not mean that it will work properly in it. The wrong lamp plugged into the wrong ballast adds up to a BURNOUT!

 Buy the entire HID system -ballast, lamp, socket, bulb and timer - all at the same time from a reputable supplier to ensure that the ballast and lamp go together. Make sure to get a written guarantee from the dealer. The system should carry a complete guarantee for at least one year.

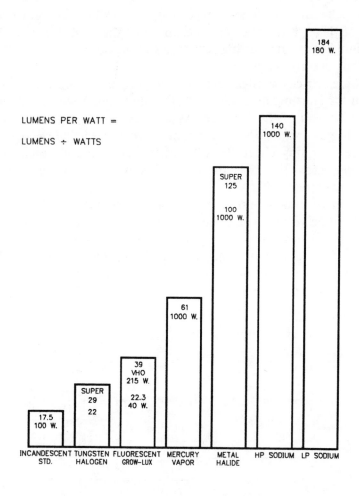

LUMENS PER WATT =

LUMENS ÷ WATTS

The efficiency of the LP sodium lamp is misleading because the largest wattage available is 180. One thousand watt HP sodium lamps are available and with a lumen-per-watt conversion of 140, the HP sodium is clearly the most efficient.

The electricity or line voltage (1) flows through the ballast (2). The ballast is the box that contains a capacitor (3) that provides a high, fast charge of electricity to start the lamps. Getting the electricity to flow between the electrodes (7) and (9) in the arc tube (10) requires a high-voltage charge or current. This current is sent through the starting mechanism of the lamp (5). In HP sodium lamps, the starting electrode and the operating electrode are one and the same.

The electricity is then arced or shot across the arc tube (10) from the starting electrode (6) to the operating electrode (9) at the other end of the arc tube. As soon as the arc is established and the gases vaporize, the arc jumps from the starting electrode to the operating electrodes (7) and (9). Once the electricity is flowing across the tube, the elements slowly vaporize into the discharge stream (8).

When the discharge stream (8) is working and the lamp warms up, the line voltage could run out of control, since there is an unrestricted flow of electricity between the two electrodes. The ballast (2) regulates this line voltage by means of a wire coil wrapped around an iron core (4). By employing this core (4) the lamp is assured of having a constant and even supply of electricity.

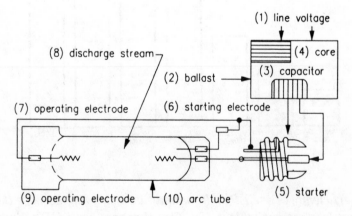

AN INSIDE LOOK AT QUALITY

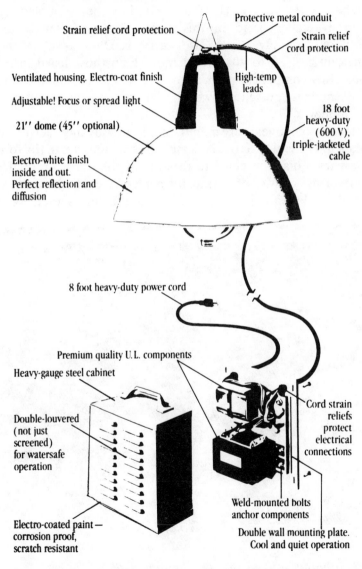

Strain relief cord protection

Protective metal conduit

Strain relief cord protection

Ventilated housing. Electro-coat finish

High-temp leads

Adjustable! Focus or spread light

21'' dome (45'' optional)

18 foot heavy-duty (600 V), triple-jacketed cable

Electro-white finish inside and out.
Perfect reflection and diffusion

8 foot heavy-duty power cord

Premium quality U. L. components

Heavy-gauge steel cabinet

Double-louvered (not just screened) for watersafe operation

Cord strain reliefs protect electrical connections

Weld-mounted bolts anchor components

Electro-coated paint — corrosion proof, scratch resistant

Double wall mounting plate.
Cool and quiet operation

About Ballasts

All HID's require ballasts. It is very important to buy the proper ballast for your HID. If possible, buy the assembled unit from a retailer listed in this book. Electrical supply and greenhouse supply stores also carry HID's; however, they generally cost 30 to 40 percent more than those listed in this book. Buy component parts if you are low on capital and want to assemble it yourself. However, you are not assured of saving any money.

Ballast components are manufactured by Advance, Jefferson, Sola and General Electric. Assembly instructions are in the form of a wiring diagram glued to the side of the transformer. The components consist of a transformer core, cooling capacitor, containing box and wire. Capacitor manufacturers are Cornell,

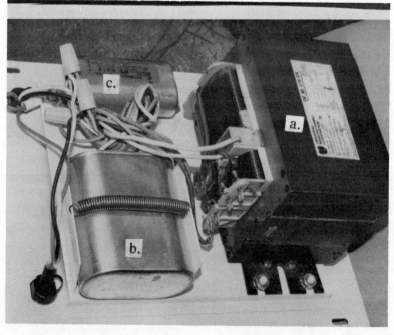

This photograph of a HP sodium ballast shows (A) the transformer (B) capacitor and (C) the ignighter or starter.

G.E., Duviler and Dayton. If you are not familiar with electrical component assembly and reading wiring diagrams, it is best to purchase the assembled ballast in a package containing the lamp and hood from one of the many HID distributors.

Do not buy used parts from a junkyard or try to use a ballast if unsure of its capacity. The fact that a bulb fits a socket attached to a ballast mean it is the proper system. The best way to grow a miserable garden is to try to save money on the ballast.

Even though HID's have specific ballasting requirements, the ballasts have a good deal in common. The transformer consists of thin metal plates that are laminated together with a sticky, tar-like resin. This transformer core is then wrapped with wire. When operated at excessive temperatures or with poor ventilation, the resin becomes thin and the metal plates will begin to vibrate or hum super loud. This steady hum can be unnerving. Ballasts operate at 90 to 150° F. Touch a *strike-anywhere* kitchen match to the side to check if it is too hot. If the match lights, the ballast is too hot and should be taken into the shop before it creates an accident or burns out. Heat is the number one ballast destroyer! Ballasts are manufactured with a protective metal box. This outer shell safely contains the core, capacitor and wiring. Always use ballasts with all the wiring and necessary parts enclosed. Never use a ballast with exposed elec-

Multi-tap ballast can be used as 110 or 220 volts. Single-tap ballasts must be either 110 volts or 220 volts.

trical connectors. Never build another box around a ballast. It will cause excessive heat and may even start a fire!

Make sure the ballast has a handle on it. A small 400-watt halide ballast weighs about 30 pounds and a large 1000-watt HP sodium ballast tips the scales at about 55 pounds. This small, heavy box is very awkward to move with no handle.

Most ballasts sold by HID stores are set up for the 110-volt current found in all homes. Some may be ready for 220-volt service. It is usually easiest to use the regular 110-volt system because its outlets are more common. The 220-volt systems are normally used when several lamps are already taking up space on other 110-volt circuits. Changing all ballasts (except for Jefferson, which are manufactured either 110 or 220 volts and are not able to change) from 110 to 220 is a simple matter of moving one internal wire from the 110-volt brad to the 220-(208)-volt brad and changing the plug to a 220 type. Consult the wiring diagram in each ballast for specific instructions. There is no difference in the electricity consumed by using either 110- or

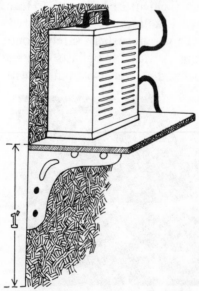

This ballast is set up off the floor on a shelf to prevent excess water from leaking in the bottom.

220-volt systems. The 110-volt system draws about 9.5 amperes and an HID on a 220-volt current draws about 4.3 amperes. Both use the same amount of electricity! To quote Ohm's Power Law: Volts × Amperes = Watts.

More expensive ballasts are equipped with ventilation fans to maintain cool operation. A fan is not necessary unless there are many ballasts in a small room and ventilation is inadequate. Air vents allow a ballast to run cooler. The vents should protect the internal parts and not be prone to letting water splash in.

Some industrial ballasts are sealed in fiberglass or similar material to make them weatherproof. These ballasts are not recommended. They were designed for use outdoors where heat buildup is not a problem. Indoors, the protection of the sealed unit from weather is not necessary and could create excessive heat.

220-volt ballasts are easy to loop together. Up to four ballasts may be wired in a *series circuit* on a 220 volt 30 ampere circuit. This is the most efficient way to use HID ballasts. There is less resistance for electricity when ballasts are wired in series. Less electricity is lost in transmission. I advise that *only* electricians try this relatively simple procedure. There is a lot more current flowing with more ballasts and *grounding* requirements increase. Any competent electrician should be able to loop them together.

The ballast has a lot of electricity flowing through it. DO NOT TOUCH THE BALLAST WHEN OPERATING! Do not place the ballast directly on the damp floor — or any floor. Always place it up off the floor and protect it from possible moisture. The ballast should be suspended in the air or on a shelf attached to the wall. It does not have to be very high — just far enough to keep it off a wet floor.

There are remote and attached ballasts. The remote ballast is the best for most indoor situations. It may easily be moved and placed near the floor to radiate heat in a cool portion of the grow room or placed outside if the room is too hot. Attached ballasts are fixed to the hood, require more overhead space, are very heavy and create more heat around the lamp.

Some ballasts are manufactured with an attached timer. These units are very convenient, but the timer should be constructed of heavy-duty heat-resistant materials. If is lightweight plastic, it could easily melt under the heat of the ballast.

A good ballast manufacturer will place a 10-ampere fuse inside the ballast. This is a double safeguard against anything happening and destroying the lamp or causing a fire.

High Intensity Discharge Lamps

Artificial light from the High Intensity Discharge (HID) lamp family may be used to stimulate growth responses induced in

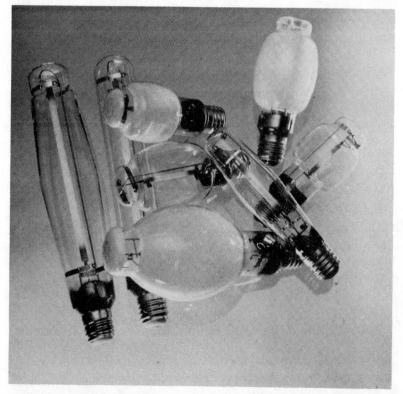

Metal halide lamps have a shapely bulbous curves while HP sodium lamps are more tubular in shape.

plants by natural sunlight. This may be seen by comparing charts on HID spectral emission (pages 54 and 62) with the chart on photosynthetic response, chlorophyll synthesis and positive tropism (page 25).

The HID lamp family contains mercury vapor, metal halide and High Pressure (HP) sodium lamps.

The two most popular HID wattages are 400 and 1000. Value is the main reason. The 1000-watt system costs about 30 percent more than the 400-watt system, but is more efficient in its lumen-per-watt conversion and produces more than twice as much light. By employing a *light balancer*, uniform light distribution is no longer a problem. The smaller 400-watt systems are great for a space that is 2 to 6 feet square or a small greenhouse. The smaller 400-watt HID's are similar to the larger 1000-watt systems, only smaller, producing less light and heat. Their color spectrum is almost identical to those of their big brothers. The 400-watt halides last about twice as long as the 1000-watt, but both have the same lumen maintenance curve!

The lettering on the dome of the Sylvania 400 watt metal halide bulb lists a C for phosphor coated and BU for base up. The Westinghouse MS 1000/C/BU lamp is a super 1000 metal halide phosphor coated, base up bulb.

Mercury Vapor Lamps

The mercury vapor lamp is the oldest and best-known member of the HID family. The HID principle was first used with the mercury vapor lamp around the turn of the century, but it was not until the mid-1930's that the mercury vapor lamp was really employed commercially on a large scale.

As the lumen-per-watt chart shows (page 48), the mercury vapor lamps produce only 60 lumens per watt. A comparison of the spectral energy distribution (chart on page 65) of the mercury vapor and the photosynthetic response chart (page 25) will show you that this is a poor lamp for horticulture. Not only is it expensive to operate, but it produces most of its color in areas that are not helpful to plant growth.

The old mercury vapor lamps produce light by arcing electricity through mercury and a little argon gas is used for starting. They come in sizes from 40 to 1000-watts. They have fairly good lumen maintenance and a fairly long life. Most wattages last up to three years at 18-hour daily operation.

The mercury vapor usually requires a separate ballast; however, there are a few low wattage bulbs that have self-contained ballast. All too often these ballasts are scrounged from junkyards or who-knows-where and used in place of halide or HP sodium ballasts. People who use or try to modify these ballasts for use with another HID have all kinds of problems and still have to buy the proper ballast in the end. Remember, trying to save money on a ballast usually costs more in produce that was not realized.

In summary, the mercury vapor lamp produces a color spectrum that is not as efficient as the halide or HP sodium for indoor cultivation. It is *NOT* the lamp to use if you want any kind of garden at all! Gardeners who have used them paid more for electricity and their gardens yielded much less.

 Metal halides and HP sodiums are the most efficient lamps for gardening indoors.

Metal Halide Lamps

The metal halide HID lamp is the most efficient source of artificial white light available to the horticulturist today. It comes in 175-250-400-1000- and 1500-watt sizes. They may be either clear or phosphor-coated, and all require a special ballast. Most gardeners do not consider using the 175- or 250-watt halides. The 1500-watt halide is also avoided due to its relatively short (2000 to 3000 hours) life and incredible heat output. Most gardeners prefer the 1000-watt halide and those with small growing areas or low-light greenhouses the 400-watt.

Metal halides are either clear or phosphor coated.

Three major metal halide manufacturers are General Electric (Multivapor)[4], Sylvania (Metalarc)[5] and Westinghouse (Metal Halide). Each manufacturer has a *super* version of the halide. The Super Metalarc, the High-Output Multivapor and the Super Metal Halide fit the standard halide ballast and fixture. They produce about 25 percent more lumens than the standard halides. These *super* halides cost about $10 more than the standard, but are well worth the money.

The *clear* halides are the most commonly used by indoor gardeners. This lamp is the brightest white lamp around. It supplies the most lumens of the best possible spectrum for plant growth. The clear halide works well for seedling, vegetative and flower growth.

Phosphor-coated 1000-watt halides emit a more diffused light and are easy on the eyes, emitting less ultraviolet light than the clear halides. They produce the same initial lumens and about 4,000 fewer lumens than the *standard* halide and have a slightly different color spectrum. Phosphor-coated halides have more yellows, less blue and less ultraviolet light. Some gardeners prefer the *phosphor-coated* halide to the HP sodium for both vegetative growth and flowering, saying it is the best all-round bulb.

The 1000-watt *super clear* and *super phosphor-coated* halides are the most common halides used indoors. Compare energy distribution charts and lumen output of all three lamps to decide which lamp offers the most desirable characteristics for your garden. Typically, the home gardener starts with the 1000-watt Super Metalarc (Sylvania), High-Output Multivapor (G.E.) or Super Metal Halide (Westinghouse).

---

[4] G.E. also produces the *I-Line Multivapor,* available in 325, 400 and 1000 wattages. They are designed to work in most mercury vapor fixtures and ballasts, but WILL NOT WORK in small mercury ballasts containing peaking capacitors or two-lamp types. The Multivapor I-Line will produce about 2,500 less lumens than the standard halide.

[5] Sylvania produces the *Metalarc Swingle,* which is very similar to the G.E. I-Line Multivapor. The swingle is made for use in many mercury vapor ballasts, and as with the I-Line, is not as efficient. I recommend neither lamp. If you must use one, write the factory for ballast specifications before buying a ballast.

Construction and Operation

Metal halide lamps produce light by passing or arcing electricity through vaporized argon gas, mercury, thorium iodide, sodium iodide and scandium iodide within the quartz arc tube (1). At the end of the arc tube is a heat reflecting coating (2) to control temperature during operation. Spring supports in the neck (4) and dome (3) of the outer bulb or envelope (5) mount the arc tube frame (9) in place. The bimetal shorting switch (6) closes during lamp operation, preventing voltage drop between the main electrode (7) and the starting electrode (8). Most bulbs

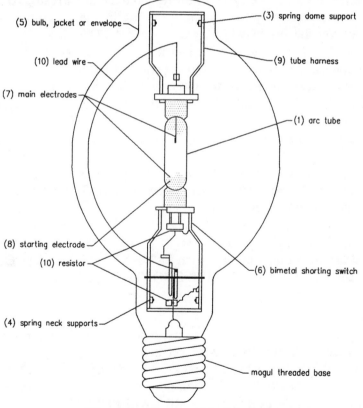

Diagram of a metal halide lamp.

are equipped with a resistor (10) that keeps the bulb from shattering under temperature stress. The outer bulb functions as a protective jacket. It contains the arc tube and starting mechanism, keeping them in a constant environment as well as absorbing ultraviolet radiation. *Protective goggles that filter out ultraviolet rays are a good idea if you spend much time in the grow room or if you are prone to staring at the HID.*

Initial vaporization takes place in the gap between the main electrode (7) and the starting electrode (8) when a high starting voltage is applied. When there is enough ionization, electricity will arc between the main electrodes (7). As the lamp warms up, the metal iodide additives begin to enter the arc stream. After they are in their proper concentrations in the arc tube, the characteristic bright white light is emitted. This process takes about 3 to 5 minutes. NOTE: The metal halide arc system is very complex and requires a seasoning period of 100 hours operation for all of its components to stabilize. At first the colors produced by the bulb may vary, but once, the system is seasoned, clear white light appears.

If a power surge occurs and the lamp goes out, or if the lamp is turned off, it will take 5 to 15 minutes for the lamp to restart. The gases inside the arc tube must cool before restarting. If the lamp is on a timer, it will restart automatically. There is no need to turn the timer on or off manually.

When the lamp is started, incredible voltage is necessary for the initial ionization process to take place. Turning the lamp on and off more than once a day causes UNNECESSARY STRESS on the HID system and WILL SHORTEN ITS LIFE.

CAUTION: If outer bulb shatters, turn off (un-plug) lamp immediately. Do not look at or get near the lamp until it cools down. When the outer bulb breaks, it is no longer able to absorb ultraviolet radiation. This radiation is very harmful and will burn skin and eyes if exposed. BE CAREFUL!

Metal halides operate most efficiently in a vertical +/- 15° position (see Diagram A). When operated in positions other than +/- 15° of vertical, lamp wattage, lumen output and life will decrease; the arc bends, creating non-uniform heating of the arc tube wall; the result is less efficient operation and shorter life. There are special lamps made to operate in the horizontal or any position other than +/- 10° (see Diagram B). These bulbs have *HOR* stamped on the crown or base. *HOR* IS NOT AN ABBREVIATION FOR HORTICULTURE! IT REFERS TO HORIZONTAL!

Metalarc Lamps - Burning Positions

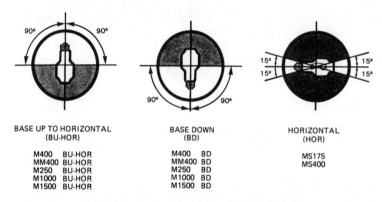

BASE UP TO HORIZONTAL (BU-HOR)	BASE DOWN (BD)	HORIZONTAL (HOR)
M400 BU-HOR MM400 BU-HOR M250 BU-HOR M1000 BU-HOR M1500 BU-HOR	M400 BD MM400 BD M250 BD M1000 BD M1500 BD	MS175 MS400

Metalarc Lamps — Burning Positions

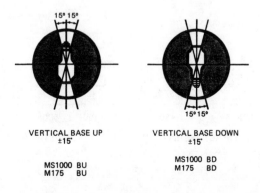

VERTICAL BASE UP ±15°	VERTICAL BASE DOWN ±15°
MS1000 BU M175 BU	MS1000 BD M175 BD

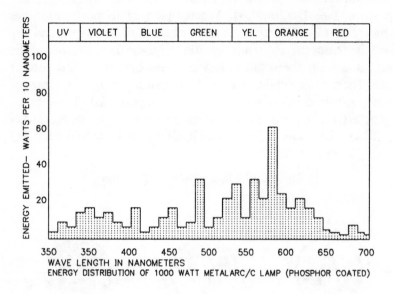

ENERGY DISTRIBUTION OF 1000 WATT METALARC/C LAMP (PHOSPHOR COATED)

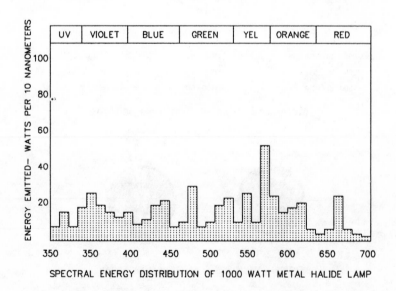

SPECTRAL ENERGY DISTRIBUTION OF 1000 WATT METAL HALIDE LAMP

Lumen Miantenance and Life

Metal halides have very good lumen maintenance and a long life. The decline in lumen output over the lamp's life is very gradual. The average life of a halide is about 12,000 hours - almost two years of daily operation at 18 hours. Many will last

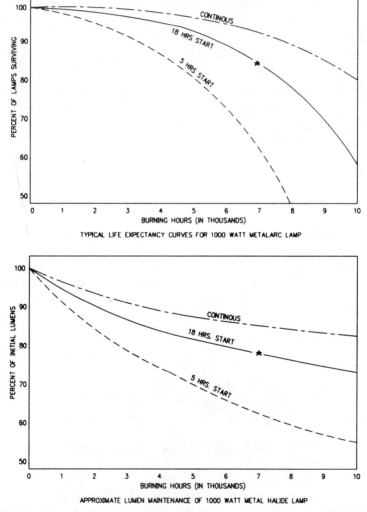

TYPICAL LIFE EXPECTANCY CURVES FOR 1000 WATT METALARC LAMP

APPROXIMATE LUMEN MAINTENANCE OF 1000 WATT METAL HALIDE LAMP

★ Successful gardeners change the bulb before it burns out. This is about every 12 to 18 months or 6,500 hours. This ensures maximum light intensity.

even longer. The lamp has reached the end of its life when it fails to start or come up to full brilliance. This is usually caused by deterioration of lamp electrodes over time, loss of transmission of the arc tube from blackening, or shifts in the chemical balance of the metals in the arc tube. I do not advise waiting until the bulb is burned out before changing it. An old bulb is inefficient and costly. Replace bulbs about every 12 to 18 months or 6,500 hours. Electrode deterioration is greatest during starting and is usually the reason for the end of lamp life. DO NOT START THE HALIDE MORE THAN ONCE A DAY, AND DO USE A TIMER!

The halide may produce a stroboscopic (flashing) effect. The light will appear bright, then dim, bright, dim, etc. This flashing is the result of the arc being extinguished 120 times every second. Illumination usually remains constant, but it may pulsate a little. This is normal and nothing to worry about.

Halide Ballasts

Read "About Ballasts" pages 42-47. The ballast for a 1000-watt halide will operate *standard, clear* and *phosphor-coated* and *super,clear* and *phosphor-coated* halides on a 110- or 220-volt current. A different ballast is required for 400-watt halides; it will operate all 400-watt halides: super or standard, clear or phosphor-coated. The ballasts *must be* specifically designed for the 400- or 1000-watt halides, since their starting and operating requirements are unique. photo and more on 400 watt horizontal lamps.

This photo of a halide ballast shows a transformer on the left and the small can on the right is a capacitor.

High Pressure Sodium Lamps

The most impressive fact about the 1000-watt **high pressure sodium** vapor lamp is that it produces 140,000 initial lumens. That's one brilliant light! The HP sodium is also the most efficient HID lamp available. It comes in 35, 50, 70, 100, 150, 200, 250, 310, 400 and 1000 wattages. All, may be either clear or phosphor-coated except the 200- and 1000-watt bulbs (which are available only clear). All HP sodium vapor lamps have their own unique ballast. HP sodium lamps are manufactured by

This horizontal 400 watt HP sodium lamp employs a beam splitter, which is hung below the bulb on a chain to split the light over the walkways.

High Pressure Sodium Lamps G.E. (Lucalox),
Sylvania (Lumalux)[6] and Westinghouse (Ceramalux)[7]. As with
the halides, most gardeners find the best value is with the
1000-watt HP sodium rather than the 400-watt.

The HP sodium lamp emits an orange-like glow that is
sometimes compared to the *harvest* sun. The color spectrum is
highest in the yellow, orange and red end. These colors promote
flower production and stem elongation.

Light from the red end of the spectrum stimulates floral hormones within the plant, promoting more flower production.
When using an HP sodium lamp, flower volume and weight may
increase 20 percent or more, depending on variety of seed and
growing conditions. Many gardeners, using a 10-by-10-foot
room, will retain the 1000-watt halide and add a 1000-watt
sodium during flowering. This not only more than *doubles*
available light, but increases the red end of the spectrum, causing flowers to form and grow like crazy. This 1:1 ratio (one
halide and one HP sodium) is a popular combination for flowering.

The HP sodium is the only practical lamp to use in a
greenhouse. Since the sun provides all the blue light necessary,
the HP sodium is used during low-light hours and during total
darkness.

Operation and Construction

The HP sodium lamp produces light by passing electricity
through vaporized sodium and mercury within an arc tube (1). A
small quantity of xenon gas, used for starting, is also included in
the arc tube. The HP sodium lamp is totally different from the
metal halide in its physical, electrical and color spectrum

---

[6] The Lumalux comes in 150, 215, 360, and 880 wattages and may be used only in certain 220-volt
mercury vapor systems. Sylvania makes a ballast tester that tests mercury vapor sockets and ballasts
for Unalux retrofit capabilities. The mercury vapor sockets and ballasts are cheaper, but the largest
Unalux (880 watts) has much lower lumen output than the standard 1000-watt HP sodium vapor. If
using a Unalux, consult the nearest Sylvania sales office for further information.

[7] The Ceramalux has a color-corrected spectrum. It produces a little more blue than other HP
sodiums.

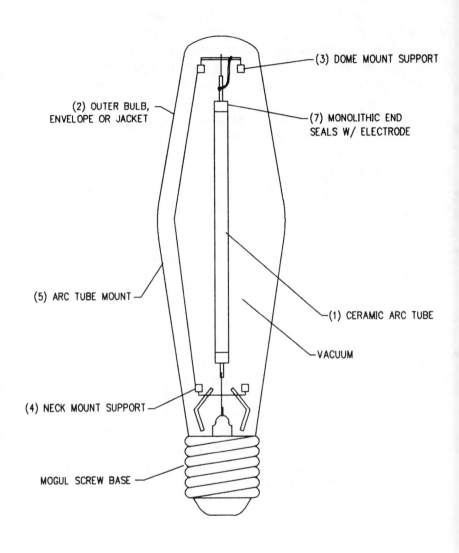

Diagram of a high pressure sodium lamp.

characteristics. An electronic starter works with the magnetic component of the ballast to supply a short, high-voltage pulse. This electrical pulse vaporizes the xenon gas and initiates the starting process, which takes 3 to 4 minutes. Electricity passes or *arcs* between the two main electrodes (6) and (7). If the lamp is turned off, or power surge occurs and the lamp goes out, the gases in the tube will usually need to cool 3 to 15 minutes before restarting is possible. As with the metal halides, if the HP sodium is on a timer, it will restart automatically.

Like the metal halide, the HP sodium has a two bulb construction, with an outer protective bulb (2) and inner arc tube (1). The arc tube's frame is mounted (5) by spring supports in the dome (3) and neck (4). The outer bulb or *jacket* protects the arc tube from damage and contains a vacuum, reducing heat loss from the arc tube. The sodium, mercury and xenon gas are contained within the arc tube and have a constant operating temperature, and the lamp may be operated in any position (360°). However, most growers prefer to hang the lamp overhead in a vertical operating position.

Life and Lumen Maintenance

HP sodium lamps have the longest life and best lumen maintenance of all HID lamps. Eventually the sodium bleeds out through the arc tube; over a long period of daily use, the ratio of sodium to mercury changes, causing the voltage in the arc to rise. Finally the arc tube's operating voltage will rise higher than the ballast is able to sustain. At this point, the lamp will start, warm up to full intensity, then go out. This sequence is then repeated over and over, signaling the end of the lamp's life. The life of a 1000-watt HP sodium lamp will be about 24,000 hours, or five years operating at 12 hours a day. As with other HID's, HP sodiums should be replaced before the end of their rated life.

HP Sodium Ballasts

Read "About Ballasts," pages 42-47. a special ballast is required specifically for the 400- or 1000-watt HP sodium lamp. The lamp has unique operating voltages and currents during start up and operation. These voltages and currents do not correspond to similar wattages of other HID lamps. As with the halide ballast, to save money and time I recommend purchasing it from an HID lamp store rather than in a component kit.

LIFE AND LUMEN MAINTENANCE

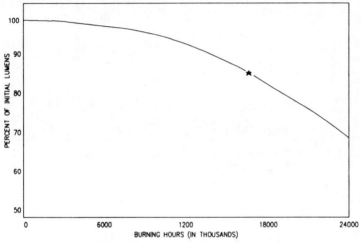

APPROXIMATE LUMEN MAINTENANCE OF HP SODIUM LAMP

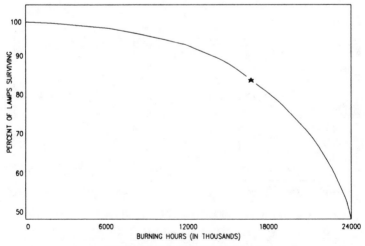

MORALITY CURVE OF 1000 WATT HP SODIUM LAMP

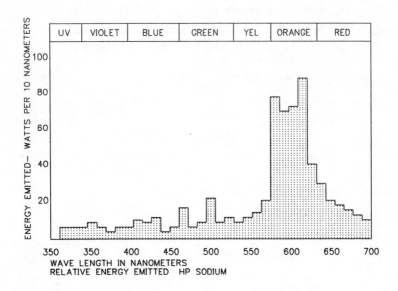

RELATIVE ENERGY EMITTED HP SODIUM

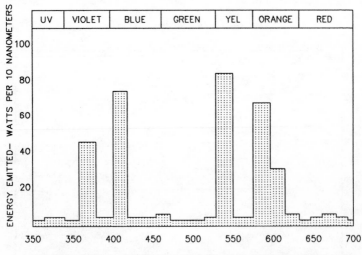

SPECTRAL ENERGY DISTRIBUTION OF 1000 WATT MERCURY VAPOR LAMP

Other Lamps

Incandescent Lamps

The incandescent lamp is the electric lamp invented by Thomas Edison. Light is produced by sending electricity through the filament, a very fine wire inside the bulb. The filament resists the flow of electricity, heating it to incandescence (causing it to glow). Incandescent bulbs work on ordinary household current and require no ballast. Filaments may be of many shapes and sizes, but are nearly always made of tough, heat-resistant tungsten. They come in a wide range of wattages and constructions for special applications. Most lamps used in homes for Christmas trees, interior lighting and refrigerators are incandescent lamps.

There are many types of incandescent lamps. They usually use a tungsten filament with a glass bulb construction and threaded base that fits household sockets. The bulb is usually under a vacuum or contains some type of gas to minimize wear on the filament.

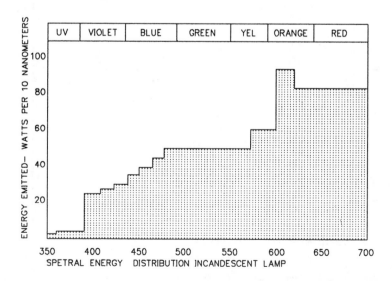

SPETRAL ENERGY DISTRIBUTION INCANDESCENT LAMP

Most incandescents have a spectrum in the far red end, but there are some incandescent grow lamps that have a more even spectrum. Incandescent lamps are expensive to operate and produce so few lumens per watt that they are not really worth using. They are most efficiently used as a source of bottom or soil heat for clones rooting under cool fluorescents. A few gardeners use incandescents during flowering to help promote more and heavier flowers.

Tungsten Halogen Lamps

The tungsten halogen lamp was originally called the *iodine quartz* lamp. This is because the outer tube is made of heat-resistant quartz and the main gas inside the quartz tube was iodine, one of the five halogens . There are many variations to this quartz halogen or quartz tungsten lamp. Today bromine, also one of the halogens, is used most often in the

TUNGSTEN HALOGEN LAMPS

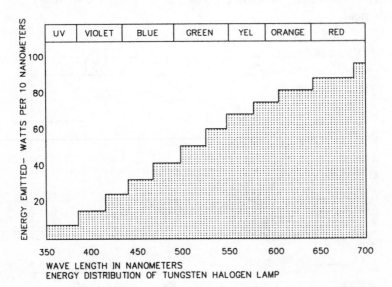

ENERGY DISTRIBUTION OF TUNGSTEN HALOGEN LAMP

lamps, so the name "halogen" covers all of the gases in the arc tube. Tungsten lamps are very similar to incandescents. They use a tungsten wire filament, use a sealed bulb and are very expensive to operate: Their lumen-per-watt output is very low. Tungsten halogens, like incandescents, run on 110-volt current and require no ballast. They are as inefficient to operate as incandescents (See Lumens per Watt graph page 39). Their color spectrum is in the far red end, with 10 to 15 percent in the visible spectrum.

LP Sodium Lamps

Low-Pressure (LP) sodium lamps come in 55, 90, 135 and 180 wattages. Their lumen per watt conversion is the highest of all lamps on the market today. More careful inspection of the color spectrum chart above shows that it is *monochromatic*, or produces light only in one very narrow portion of the spectrum, at 589 nm. The LP sodium lamp emits a yellow glow. Colors are not distinguished and appear as tones.

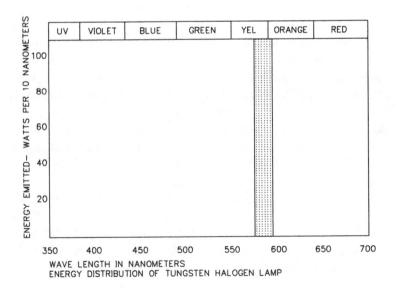

ENERGY DISTRIBUTION OF TUNGSTEN HALOGEN LAMP

LP sodium lamps are supplied by Westinghouse. Their main use in industry has been for security or warehouse light.

Each wattage requires its own unique ballast and fixture. The ballast or transformer regulates electric current and is located inside the fixture. The fixture for a 180 watt lamp is just a little larger than a fixture for two 40 watt 4-foot fluorescent tubes.

Westinghouse (Philips Corp.) is the only supplier of LP sodium lamps. The ballast and fixture for an LP sodium cost about $200. As with other lamps, I advise purchasing the lamp, ballast and fixture from a reputable supplier and in the same package.

The LP sodium must be used with a metal halide lamp to stimulate photosynthesis and chlorophyll synthesis. LP sodium lamps work well for side lighting or in areas with high electrical rates.

This lamp has the unique quality of maintaining 100 percent of its lumen output throughout its life. There is no gradual decrease in the lumen output over time as with other discharge lamps. The LP sodium lamp will burn out all at once; this happens at about 18,000 hours.

The basic design of the LP sodium lamp is essentially the same as it was when first introduced to the market in 1932. Like HID lamps, the LP sodium has a two-bulb construction. The arc tube is made of lime borate glass and contains a mixture of neon, argon and pure sodium metal. The neon and argon begin to glow after electricity enters the arc tube. As the gas mixture gives off increasing amounts of heat, the sodium metal, which is still in the solid form, begins to vaporize. A yellowish glow is soon emitted from the vaporized sodium.

Fixtures can be lightweight plastic due to low outside bulb temperatures. The LP sodium lamp conserves energy by keeping heat inside the lamp. A special reflective coating on the outer tube allows light to pass out while heat remains inside. A vacuum is formed between the outer and inner tubes, conserving heat even more.

To ensure long life of the lamp, it should be operated horizontally. Do not let it operate at more than 20 percent + /- off horizontal.

Pure sodium metal will react with air or water and explode. There is about one gram of sodium in a 180 watt LP sodium lamp - not enough to cause a big explosion, but enough to warrant careful handling. When disposing of an LP sodium bulb, place it in a dry, plastic garbage can and break it.

Fluorescent Lamps

Until HID's were developed, fluorescent light was the most efficient and widely used form of artificial light available to the indoor gardener. Some fluorescents boast a spectrum almost

This orchid grower uses fluorescent lamps to help illuminate her greenhouse.

identical to that of the sun, but they are not bright enough to grow high-light plants efficiently. Today, these lamps are most efficiently used as a light source to root cuttings. Fluorescent lamps are manufactured in long glass tubes or circle-line tubes, and are used in many commercial and residential buildings. They come in a wide variety of sizes: lengths of 18 inches 24 inches 36 inches, 48inches, 72 inches and 96 inches, and standard circline-tube diameters of 8 ¼ inches, 12 inches and 16 inches. Longer tubes are better to use than short ones since there is a light loss at the ends of tubes. The 4-foot and 8-foot tubes and the easiest to handle and most readily available.

Fluorescent tubes come in several wattages or outputs, and ballasts have different wattages. Both tubes and ballasts are made by several companies. The *standard* or *regular* tubes use about 10 watts per linear foot. A 4-foot tube uses about 40 watts, 8-foot, 80 watts, etc. High-Output (HO) tubes use about 50 percent more watts per linear foot and emit about 40 percent more light than the *standard*. These fluorescents require a special ballast and end caps. Very High Output (VHO) use almost three times as much electricity, and produce more than twice as much light as the *standard* fluorescent. VHO fluorescents are more expensive and more difficult to find. VHO tubes also require a special ballast. They may be ordered from the manufacturer or purchased from the wholesaler.

Fluorescent lamps work very well to root cuttings. They supply cool, diffused light in the proper color spectrum to promote root growth. The VHO are more expensive, but are preferred for their high lumen output. None the less, if low on capital, a gardener may use any fluorescent lamp to root cuttings. The only drawback to using the less luminous *standard* or HO fluorescents is that cuttings may take a few days longer to root. Fluorescents, like HID's, diminish in intensity with distance from the light source. Since fluorescents produce much less light than HID's, they must be very close 2 to four inches to the plants for best results.

In many cases as when there are many plant varieties and ages of plants under a fluorescent, it is easier to retain the lamp at one overhead level and move the plants closer to the lamp by placing them on a block to elevate then.

A few gardeners hang extra fluorescent lamps with HID's to increase light intensity. This works well, but I have found fluorescents to be more trouble than they are worth for anything but rooting cuttings. Fluorescent tubes are most effective when mounted above plants if they are the sole source of light. When tubes are placed vertically around plants, they do not promote straight, even growth. If used with bright halides, fluorescents can be used as side lighting for lower leaves, but it is a difficult job to mount the fluorescents close enough to the plants to do any good. Fluorescents may also shade plants from HID light and generally get in the way.

Fluorescents have a wide variety of spectrums. Sylvania makes the Gro-Lux and the Wide Spectrum Gro-Lux. The Standard Gro-Lux is the lamp to use for starting clones or seedlings. It is designed to be used as the *only* source of light, having the full spectrum necessary for photosynthesis and chlorophyll production. The Wide Spectrum Gro-Lux is designed to supplement natural light and covers the blue to far red regions. Westinghouse makes the Agro-Light, which produces a very similar spectrum to the sun's. Warm White and Cool White bulbs used together, make excellent lamps to root clones under, especially if they are VHO.

Power twist or groove type lamps offer additional lumens in the same amount of linear space. The deep, wide grooves (See drawing page 69) give more glass surface area and more light output. Several companies market *power-twist* fluorescents.

Fluorescent bulbs and fixtures are relatively inexpensive. Two, 4-foot bulbs and a fixture will usually cost from $20 to $30. Clones root best with 18 hours of fluorescent light.

"Side mount" reflectors have a partition between the light tubes. This partition eliminates the other and subsequent light loss that occurs when the tubes are side by side.

Construction and Operation

Like the HID family, fluorescents require an appropriate fixture, containing a ballast (much smaller than the HID ballast) and the ordinary 110-or 120-volt house current. The fixture is usually integrated into the reflective hood. There are several types of fixtures. Some have one pin on each end; others are two pin types. If purchasing new tubes, make sure -the bulb fits the fixture. The fixture may contain one, two or four tubes.

The ballast, which is contained in the fixture, radiates almost all of the heat produced by the system. The ballast is located far enough away from *standard* tubes that plants can actually touch them without being burned. VHO tubes may burn tender plants if they get too close.

The **ballast** or transformer regulates electricity. Most ballasts and fixtures are for use with *standard* 40- or 80-watt tubes. *Special ballasts are required for VHO* fluorescent tubes. The operating requirements of *VHO* lamps are greater, due to the in-

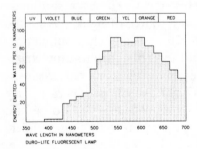

DURO-LITE FLUORESCENT LAMP

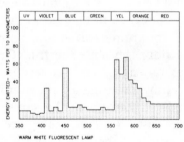

WARM WHITE FLUORESCENT LAMP

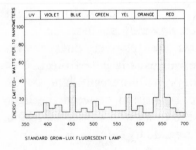

STANDARD GROW-LUX FLUORESCENT LAMP

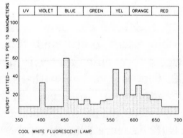

COOL WHITE FLUORESCENT LAMP

crease in current, than for standard fluorescents. I advise ordering the *VHO* ballast, fixture and tubes at the same time and from a reputable supplier.

The ballast reduces the current in the tube to the operating voltage required by a particular lamp. The ballast will normally last 10 to 12 years. *Used* fluorescent fixtures (unlike *used* mercury vapor ballasts) are generally acceptable. The end of life is usually accompanied by smoke and a disagreeable chemical odor. When the ballast burns out, remove it (or take the entire fixture to the nearest electrical supply store) and buy a new one to replace it. Be very careful if the ballast has brown slime or sludge on or around it. This sludge could possibly contain PCB's. If the ballast contains the sludge, throw it away! Most modern fluorescents are self-starting, but older fluorescents require a special starter. This starter may be integrated into the body of the fixture and hidden from view, or be a small metal tube (about an inch in diameter and half an inch long), located at the end of the fixture on the underside. The latter starters are replaceable; the former require a trip to the electrical store.

If the ballast creates too much heat, remove it from the fixture and place it in a remote location. Just splice the wires. Secure the remote ballast away from water and where heat will not cause damage.

Most electrical supply stores are able to test starters. If your fluorescent fixture does not work, and you are not well versed in fluorescent troubleshooting, take it to the nearest electric store and ask for advice. Make sure they test each component and tell you why it should be replaced.

The tubular glass bulb is coated on the inside with phosphor. The mix of phosphorescent chemicals in the coating and the gases contained within determine the spectrum of colors emitted by the lamp. The bulb contains a blend of inert gases: argon, neon or krypton and mercury vapor, sealed under low pressure. Electricity arcs between the two electrodes, located at each end of the tube, stimulating the phosphor to emit light. The light emission is strongest near the center of the tube and somewhat less at the ends. If rooting just a few cuttings, place them under the center of the fixture for best results.

Once the fluorescent is turned on, it will take a few seconds for the bulb to warm up before an arc can be struck through the tube. Fluorescents blacken with age, losing intensity. I recommend replacing bulbs when they reach 70 percent of their stated service life listed on the package or label. A flickering light is about to burn out and should be replaced. Life expectancy ranges from 9,000 hours (1 1/4 years at 18 hours daily operation) with *VHO* tubes to 18,000 hours (2 ½ years at 18 hours daily operation) with the *standard*.

Change fluorescents every 9 to 12 months. Use a grease pencil to mark the date that you install any light. mark the bulb or tube near the end or base.

About Bulbs

HID bulbs are tough and durable. They survive being shipped many miles by uncaring carriers. Once the bulb has been used a few hours, the arc tube blackens and the internal parts become somewhat brittle. After a bulb has been used several hundred hours, a good bump will substantially shorten its life and lessen its luminescence.

Never remove a warm lamp. The heat makes them expand in the socket. A hot bulb is more difficult to remove and must be forced. *vaseline or a special electrical lubricant may be smeared lightly (it takes only a dash) around the mogul socket base to facilitate screwing it in and out.

Always keep the bulb clean. Wait for it to cool and wipe it off every 2-4 weeks with a clean cloth. Dirt will lower lumen output.

Store HID's that are not being used in the same box they came in.

Please read the following rules of disposal before laying a faithful HID to rest:

1. Break the lamp outdoors in a container. Hit it a couple of inches from the base with a hard object. Take care to avoid shattering glass, as the bulbs are under vacuum.

2. The lamps contain materials that are harmful to the skin, so contact should be avoided and protective clothing should be used.

3. Once the lamp is broken, place it in a plastic bag, then throw it away.

4. Under no conditions place the bulb in a fire.

Reflective Light

Reflective light may also increase light intensity by as much as 30 percent. A large white 4-foot reflective hood over the lamp and flat white walls will triple the growing area. EXAMPLE: Using a 1000-watt *super* metal halide with a small, 2-foot hood and no reflective walls and ceiling, the effective growing area is only 36 square feet. When a large 40-foot white reflective hood and flat white walls and ceiling are added, effective growing area is increased to 100 square feet.

Marty from Light Manufacturing assembles a new parabolic hood with a power screwdriver.

Reflective hoods come in all shapes and sizes. The main things to look for in a hood are the size, the reflective ability and the specific application. Large, 4-foot hoods work very well. The light has a good chance to spread out and not be reflected around within the walls of the hood. These hoods are very popular because they are inexpensive and provide the maximum amount of reflection for the least amount of money. The polished parabolic reflectors are dome-shaped. They tend to concentrate the light directly under the source. They work well with *light balancers* that concentrate intense light directly over plants.

HP sodium lamps mounted horizontally use a small, very effective hood for greenhouse culture. The hood is mounted just a few inches over the long horizontal HP sodium so that all the light is reflected down toward the plant beds but the small hood creates a minimum shadow. One manufacturer's hood for its HP sodium closes to protect the lamp from water spray when irrigating.

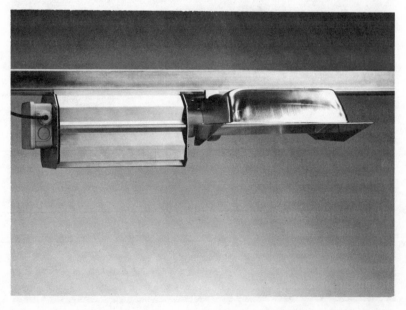

The reflective hood on this horizontal 400 watt HP sodium lamp spreads out the light into a broad beam.

There are many things the hoods may be covered with or constructed from. First and foremost, they should be made of a material that is lightweight, since they will be hanging from the ceiling. The hood should have a heat vent outlet around the bulb so it will not tend to collect heat. Excessive heat around the bulb could cause premature burn-out.

The hoods may be made of galvanized steel, polished or painted aluminum. The color is usually flat white, but some companies paint them glossy white (see discussion below on "Flat White"). Sheet metal hoods tend to be much less expensive than aluminum or stainless steel. The other differences are similar to the differences between flat white paint and reflective Mylar, discussed later. Polished aluminum hoods scratch easily and are expensive. Another type of hood that is increasing in popularity has many triangular facets for the light to bounce off. Here again the hood cost far outweighs the benefits.

The 4-foot hoods are usually manufactured in two or four parts. The smaller size facilitates shipping and handling. The customer assembles the hood with small screws and nuts.

This hood is a cross between the parabolic and the cone shaped reflective hoods.

One option is to remove the reflective hood if the garden is too tall. With no hood, the lamp burns cooler, and the white ceiling provides reflection, but somewhat less than a reflective hood. If the lamp is too close to the ceiling (less than 24 inches) install a non-flammable heat shield to protect the ceiling. See instruction No. 2 in "Setting Up the Lamp" page 92.

White, reflective walls should be 12 inches or less from the plants for optimum reflection. Ideally, the walls should be taken to the plants. This way, the walls *always* provide the optimum amount of reflection. The easiest way to install mobile walls is to hang the lamp near the corner of a room. Use the two walls in the corner as reflective walls. The two outside walls are mobile. They will need to be fabricated out of light plywood, sheet rock, or white Visqueen plastic.

White Visqueen plastic is a great way to white out a room. People use it for several reasons: It is inexpensive, expandable, removable and reusable. It may also be used to construct walls. This is very handy when a gardener wants to partition off one or several rooms. The walls can expand as the garden grows. The plastic is waterproof, so it may be used on the walls as well as the floor. It is easy to work with. It may be cut with scissors or a knife, stapled, nailed or taped. Generally, people hang the

The small vertical reflectors on the far right direct the light down towards the plants and away from the greenhouse windows.

plastic sheets wrapped around a 1-by-2 nailed to the ceiling. The white Visqueen actually forms a *mobile* wall around the garden. It is easy to keep the walls close to the plants for optimum reflection. To make the white walls opaque, hang black Visqueen on the outside. The dead air space between the two types of Visqueen increases insulation.

The only disadvantages of white Visqueen plastic are that it is not as reflective as flat white paint, it may get brittle after a couple of years of use under an HID lamp, and it is difficult to find at retail outlets.

Whitewash is an inexpensive alternative to white paint. It is a little messy to apply, and it is thin, so several coats will have to be applied. If fungus or moisture is a problem, like the kind found on *wet* concrete basement walls, the mess is worth the trouble. For mixing directions, see page 110.

Using **flat white paint** is one of the simplest, least expensive, most efficient ways to create optimum reflection. Artist's white paint is more expensive, but *very* reflective. It is recommended for reflective hoods. Semi-gloss white is not quite as reflective as flat white, but it is much easier to wash and keep clean. Whatever type of white is used, a fungus-inhibiting agent should be added before the paint is mixed. A gallon of good flat white paint costs $15 to $20. One gallon should be enough to *white out* the average grow room. Use a primer to prevent *bleed through* of stains or if walls are rough and unpainted. The vent fan should be installed before painting. Fumes can cause headaches and nausea.

REFLECTIVE CHART

Material	Percentage of Light Reflected
Reflective Mylar	90 - 95
Flat white paint	85 - 93
Semi-gloss white	75 - 80
Flat yellow	70 - 80
Aluminum foil	70 - 75
Black	less than 10

Why is flat white so reflective? When light shines on a green object, green pigment in the object absorbs all colors but green from the spectrum and the green light is reflected. This is why we see the color green. Flat white contains little or no light-absorbing pigment. Flat white essentially absorbs no light; it is almost all reflected, except for a small amount that somehow gets lost. Flat white is whiter and reflects better than glossy white. Glossy white is manufactured with more light-absorbing varnish. The glossy surface lends itself to bright spots and glare. Flat white contains less varnish and inhibits the path of reflective light much less. It also has a mat texture, actually providing more reflective surface.

Reflective Mylar provides one of the most reflective surfaces possible. It looks like a very thin mirror. Unlike light absorbing paint, reflective Mylar reflects almost all light. It is simply taped or tacked to the wall. The trick to setting it up is to get it flat against the wall. When it is loose or wavy, light is reflected poorly.

Aluminum foil is one of the worst reflective surfaces possible. The foil always crinkles up, reflecting light in the wrong directions, actually wasting light. It also reflects more ultraviolet rays than other surfaces. Take a look at the reflective chart. Aluminum foil is not very reflective!

More Growing Light for Less Money

There are several ways of getting a more *even* distribution of light in the garden. This can be accomplished by using several 400-watt HID's, installing side lighting or rotating the plants. The most efficient way is to replicate the movement of the sun through the sky. This is done two basic ways. Both methods move the lamp back and forth overhead so it covers more area. The advantages to this are:

1. The plants get a more even distribution of light and grow more evenly. When the HID is stationary, plants tend to grow

toward the lamp. When the lamp is always in the same place, the plants grow up around it, severely shading the rest of the garden. Rotating the plants every few days so they receive more even light distribution would solve this problem. It is much easier to employ one of the following methods to move the *lamp* rather than the *plants*.

2. A lamp moving overhead increases the *intense* light that the majority of plants receive. This is not a substitute for more lumens from an additional lamp. It is a more efficient way to use an HID. Since the lamp will be directly above more plants, they all will receive more direct, intense light. Young clones and seedlings may s-t-r-e-t-c-h, becoming leggy, to get more light if the lamp travels too far away. Start using the *light balancers* after the plants are 12 inches tall and have several sets of leaves.

3. Light is received by the plants from more directions. Total light energy is optimum for all plants, as long as one plant is not shading another. This promotes even growth.

Light Balancers

A light balancer is a device to move a lamp back and forth across the ceiling of a grow room to provide more *balanced* light coverage. The methods employed to move the lamp across the ceiling may be motorized or manual, fast moving or moving on- ly once or twice a day. The speed at which the lamp moves is of

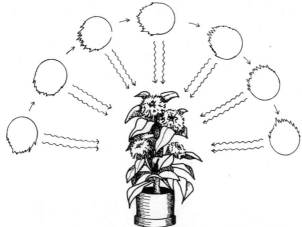

This drawing simulates the path of the sun over a single plant.

minimal importance. But the more often it traverses the garden, the more even the profile of the garden will be and the closer plants can be to the lamp. The unit should not move so fast that the lamp wobbles, making it unstable. It is not necessary for the lamp to move exactly like the sun; whether the lamp moves from east to west is of no consequence. The path it takes should be a consistent one that distributes light evenly. If the lamp is allowed to stay in the same position for two or three days before it is moved, plants will get uneven light distribution. Motorized units have an advantage in this respect, since they are moving at a constant rate all the time.

These *light balancers* may be purchased from an ever-increasing number of suppliers or constructed by the gardener. There are only two things to be on the lookout for when constructing your own. (1) strength and (2) ease of movement. First and foremost, the rigging overhead must be able to support the weight of the lamp and hood. If the system were to come crashing down on the garden it could cause a real problem. Besides wrecking your precious garden, it very well could start a fire. Make sure the thing is secured to the ceiling! The electric cord should not slow down or affect the movement of the light balancer in any way. Second, the system should be easy to move. If it is easy to move, chances are that you will move it. Homemade made *light balancers* work best for gardeners who are able to look after their garden two or three times a day, moving the lamp every time.

There are two basic kinds of *light balancers*. (1) The first is a *linear* system. These systems move in a straight line simulating the sun's path through the heavens. This system increases the intense light to plants in a *linear* oval. The square footage covered by the system depends on the length of the track and the number of lamps employed. The system uses a track affixed to the ceiling. The lamp moves back and forth across the ceiling, guided by the track. The lamp is hooked to the *balancer* with an extendible chain or cord so it can be as close as possible to the plants. These units vary as to the length and speed the lamp travels. Some are designed for one lamp, while others are able to move

The Solar Shuttle was the first light track on the market.

Close up of the clutch and brushes of the Sun Circle.

Close up of the motor and transporting chain of the Solar Shuttle.

LIGHT IS THE MOST CRITICAL LIMITING FACTOR TO PLANT GROWTH.

The Sun Circle is the only light balancer that rotates lamps in a complete 360° circle.

six lamps efficiently. A 6-foot *linear light balancer* increases optimum coverage of light from 36 to 72 square feet.

A homemade alternative to the commercial *linear* unit is the
clothesline unit. It is simple to construct. Eyebolts are attached
at opposite ends of the ceiling or ceiling corners. Pulleys are attached to the eyebolts. Between the pulleys, a small diameter,
heavy-duty nylon cord is strung in a loop. The HID is attached
to the bottom of the loop. This is just like many clotheslines used in the city, with access from only one end. After the lamp is
mounted on the looped cord, it may be moved back and forth as
often as desirable - the more often the better. Another variation
of the principle stretches a nylon cord across the ceiling with a
single pulley attached to it. Attach the lamp to the pulley, then
move the lamp back and forth on the pulley overhead. One in-
dustrious person made a *balancer* out of an old garage door
opener. The possibilities are endless. When using these types of
units, make sure to watch the plant profile. Try to give the
garden the most even distribution of light possible.

The second type is the *arc* method. It rotates in a pivoting motion. The unit swivels from a boom on a wall or the ceiling
overhead. The lamp(s) take an *arc*-shaped path, covering a little
more area than the linear method.

There are two basic types of *arc* method: (1) wall mount units
that swing back and forth in a partial arc on a motorized hinge.
(2) ceiling mount units that swivel back and forth on a full or
partial arc. The lamp(s) in both types are suspended by an adjustable chain attached to a telescoping boom(s).

Another type of *arc* method is a homemade model employing
1 inch plumbing pipes. It bolts to the ceiling or is mounted on a
wooden frame that is in turn affixed to the ceiling. This unit,
like the clothesline unit, is non-motorized. The gardener simply
moves the lamp to a different location daily or as often as
necessary to maintain an even garden profile.

Some of the advantages to using a commercial *light balancer*
are that it gives more *intense* light to more plants for less money.
Light balancers make it possible to use fewer lamps and get the
same yield. An increase of 25 to 35 percent in intense light

coverage is afforded by light balancers. Two lamps mounted on a motorized *light balancer* will do the job of three stationary lamps. I prefer motorized *light balancers* because they keep an even garden profile. Since the HID is already drawing about 9.2 amperes, and it is hooked up to a 15- or 20-ampere circuit, it would take a new circuit to hang up another HID. The commercial *balancer* is easily plugged into the same timer and socket as the lamp. Since the motor for the *balancer* uses about one ampere (75 to 100 watts) of current, it may be attached to the same circuit as the lamp with little risk of overload.

Light balancers are normally used for only part of a plant's life. When there are just a few plants, they are huddled directly under the lamp. Using a *balancer* on too many seedlings or clones causes them to s-t-r-e-t-c-h. One of the good things about homemade units is they do not have a particular cycle they must complete. They are operated by hand and may be placed in any location for as long as desired.

Planter boxes or containers on wheels offer a good alternative to *light balancers*. The containers are rotated daily. The wheels make this job easy. The light reaches every corner of the garden without having to move the lamp. This method has essentially the same effect as moving the lamp overhead, but is more work because *all* plants have to be moved, rather than only one or two lamps.

The 400-watt bulbs offer more even light distribution and the lamp can be closer to the plants since they have less heat buildup than 1000-watt HID's. The 400-watt bulbs offer certain advantages, especially if space is a problem. One gardener uses two of them in a narrow 4-by-8-foot room with amazing success. Another gardener has the brightest closet in town! The 400-watt halides do have a longer life than the 1000-watt lamps, but share the same lumen maintenance curve. For the amount of lumens produced, their initial cost is much higher. However, their life is twice as long - about 20,000 hours. If the 400-watt HID's give you the best value for *balanced light*, several ballasts may be looped together on the same 220 volt circuit. Ask an electrician for help. Do not use a 400-watt lamp in a 1000-watt system! It will work for the first 24 to 48 hours, then BOOM! The lamp and maybe the ballast will stop working and who-knows-what else!

Side lighting is another way to *balance* light. Of course this uses more electricity, but it increases the amount of light available to the plants. Probably the most efficient lamp to use in this case is the low-pressure LP sodium, since its lumens-per-watt conversion is the best there is. The lamps are mounted where light intensity is marginal, along the walls, to provide side light. Fluorescent lamps could also be used, but the lumens-per-watt conversion is much less. Remember the LP sodiums must be used with the halide, which supplies all the blue light the plants need to balance the spectrum. If you really want to get the most intense light possible in the garden, you may want to employ all of these methods: side lighting and a *light balancer*.

Cuttings and young seedlings are huddled below the HID when small and moved into larger containers when they are crowding one another. When they are far enough apart that the light does not afford complete coverage, it is time to employ a *light balancer*. Before this time, a *light balancer* might not give them enough intense light and they may get leggy. However check with a light meter to make sure each plant variety gets an adequate light.

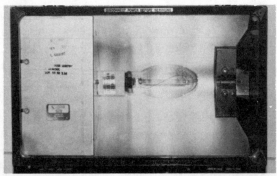

A small 250 watt HP sodium lamps will provide enough light for very small gardens or can be used for side lighting in larger gardens.

About Electricity

The basics of electricity really do not need to be understood for growing indoors, but understanding the basics may save you money, time and the shock of your life. First, simple electrical concepts and terms are defined and briefly discussed. Once these terms are understood, you will be able to see the purpose of fuses, wire thickness (gauge), amperes on a circuit, the importance of ground and the necessity to develop *safe* habits.

Before anything electrical is touched, please remember the rule below.

Alternating-Current — an electric current that reverses its direction at regularly occurring intervals.

Ampere (amp) — the measure of electricity in motion. Electricity can be looked at in absolute terms of measurement just as water can. A gallon is an absolute measure of a portion of water; a coulomb is an absolute measure of a portion of electricity. Water in motion is measured in gallons per second and electricity in motion is measured in *coulombs per second*. When an electrical current flows at one coulomb per second, we say it has *one ampere*. (I guess we could say coulomb per second, but it would sound a little weird, because everybody uses amperes!)

Breaker box — an electrical circuit box containing breaker circuit switches.

Breaker switch — an ON/OFF safety switch that will turn the electricity OFF when the circuit is OVERLOADED.

 Work backward when installing electrical components or doing wiring. Start at the bulb and work toward the plug-in. Always plug in the cord last!

Circuit — the closed path that electricity travels. If this path is interrupted, the power will go off. If this circuit is given a chance, it will travel a circular route through your body! Never give it a chance!

Conductor — something that is able to carry electricity easily. Copper, steel and water are good electrical conductors.

Direct Current – an electric current that flows in only *one* direction.

Fuse — an electrical safety device consisting of a fusible metal that MELTS and interrupts the circuit when OVERLOADED. NEVER REPLACE FUSES WITH PENNIES OR ALUMINUM FOIL! They will not melt and interrupt the circuit when overloaded. This is an easy way to start a fire!

Fuse box — an electrical circuit box containing fuses.

CAUTION! The HID lamp operated on an overloaded circuit will blow fuses, switch off breakers or burn wiring. It could wreck the HID system, even start a fire. PAY ATTENTION!

 Use only one 1000-watt HID for each 15 to 20 ampere circuit.

AMP RATING	AMPS AVAILABLE	OVERLOAD
15	13	14
20	16	17
25	20	21
30	24	25
40	32	33

Ground — a means to connect electricity to the ground or earth. Safety is the reason for ground. If a circuit is properly grounded, and the electricity travels somewhere it is not supposed to, it will go via the ground wire into the ground and be rendered harmless. Electricity will travel the path of least resistance. This path must be along the ground wire. It is all right to have several ground wires if you are really paranoid.

This drawing speaks for itself.

The ground is formed by a wire (usually green or bare copper) that runs parallel to the circuit and is attached to a metal ground stake. All the circuits in the home are then attached to the ground stake. Metal cold-water pipes serve as excellent conductors for the ground. They are all attached to one another. Water

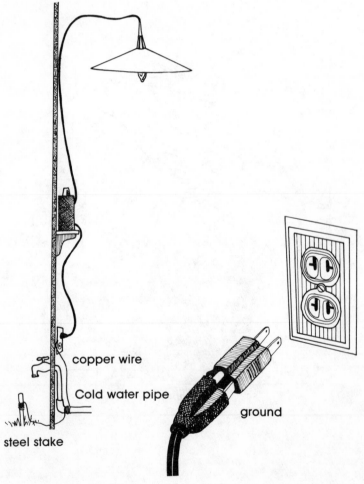

copper wire

Cold water pipe

ground

steel stake

A complete grounded circuit is essential for safety. If you use a ground adaptor, make sure the socket is grounded separately.

pipes conduct electricity well and are all in good contact with the ground.

The entire system - pipes, copper wire and metal ground stake - conduct any *misplaced* electricity safely into the ground.

The ground wire is the third wire with the big round prong on a male plug. The ground runs through the ballast all the way to the hood.

HID systems must have a ground that runs a continual path from the socket through the ballast to the main fuse box, then to the house ground. See drawing above.

Hertz — fluctuations or cycles in electricity within a conductor (wire). In the United States, alternating-current electricity runs at 60 HERTZ or cycles per second.

Ohm's Power Law — law that expresses the strength of an electric current: Volts × Amperes = Watts.

Short circuit — side or unintentional circuit formed when conductors (wires) cross. A short circuit will normally blow fuses!

Volts — air, water, gas - virtually anything can be put under pressure. Pressure is measured in pounds per square inch (PSI). Electricity is also under pressure or electrical potential; this pressure is measured in volts. Most home wiring is under the pressure of approximately 110 or 220 volts.

Watt — a measure of work. Watts measure the amount of electricity flowing in a wire. When amperes (units of electrons per second) are multiplied by volts (pressure) we get watts. 1000-watts = 1 kilowatt.

A halide lamp that draws about 9.2 amperes × 120 volts = 1104 watts. Remember Ohm's Power Law: Amps × Watts = Volts. This is strange; the answer was supposed to be 1000-watts. What is wrong? The electricity flows through the BALLAST, which takes energy to run. The energy drawn by the ballast must then amount to 1104 watts.

Watt-hours — the amount of watts used in an hour. One watt-hour is equal to one watt used for one hour. A kilowatt-hour is 1000 watt-hours. A 1000-watt HID will use one kilowatt per hour and the ballast will use about one watt. Electrical bills are charged out in KWH (See chart on Cost of Electricity, page 92).

Wire and Wiring

Electrical wire comes in all sizes (gauges), and they are indicated by number. In measuring the wire, the higher the number the smaller the wire, and the lower the number the larger the wire (See drawing below). The standard wire in most homes is 14-gauge. Wire size is important for two reasons (1) *ampacity* (2) *voltage drop. Ampacity* is the amount of amperes a wire is able to carry safely. Electricity flowing through wire creates heat. The more amps flowing, the more heat created. This heat is wasted power! To avoid this wasted power, the proper thickness of wire must be used: at least 14 gauge. It must be well insulated and must have a ground wire.

In addition, forcing too much power (amperes) through a wire also creates *voltage drop.* Voltage (pressure) is lost in the wire. For example: if you force an 18-gauge wire to carry 9.2 amperes at 120 volts not only would it heat up, maybe even blowing fuses, but the voltage at the outlet would be 120 volts while the voltage 10 feet away could be as low as 108. Would you like to pay for this unused 12 volts? The farther electricity travels, the more heat is generated and the more voltage drops.

Voltage drop not only is wasteful, but causes lamps to function very inefficiently. *A lamp designed to work at 120 volts that receives only 108 volts (90 percent of the power it was intended to operate at) would produce only 70 percent of the normal light.* ALL THIS MEANS: Use at least 14-gauge wire for any extension cords and if the cord is to carry power over 60 feet, use 12-gauge wire.

● ● ● ● ● ·
8   10 12 14 16 18

Wire is rated by number; the smaller the number, the larger the wire.

Show chart that gives wire and amp ratings

A simple electrical circuit requires two wires. One wire runs from the source of power to the load (from the electrical outlet to a ballast for example), and the other wire completes the circuit back to the source of power. There always should be a third or ground wire along with the circuit wires.

Voltage in homes ranges from 110 to 125. Most calculations use 125 volts. The only way to tell the exact voltage available at the outlet is to measure the electricity with a voltmeter.

Wires are usually
BLACK = HOT
WHITE or RED = COMMON
BARE, BLUE or GREEN = GROUND.
When wiring a plug-in or socket:

1. The HOT wire attaches to the BRASS or GOLD screw.

2. The COMMON wire attaches to the ALUMINUM or SILVER screw.

3. The GROUND wire always attaches to the ground prong.

4. TAKE SPECIAL CARE TO KEEP THE WIRES FROM CROSSING AND FORMING A SHORT CIRCUIT.

Inadequate wire and poor connections almost caused a fire.

Plug-ins and sockets must have a solid connection. If they are jolted around and the electricity is allowed to jump, the prongs will burn and a fire could result. Check plug-ins periodically to ensure that they have a solid connection.

If a new circuit or breaker box is desired, hire an electrician, or purchase *WIRING SIMPLIFIED* by H.P. Richter and W.C. Schwan. It costs about $3 and is available at most hardware stores. Installing a new circuit in a breaker box is very easy, but installing another fuse is more complex. Before trying anything of this scope, read up on it and discuss it with several professionals. You could be in for the shock of your life!

About Electricity Consumption

There are many ways to deal with the *increase* in consumption of electricity. One friend moved into a home that had all electric heat as well as a fireplace. He installed three HID lamps in the basement that generated quite a bit of heat. The excess heat was dispersed by using a vent fan attached to a thermostat/humidistat. He turned off the electric heat, bought a fireplace insert and started heating with wood. Even running three lamps, consuming three kilowatts per hour, the electric bill was less than it had been with electric heat!

A-one-to-three-bedroom home can run two or three 1000-watt lamps and a four-or-five-bedroom home can operate three to five lamps with little or no problem. Any more lamps usually re-

Price per KW hr.	12 Hour Days		18 hour Days	
	Day	Month	Day	Month
$.02	.24	7.20	.36	10.80
$.03	.36	10.80	.54	16.20
$.04	.48	14.40	.72	21.60
$.05	.60	18.00	.90	27.00
$.06	.72	21.60	1.08	32.40
$.07	.84	25.20	1.26	37.80
$.08	.96	28.80	1.44	43.20
$.09	1.08	32.40	1.62	48.60
$.10	1.20	36.00	1.80	54.00

quire new incoming circuits or the use of present circuits is severely limited. Some friends bought a new, efficient water heater and saved $17 a month! Another indoor gardener set her water heater for 130° instead of 170°. This simple procedure saved about 25 kilowatt-hours per month! DO NOT TURN THE WATER HEATER ANY LOWER THAN 130° F. HARMFUL BACTERIA CAN GROW BELOW THIS SAFE POINT!

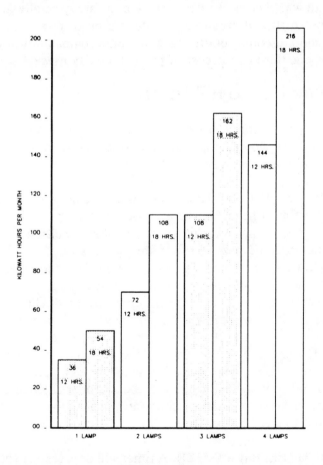

HID lights are most likely to be used economically where hydroelectric power is plentiful such as the West Coast and the Tennessee-Kentucky area. Some power companies are not able to sell all the power they generate during certain hours of the day. These power companies use coal-fired generation or nuclear generation. Many of these companies generate electricity during the daylight hours for factories and office buildings, but after 4 or 5 p.m. the power plant will not need to generate electricity; however, it is impractical and uneconomical to shut the plant down. Electrical rates after 4 p.m. are generally greatly discounted. It will probably take quite a bit of power usage to get a good discount, but the rates of some companies will be as low as one-third of the cost of prime-time day usage.

Setting Up the HID Lamp

STEP ONE: Before setting up the HID system, read "Setting Up the Grow Room" in Chapter 1, pages 17-22, and complete the step-by-step instructions.

STEP TWO: Both the lamp and ballast radiate quite a bit of heat. Care must be taken when positioning them so they are not so close 6 to 12 inches) to plants or flammable walls and ceiling that they become hazardous. If the room is limited in space, with a low ceiling, placing a protective, non-flammable material, such as metal or asbestos, between the lamp and ceiling will give much more space. If the room is 6-by-6-feet or smaller, an exhaust fan will be necessary to keep things cool. It is most effective to place the remote ballast near the floor to keep things cool. It may also be placed outside the grow room if the temperature is too high, which is unlikely when a good vent fan is used. When hanging the lamp on the overhead chain or pulley system, make sure electrical cords are unencumbered and not too close to any heat source.

STEP THREE: **Buy a TIMER!** A timer will be necessary for you to play Mother Nature successfully. The reasons for having a timer are obvious. If the HID system is not equipped with a timer, the only way to turn it on and off is to plug and unplug it, a shocking and colorful experience. *Mother Nature* provides a rigid schedule for plants to count on and live by. When the horticulturist assumes her role, will he or she remember to turn the lamp on and off at exactly the same time each and every day for several months? Or will he or she even be there each and every day, at the same time, twice a day, all year round? (see: photos of various timers.)

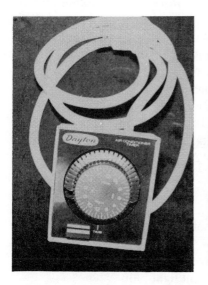 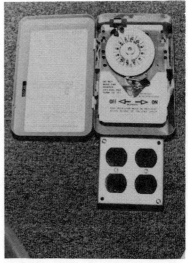

The grounded timer on the left is rated at 15 amps and is perfect for one lamp and a light balancer. The grounded timer on the right is rated at 40 amps and is designed for up to three lamps and a light balancer.

STEP FOUR: To plug in the HID lamp, it will be necessary to find the proper outlet. A 1000-watt HID lamp will use about 9.5 amperes (amps) of electricity on a regular 110 to 120 volt house current.

A typical home will have a fuse box or a breaker box. Each fuse or breaker switch controls an electrical circuit in the home. The fuse or breaker switch will be rated for 15, 20, 25, 30 or 40 amps of service. These circuits are considered overloaded when more than 80 percent of the amps are being used. (See Overload Chart, page 86).The fuse will have its amp rating printed on its face, and the breaker switch will have its amp rating printed on the switch or on the breaker box. To find out which outlets are controlled by a fuse or breaker switch, remove the fuse or turn the breaker switch off. Test every 110-volt outlet in the home to see which ones *do not work. All the outlets that do not work are on the same circuit.* All outlets that work are on another circuit. When you have found a circuit that has few or no lights, radios, TV's, stereos etc. plugged into it, look at the circuit's amp rating. If it is rated for 15 amps, just plug one 1000-watt HID in-to it. A leeway of 5.5 amps is there to cover any power surges or incongruences in electricity. If the circuit is rated for 20 or more amps, it may be used for the HID lamp as well as a few other low-amp appliances and lights. To find out how many amps are drawn by each appliance, add up the number of watts drawn by each appliance, then divide by 120.

EXAMPLE:

A circuit with a 20-amp fuse containing the following items

> 1400-watt toaster oven
> 100-watt incandescent light bulb
> + 20-watt radio
> 1520 total watts divided by 120
> = 12.6 amps in use.

This simple example shows 12.6 amps are being drawn when everything is *on*. By adding 9.2 amps, drawn by the HID to the circuit, we get 21.8 amps drawn - *AN OVERLOADED CIR-CUIT*. There are three solutions to this problem: (1) Remove one or all of the high amp drawing appliances and plug them into another circuit. (2) Find another circuit that has few or no amps drawn by other appliances. (3) Install a new circuit. A 220-volt circuit will make more amps available per circuit if using several lamps.

Never replace a smaller fuse with a fuse that has a higher amperage rating. The fuse is the weakest link in the circuit. If a 20-amp fuse is placed into a 15-amp circuit, the fuse is able to conduct more electricity than the wiring. When this happens, the wires burn, rather than the fuse. An overloaded circuit may result in a house fire. Please be careful.

Use an extension cord that is at least 14-gauge wire or heavier if the plug will not reach the outlet desired. The thicker 14-gauge extension cord is more difficult to find and may have to be constructed. A smaller 16- or 18-gauge cord will not conduct adequate electricity and will heat up, straining the entire system. Cut the 14 gauge extension cord to the exact length; the farther electricity travels, the weaker it gets and the more heat it produces, which also strains the system.

STEP FIVE: Always use a *three-prong grounded plug*. If your home is not equipped with working *3-prong grounded outlets,* buy a *three-prong grounded plug and outlet adaptor.* Attach the ground wire to a grounded ferrous metal object, such as a

CAUTION! An HID lamp operated on and overloaded circuit will blow fuses, switch off breakers or burn wiring. It could wreck the HID system, even start a fire. PAY ATTENTION!

 Use only one 1000-watt HID per 15 to 20 amp (110-volt) circuit. DO NOT BREAK THIS RULE!

grounded cold-water pipe, or a heavy copper wire driven into the earth to a form a ground, or screw the ground into the plug-in face. You will be working with water under and around the HID system. Water conducts electricity about as well as the human body . . . guaranteed to give you a charge!

STEP SIX: Once the proper circuit is selected, the socket and hood mounted overhead and the ballast in place on the floor (but not plugged in), screw the HID bulb finger-tight into the socket. Make sure the bulb is secured in the socket firmly. The threaded metal base of the bulb should not be seen from under the socket, to make certain there is a good connection. When secure, wipe off all smudges on the bulb to increase brightness.

STEP SEVEN: Plug the three-prong plug into the timer that is in the OFF position. Plug the timer into the grounded outlet, set the timer at the desired photoperiod and turn the timer on. *Shazam!* the ballast will hum, the lamp will flicker and slowly warm up, reaching full brilliance in about five minutes.

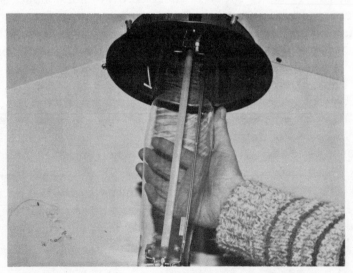

When installing the bulb, make sure that it is screwed securely into the socket.

STEP EIGHT: When using more than one HID, it is easiest to plug in each lamp individually. This way flexibility is maintained. If another lamp needs to be hung up or removed, it is easy and does not require more wiring into a central system.

This grow room is equipped with a CO_2 enrichment system, white walls and a vent fan.

Troubleshooting the Lamp

When your light does not shine, your garden does not grow. Finding the reason a HID system does not work is simple and easy when the steps below are followed.

STEP ONE: First, the problem must be isolated. Is the ballast receiving electricity? Plug the ballast in. If it humms, it is receiving electricity. If there is no humm, check the plug and outlet for a firm connection. Check the timer on another light to ensure it functions properly. If there is still no humm, remove the covering over the ballast; check for solid wire connections. The transformer is the big dark steel box; check it for burns. If you see any burns, take the transformer to a halide dealer for replacement. The starter (HP sodium only) and capacitor look like an oblong tin can. They are burned out if the sealed lip around each end is pinched out. The lip should be completely smooth and unwrinkled. When a starter or capacitor is burned out, it must be replaced. See ballast photos on pages 42-43 and page 56.

STEP TWO: If the ballast works, the problem must be in the bulb or the wiring between the ballast and the bulb. First check to make sure the bulb is screwed firmly into the socket. This is the most common reason the bulb will not work. Once the bulb is securely screwed into the socket, check all the connections for heat and firm contact. Always un-plug the ballast before touching bare wire or connections. Check the arc tube in bulb for darkness. If the bulb is two to five years old, it could be burned out.

STEP THREE: If a fuse burns out or a breaker switche turns off, there is an overloaded circuit. See information about Setting Up the HID Lamp on pages 96-97.

STEP FOUR: If the lamp flickers or pulsates, do not worry. After about 100 hours of operation, the lamp halogens in the arc tube will stabilize and appear to pulsate less. Color changes may also occur. Color changes are normal and will not effect the life or the brilliance of the bulb.

STEP FIVE: HID bulbs become brittle after several hours of use. Handle used bulbs as little as possible to avoid breakage. Wipe finger prints from the bulb after handling to retain full brilliance. When restarting lamp, wait about 15 minutes for the bulb to cool before it will restart.

CHAPTER THREE

Soil and Containers

Flowers and vegetables flourish in rich organic soil as well as soilless mixes. Outdoors, when planted in the earth, roots will branch out and penetrate deep into the soil, in search of water and nutrients. Outdoors, many plants tend to grow above ground at the same rate as they grow below the surface. The roots spread out as far as the *drip line* (page 123). If the root system is inhibited from growing and finding water and nutrients, the entire plant's growth is inhibited. An outdoor plant will have lateral branches spread out about as far as its roots are able to spread out. It is important to remember how much root space vegetables and flowers need and provide adequate soil or growing medium to meet those needs. In the indoor environment, roots must be contained in a pot or planter box. It is virtually impossible to provide an indoor soil environment exactly like that found outdoors. This is why extreme care must be taken when selecting soil and containers.

SOIL

Soil is made up of many mineral particles mixed together with living and dead organic matter that incorporates air and water. Three factors contribute to the root's ability to grow in soil: (1) texture (2) pH and (3) nutrient content.

Texture is governed by the size and physical make up of the mineral particles. The proper soil texture is required for adequate root penetration, water and oxygen retention and drainage, as well as many other complex chemical processes. Clay or adobe soil is made up of very small flat mineral particles. When it gets wet, these minute particles pack tightly together, slowing or stopping root penetration and water drainage. Roots are unable to breathe because very little or no space is left for oxygen. Water has a very difficult time penetrating these tightly packed soils, and once it does penetrate it, drainage is slow. Sandy soils have much larger particles. They permit good aeration (supply of air or oxygen) and drainage. Frequent watering is necessary, as water retention is very low. The soil's water- and air-holding ability, as well as root penetration, are a function of texture.

Soil texture is easily checked by picking up a handful of moist (not soggy) soil and gently squeezing it. The soil should *barely* stay together and have a kind of *sponge effect* when the hand slowly opens up to release pressure.

Soil amendments increase the soil's air- and water-retaining ability. Soil amendments fall into two categories: (1) mineral (2) organic.

The amendments in the **mineral** group are all near neutral on the pH scale and essentially contain no nutrients of their own. Mineral amendments decompose through weathering and erosion, which does not effect soil pH. The amendments are also very lightweight. This is a good point to consider when containers have to be moved much.

Perlite (sand or volcanic glass expanded by heat like popcorn) holds water and nutrients on its many irregular surfaces and works especially well for aerating the soil. This is a good medium for people planning to *push* plants with *heavy* fertilization. It drains fast and does not promote salt buildup. Perlite comes in three grades: fine, medium and coarse. Medium and coarse are the choice of most gardeners for a soil amendment.

Pumice (volcanic rock) is very light and holds water, nutrients and air, in its many catacomb-like holes. It is a good amendment for aerating the soil and retaining moisture evenly. Pumice is a favorite hydroponic growing medium.

Vermiculite (mica processed and expanded by heat) holds water, nutrients and air within its fiber and gives body to fast draining-soils. Fine vermiculite also works very well as a medium in which to root cuttings. This amendment holds more water than perlite or pumice. It works best for water retention in small pots or for people who do not like to water. Vermiculite is used for hydroponic wick systems since it holds so much moisture. Vermiculite comes in three grades: fine, medium and coarse. Always use the fine to root cuttings. If fine is not available, crush coarse or medium between the hands, rubbing the palms back and forth. As a soil amendment, coarse is the best choice.

Organic soil amendments break down through bacterial activity, slowly yielding humus. Humus is a soft, spongy material that binds minute soil particles together, improving the soil tex-

Vermiculite, sand and manure is a popular and inexpensive mix.

ture. Young, composting, organic soil amendments require nitrogen to carry on their bacterial decomposition. If they do not contain at least 1.5 percent nitrogen, the organic amendments will get it from the soil, robbing roots of nitrogen. When using organic amendments, make sure they are thoroughly composted (at least one year) and releasing nitrogen rather than using it from the soil. A good sign of soil fertility is a dark, rich color.

I prefer to use mineral amendments because there is no bacterial activity that alters nutrient content and pH. Others prefer rich, thoroughly composted organic matter that not only amends texture, but supplies available nutrients as well. Leaf mold, garden compost (at least one year old) and many types of thoroughly composted manure usually contain enough nitrogen for their decomposition needs and are releasing, rather than using, nitrogen. When using organic amendments, it is best to pur-

Orchids thrive in mineral amendments like pumice and ver-miculite.

chase them at a nursery to help control quality. Carefully look over the bag to see if it guarantees that it contains no harmful insects, larva eggs, fungus or bad micro-organisms.

Garden compost and leaf mold may be rich and organic, but are usually full of insects and who-knows-what-else. For example, the compost pile is a favorite breeding ground for cutworms. Just one cutworm in a 5-gallon pot means certain death for the defenseless flowers.

Barnyard manure may contain toxic levels of salt and copious quantities of weed seeds and fungus spores. If using manure, purchase it in bags that guarantee its contents. There are many kinds of manure: cow manure[1], horse manure, rabbit manure, chicken manure and the less common pig and duck manure. All of these manures are bulky and can be used as soil amendments. Their nutrient content varies, depending on the diet of the animal and the decomposition factors.

"Peat" is the term used to describe partially decomposed vegetation; the decay has been slowed by the wet and cold conditions of the Northern U.S. and Canada, where it is found. The most common types of peat are formed from *sphagnum and hypnum mosses.*

Sphagnum peat moss is light brown and the most common peat found at commercial nurseries. It works well for water retention, absorbing 15 to 30 times its own weight, and giving the soil body. It contains essentially no nutrients of its own and the pH ranges from 3 to 5. After decomposing several months, the pH could get very acidic. However, fine dolomite lime may be added to compensate and stabilize pH.

Hypnum peat moss is more decomposed, darker in color, with a higher pH (5 to 7). This peat moss is less common and contains more nutrients than sphagnum peat moss. This type of peat works well for a soil amendment; however, it cannot hold as much water as sphagnum moss.

Peat moss is very dry and difficult to wet the first time, unless you bought it wet, which makes it really heavy. When using peat moss as a soil amendment, it is easiest to dry-mix all of the components, then wet the mix using a wetting agent such as liquid concentrate soap (2 or 3 drops per gallon). Another trick to mixing peat moss is to squarely kick the sack a few times before opening. The few kicks help break up the bail much faster and with less mess.

PH

pH is a scale from 1 to 14 that measures acid-to-alkaline balance. 1 is the most acidic, 7 is neutral and 14 is most alkaline. Most plants will grow best in soil with a pH from 6 to 7. Within this range, most vegetables and flowers can properly absorb and process available nutrients. If the pH is too low (acidic) the nutrients are chemically bound by acid salts and the roots are unable to absorb them. An alkaline soil, with a high pH, will

This digital pH meter helps keep the pH in the safe range.

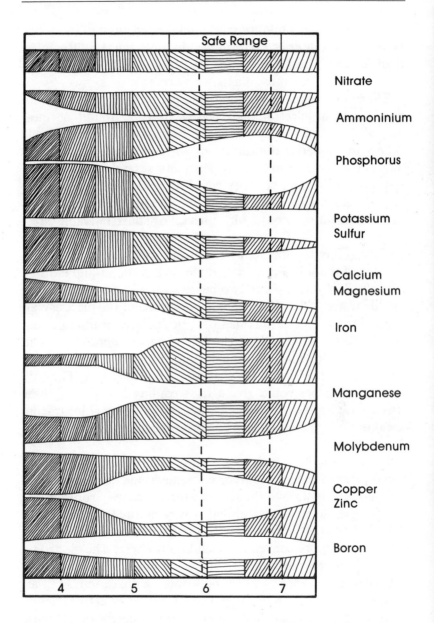

cause toxic salt buildup and limit water intake by roots. Hydroponic solutions perform best in a pH range a little lower than for soil. The pH range for hydroponics is from 5.8 to 6.8, 6.3 being ideal for most plants.

There are several ways to measure pH. A pH soil test kit, litmus paper or electronic pH tester may be found at most nurseries. When testing pH, take two or three samples and follow to the letter the directions for the soil test kit, litmus paper or electronic pH tester. There are several brands of soil test kits on the market. They cost $10 to $30 and will measure soil pH and N-P-K content by mixing soil with a chemical solution. Make sure you buy a kit with a set of understandable directions.

If using litmus paper, collect soil samples that demonstrate an average of the soil. Place the samples in a clean jar and moisten with *distilled* water. Place two pieces of the litmus paper in the muddy water. After 10 seconds, remove one of the pieces. Wait a minute and remove the other one. Both pieces of litmus paper should be the same color. The litmus paper container should have a pH color chart on the side; match the color of the litmus paper with the colors on the chart to get a pH reading. The only way litmus paper could give a false reading is if the fertilizer (Peters, Ra-Pid-Gro, Miracle-Gro etc.) contains a color tracing agent or the *distilled* water pH used for the test was not a neutral 7.

There are many brands of electronic soil pH testers. They are inexpensive ($15 to $30), very convenient and fairly accurate. Pay special attention to the soil moisture. Most electronic testers are designed to work in soil that is *very* moist. When checking pH regularly, the electronic tester is much more economical than test kits and more convenient than litmus paper. The electronic unit will test pH an infinite number of times, while the small chemical test kits are good for only about a dozen tests. For an accurate test: (1) clean the probes of the pH meter after each test with an abrasive agent that wipes clean any corrosion (2) pack the soil tightly around the probes (3) water soil with distilled or neutral pH water before testing.

Check the pH of the *water* being used. Sometimes the water pH is too low or too high. After repeated watering, this can substantially alter the pH, especially with soils high in organic amendments. Coastal, rainy climates generally have acidic water, while desert regions are prone to alkaline water. A pH problem may surface in the late autumn, when all the leaves fall and vegetation is decomposing. This biodegradation process is very acidic and may create an artificially low pH. The acidic leaves lower the pH of the outside soil and in turn the pH of the ground water. This problem is most common among smaller municipal and well-water systems. Generally, larger water facilities carefully monitor and correct pH so there are fewer problems for the gardener. Be on the lookout for any major environmental changes that could affect the water pH. It is very important to keep an eye on the pH at all times. Check pH at least once every two weeks.

Soil pH should be between 6 and 7 for maximum growth and nutrient uptake in most plants. Commercial potting soil almost never has a pH over 7.5. A lower pH is more usual - even as low as 5.5. The ideal range would be between 6 and 6.5. Most potting soils have a tendency to be a bit acidic since they are generally used for indoor, perennial, acid-loving plants. The easiest way to maintain and/or raise the pH is to mix in one cup of *fine dolomite lime* per cubic foot of potting soil. Mix *dolomite lime* thoroughly into dry soil. Mix the soil again in the container after it has been watered. This ensures a thorough, even mix.

Fine dolomite lime has been a favorite pH stabilizer of gardeners for many years. It is virtually impossible to apply too much as long as it is thoroughly mixed in. It stabilizes the pH safely. That is, by adding dolomite to the soil when planting, the pH is guaranteed to remain stable, even with changes in the water supply and acidic fertilizers. Dolomite lime is a compound of magnesium (Mg) and calcium (Ca), which accounts for its immense popularity among indoor gardeners. Both of these secondary nutrients are needed by flowering fruits and vegetables, but many fertilizers do not supply adequate amounts of them.

Dolomite does not save the soil from excess salt buildup; only you, Mother Nature, and regular leaching will take care of toxic salts. When purchasing dolomite, ask for the finest (dust-like) grade available. Since it will be used for only a few months, the dolomite should be as fine as possible so it is readily assimilable. Coarse dolomite could take as long as a year before it breaks down enough for the plants to assimilate it.

Make sure to mix the fine dolomite thoroughly with the soil when planting. Improperly mixed, the dolomite will form a cake or layer that burns roots and deflects water.

Hydrated lime is very similar to dolomite lime, but as the name *hydrated* implies, it is *very* soluble. Hydrated lime works acceptably to alter pH after planting. Mix it thoroughly with warm water and apply with each watering. Many horticulturists use a mix of one fourth hydrated lime and three fourths dolomite lime. This mix provides lime that is immediately available to neutralize the pH and the dolomite lime has a long-lasting effect. It is not advisable to use more than one cup of hydrated lime per cubic foot of soil. With only hydrated lime in a soil mix, it is released so fast that it may be toxic to plants at first but will be washed out within a couple of weeks.

Whitewash is made from hydrated lime and table salt. The recipe is printed on sacks of hydrated lime. Whitewash is not as viscous as latex paint and may require a few coats. I really like whitewash because and it is *antiseptic* against fungus.This is the most effective way to safely *white out* damp, sweaty walls.The famous *Bordeaux* fungicide mix uses hydrated lime and copper sulfate. Hydrated lime may also be used as a grow room fungicide. Just sprinkle it on the floor and around the room. It will kill fungus on contact.

Use quicklime only in small doses; it can be toxic to plants. Calcic lime contains only calcium and is not a good choice for plant growth. It does not have the buffer qualities of dolomite,

 When planting, add one cup of fine dolomite lime to each cubic foot (or one ounce per gallon) of planting medium to stabilize the pH and provide Ca & Mg.

nor does it contain any magnesium (Mg).

There are several ways to raise the pH. Each requires putting some form of alkali in the growing medium or water, such as calcium carbonate, potassium hydroxide, sodium hydroxide or several other compounds. Both hydroxides are caustic and require special care when handling. They are normally used to raise the pH of hydroponic nutrient solutions. The easiest and most convenient way to raise the pH and/or stabilize it is to add *fine dolomite lime* and hydrated lime before planting.

There are many ways to lower the pH. If the water has a high pH, distilled white vinegar will solve the problem. Calcium nitrate or nitric acid, used mainly in hydroponic units, and sulfur also work very well to lower pH. If using fertilizers containing these nutrients, keep close watch on the pH; they could lower it substantially[2].

Aspirin is one household remedy to lower pH. Just add about two per quart of water to lower the pH one point.

If uncertain how much solution to apply to alter the pH, give a dosage of half as much as recommended, then check it. Wait about 15 minutes and check it again. Now add the balance of the chemical or as much as needed to achieve the desired result.

After altering the pH, check it, then check it again several days later, and once or twice the following weeks to make sure it remains stable.

 To raise the pH one point, add three cups of **fine dolomite lime** to one cubic foot of soil. An alternate fast-acting mix would be 2 ½ cups of dolomite and half a cup of hydrated lime to one cubic foot of soil.

 To lower the pH of water one point, add one teaspoon of white distilled vinegar per gallon of water. Check pH of the solution before watering because the pH of vinegar varies according to type and manufacturer.

 If soil pH is under 5 or over 8, it is easiest, and less expensive in the long run, to change soil rather than experimenting with changing the pH.

Pulverized eggshells, clam or oyster shells and wood ashes have a high pH and work to raise pH. It takes many, many eggshells to fill a cup and it takes a long time for the shells to break down and affect the pH; wood ashes usually have a pH of about 11 and are easy to over-apply. Many times ashes come from fireplaces or wood stoves that have been burning all kinds of (plastic) trash and are therefore unsafe. Do not use wood ashes!

Potting soil, fresh out of the bag, generally supplies rapid-growing annuals with enough N-P-K for the first month of growth, before supplemental fertilization is necessary. Secondary and trace elements are usually found in sufficient quantities and unnecessary to add, except for *fine dolomite lime*. If you are totally into organic horticulture, supplemental fertilization may be replaced by organic soil amendments and fertilizer. See Chapter 4: "Gradual Release Organic Fertilizers" pages 142-146.

Potting soil from a nursery is the easiest soil to use for indoor cultivation. It is usually pH balanced, contains adequate levels of most nutrients, retains water and air evenly, drains well, and allows easy root growth. Most potting soils, except those containing unusually large amounts of organic fertilizer amendments, will be depleted of nutrients within three or four weeks. After this time, supplemental fertilization will usually be necessary. Potting soils tend to be very localized, since they are so heavy and shipping costs prohibitive. There are many good brands to choose from. Ask your nurseryperson for help in selecting one. None the less, make a point of checking the pH yourself.

Potting soils containing more than 50 percent vermiculite, pumice or perlite may tend to stratify when heavily saturated with water before planting. The light mineral amendments tend to float, with the heavier organic matter settling to the bottom. If this happens, mix the water-saturated soil thoroughly with your hands until it is evenly mixed before planting or transplanting.

Mushroom compost is an inexpensive potting soil that is high in organic amendments. Frequently mushroom compost has been sterilized chemically for several years so that only mushrooms would grow in it. The law usually requires that after mushroom gardeners discard the rich compost, that it sit fallow for two or more years before it is can be The fallow time allows for all the harmful sterilints to leach out. The compost is very fertile since it has been allowed to decompose for many years. Check at your local nursery or extension service for a good source of mushroom compost. Some of the most abundant vegetable harvests I have seen used mushroom compost for the growing medium.

Potting soil can get somewhat expensive when used only once, then discarded. If it is used for more than one crop, undesirable micro-organisms and insects may have time to get started, nutrients are depleted, water and air retention are poor and compaction leads to poor drainage. There is an inexpensive alternative to potting soil: soilless mix.

Mushroom compost is an excellent organic amendment to soil and soilless mixes. Most growers use about one third mushroom compost with two thirds soil.

Soilless Mix

Soilless mix is a very popular, inexpensive, lightweight sterile growing medium that has been used in nurseries for many years. It is generally made from one or all of the following: pumice, vermiculite, perlite, sand and sphagnum peat moss. Soilless mix is one of my favorites. It allows for good, even root growth. It can be *pushed* to amazing lengths with total control; and best of all, it is very inexpensive!

Soilless mix is preferred by commercial nurserypeople and indoor gardeners alike. It has good texture. It contains essentially no nutrients of its own, unless fortified with nutrients, and is generally at or near 7 on the pH scale. Soilless mix works very well for gardeners who tend to over-water or over-fertilize or like to *push* plants with heavy fertilization. It drains fairly rapidly and may be leached efficiently and there is little buildup of nutrients to toxic levels. Soilless mix may be purchased ready-mixed in bags of Jiffy Mix, Ortho Mix or Terra-lite. Some gardeners say these mixes hold moisture too long and they add 10 to 50 percent perlite for better drainage. These commercial soilless mixes are fortified with small amounts of all necessary nutrients. The fortified nutrients generally last for about a month. None the less, it is a good idea to use a fertilizer containing trace elements. After that, supplemental fertilization will be necessary to sustain vigorous growth in annuals.

Soilless components may be purchased separately and mixed to the desired consistency. Mix small amounts right in the bag. Larger batches should be mixed in a wheelbarrow or on a concrete slab. NOTE: Mixing soil or soilless mix is a dusty, messy, miserable job; it is best to do it outdoors and wear a respirator. A light misting of water will help quell dust.

 Mix soilless amendments outdoors and when they are dry. Use a respirator to avoid dust.

Coarse sand, fine vermiculite or perlite works well for rooting cuttings. Sand and perlite are fast draining, which helps prevent damping-off. Vermiculite holds water and air longer and makes cloning easier. Soilless mix also allows for complete control of critical nutrient and root-stimulating hormone additives, essential to asexual propagation.

Texture of soilless mix should be coarse, light and spongy. This allows drainage with sufficient moisture and air retention, as well as providing good root penetration qualities. Fine soilless mix holds more moisture and works well with smaller containers. Soilless mixes using more *perlite* and *sand* drain faster, making it easier to *push* with fertilizer and not lead to excessive salt buildup. *Vermiculite* and *mosses* hold water longer and are great for small pots, rooting cuttings or situations that require good water retention.

pH is generally a neutral 7. If using more than 15 percent moss in your mix, add appropriate *dolomite* or hydrated lime to correct and stabilize pH. Check the pH every week or two; continued watering will promote a lower pH. Soilless mix tends to maintain a neutral pH easily; it is mainly composed of mineral particles that are not affected by organic decomposition, which could change pH. The pH is affected very little by acidic fertilizers or by water with a high or low pH.

Here are a few examples of the many soilless mixes:

1. ⅛ peat moss
⅛ coarse sand
¼ vermiculite
½ perlite

2. ⅛ sphagnum moss
⅛ coarse sand
¼ perlite
½ vermiculite

3. ⅓ peat
⅓ pearlite
⅓ vermiculite ★

4. ½ peat
½ perlite ★

★amount of dolomite or hydrated lime to bring pH up to neutral. See RULE OF THUMB page 111

Nutrients are not contained in soilless mix unless they are fortified or added by the gardener. Regular frequent feeding with a soluble N-P-K fertilizer containing trace and secondary elements, such as Miracle-Gro, Ra-Pid-Gro or Peters, is necessary, even if the mix is fortified!. (See "Trace Element Fertilizers," page 146.

Rockwool root cubes or Jiffy 7 Pellets and Oasis cubes are the neatest invention since the crutch. These root cubes and peat pots are very convenient and lend themselves to promoting cuttings or seedlings with a strong root system. Peat pots are small compressed peat moss containers with an expandable outside wall. The flat pellets pop up into a seedling pot when watered. They work very well for sowing seeds or even rooting cuttings. Just place the seed or cutting in the wet peat pot or root cube and keep it evenly moist. For cuttings, make sure to crimp the top in around the stem so constant contact is made between the stem and the root cube or peat pot. When roots show through the side, set pot or cube into a larger pot. There will be virtually no transplant shock. They do tend to dry out and contract, which exposes stems. Be sure to check peat pots or root cubes daily, keeping them evenly moist but not drenched. Root cubes and peat pots do not any nutrients. Seedlings do not require any nutrients for the first week or two. Feed seedlings after the first week or so and cuttings as soon as they are rooted. I like to feed cuttings and seedlings Up-Start when they are planted and with each watering for the first two weeks.

Small tomato seedlings are emerging from Jiffy-7 pellets.

Soil Mixes

Some gardeners like to mix their own soil. Many of them go out to the back yard and dig up some good-looking DIRT that drains poorly and retains water and air unevenly. This DIRT is then mixed with garden compost, full of micro-organisms and bugs. They think this unique organic soil mix will grow the best produce possible and besides, it is much cheaper than buying it! The truth of the matter is that by saving $10 on soil, they will pay for it many times over in fruit and flowers that were not produced. If you choose to mix your own soil, buy all of the components at the nursery. Alternatives that require more work are to sterilize them by baking in the oven at 160° F for 30 to 45 minutes, or following the *solarizing* technique below. This bakes all the bad bugs, but leaves most of the good ones. The stench is horrible (you are cooking bugs), not to mention the mess. If using garden soil, be sure to find the richest, darkest soil with a good texture. As much as 30 to 70 percent perlite and/or vermiculite will probably be necessary as a soil amendment. Even well-draining garden soils tend to compact and need more *fluff* for good drainage and water and air retention. Check the pH before digging soil to make sure it is within the acceptable 6 to 7 range. Add fine dolomite regardless of the pH. Check it two or three times after mixing to ensure that the pH has stabilized.

Compost

Many gardeners have no trouble with organic composts, but some of them lose their entire garden or have poor yields due to disease in the soil. Many good compost recipes are available from monthly publications such as *Sunset, Organic Gardening, Mother Earth News* or from the companies specializing in

NOTE: When using sand to root cuttings or as an additive to soil or soilless mix, make sure it is washed, coarse sand; it will drain much better than fine sand. *Do not use beach or ocean sand* it contains toxic levels of salt. Sand is the heaviest soil amendment; if too much is used, it will settle to the bottom, while the perlite and vermiculite remain on top.

organic composts.

A good compost pile would have cow manure - the older the better - or any kind of manure that is handy.(See box page 119). Manure from horse stalls or feed lots is mixed with straw or bedding. Make sure the bedding is not sawdust. Sawdust is very acidic and will leach all of the nitrogen out of the pile as well. The best kind of manure to acquire is the oldest, rottenest possible. It is less prone to have any weed seeds that are still alive. Fresh grass clippings are one of my favorites to use in a compost pile. The clippings are full of nitrogen, which speeds decomposition. Put your hand down deep into a pile of grass clippings that has been in the sun for a couple of hours . . . Now, that's hot!

The best way to build a compost pile is high, and keep turning it. Good compost pile recipes include the addition of organic trace elements, enzymes and the primary nutrients. Retail nurseries generally sell compost starter with all the necessary ingredients for a healthy compost pile. The organic matter used should be ground up and in the form of shredded leaves and grass. Do not use large woody branches that could take years to decompose.

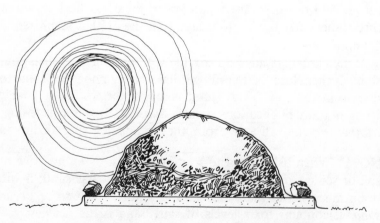

The ultimate compost pile is covered with black plastic visqueen and rests on a concrete slab.

The easiest and most effective way to rid soil and compost of bad bugs, larva, weed seeds and fungi is to let the sun do it for you. This technique is called *solarizing* (see drawing above). The principle is simple: Just place a piece of *clear* plastic (black plastic will retain the heat and not let it pass into in the compost pile) over the compost pile or soil. The heat from the sun will cook all the bad stuff out. Use a piece of plastic 2 to 6 mils thick; the thicker the plastic, the longer it will last under the sun's destroying rays. The compost pile should be in a sunny location. The more sun it gets, the more heat is generated. The sun's rays pass through the clear plastic, heating up the interior of the pile. This heat is then trapped below the plastic. This trapped heat develops 100 percent humidity and the temperatures often reach 140°! The plastic must completely cover the pile. Hold it down with a continuous pile of dirt around the entire outside perimeter. The soil or compost will be clean of all harmful bugs, larva, weed seeds and fungi in one to three months, depending on the intensity and the amount of sun the pile receives. Remember, the sun is the most intense when it is nearly or directly overhead. So the best time for the pile to receive sunlight is between 10 a.m. to 3 p.m. If the pile is located on a slab of concrete, or on a platform that is able to heat up, the heat builds up from both directions rapidly.

Horse and sheep manures are *hot* because they contain little water and lots of air. They heat up readily in a compost pile. Cow and pig manures are *cold* because they hold a lot of water and can be compacted easily, squeezing out the air. Worm castings and bat guano are considered *sweet* because their nutrients are immediately available to plants and they will not burn. Most city zoos offer the manure and bedding from the animals at the zoo. This *Zoo Doo*, as it is called in Portland, is full of nutrients, and weed seeds, It should be composted for at least a year before it is used indoors.

One of the few pests that can make it through the intense heat of the plastic coated compost pile is the cutworm. They are most common in compost piles with a dirt foundation. There are several different cutworms. It is most common in compost piles with a dirt foundation. There are several varieties of cutworm. They live in the soil, flourish in compost piles and curl up for protection when exposed. Cutworms are ¼ inch to 1 inch in length and may easily be spotted with the naked eye. If these pests make it to the soil where the crops are growing, just one cutworm per pot could destroy the entire garden.

Before using compost, pour it through ¼-inch-mesh hardware cloth (screen). Place a heavy duty framed screen over a large garbage can or a wheelbarrow to catch the sifted compost. This will break the up humus before it is mixed with the soil. After adding soil, the mix may be resifted for additional mixing. Earthworms found on the screen may be returned to the medium, while cutworms are promptly squished.

Gardeners using one-third worm castings one-third perlite and one-third organic matter have had excellent results. Many gardeners mix a third to a half perlite to a bag of rich potting soil that has lots of worm castings. Worm castings are heavy, compacting the roots, and leave little or no space for *air* to the roots. Adding perlite aerates the soil.

Here are just three examples of the many possible combinations of soil mixes. NOTE: No DIRT is used.

1. ⅓ worm castings
    ⅓ manure
    ⅓ coarse sand

2. ⅓ worm castings
    ⅓ perlite
    ⅓ vermiculite

3. ⅓ peat
    ⅓ vermiculite
    ⅓ worm castings
    Dolomite or hydrated
    lime to correct pH.

Add fine dolomite lime to each one of these soil mixes, whether or not the pH is off. See RULE OF THUMB, page 111.

Soil Termperature

Raising the soil temperature makes the chemical process faster and hastens nutrient uptake. Ideally, the soil temperature should range from 65 to 75° F. The soil may be heated by means of heat tape placed in or under soil. Heat tape may be purchased at most nurseries. Some gardeners use a waterbed heating pad to heat a large bed. It is an inexpensive alternative to heating the air. Soil may also be heated by placing the container up off the floor on blocks to allow the flow of warm air underneath. Using this method, an additional heat source may not be needed. Do not heat the soil or nutrient solution over 75° F. It will dehydrate and cook the roots!

This lime tree needs to be flushed with water. Note the cut in photo on the left that shows the excess salt build-up on the side of the pot.

Containers

Containers come in all shapes and sizes. They may be constructed of almost anything; clay, metal, plastic, wood and fiber are the most common. Just about any kind of container will do, as long as it is thoroughly clean and has not been used for any petroleum products. See Chart on "Potting," page 125, Clay, fiber and wood containers *breathe* better than plastic or metal ones. Clay pots are heavy and notorious for absorbing moisture from soil inside, causing soil to dry out quickly.

Grow bags are a good, inexpensive, long-lasting alternative to rigid containers. In fact, some people use the sack the potting soil came in as a container. Once the soil is inside and moist, the bag holds its shape well. The bags tend to expand and contract with the soil, lessening the chance of burned root tips that grow down the side of the pot.

Fiber or pulp pots are very popular and inexpensive, but their bottoms frequently rot out. Painting the inside of the fiber container with latex paint will extend the life.

A bright halide and coarse, fast draining soil help create a perfect natural environment for this corp of cacti.

Automatic self-watering pots are used for African violets and most other gesneriads. These kind of pots work very well for slower-growing perennials. Elaborate about placing charcoal in the bottom

Other than making sure containers are clean, there are two important factors to consider: (1) drainage holes (2) size.

Drainage holes should let the excess water drain easily, but not be so big that soil in the bottom of the container washes out onto the floor. Pots may be lined with newspaper if drainage is too rapid or soil washes out drain holes. This will slow drainage, so be wary!

The size of container is of utmost importance. Most flowers and vegetables are annual plants that grow very rapidly, requiring a lot of root space for vigorous growth. If the roots are confined, growth slows to a crawl. A good example may be found at most retail nurseries about midsummer. Tomato plants that are still in small 4-inch or gallon pots that will be fully mature and have a few ripe tomatoes. Notice the branches do not extend much beyond the sides of the container and *dripline*; the plants are tall and leggy with curled-down leaves. They have an overall stunted sickly appearance. These plants are pot- or root-bound. Sure, they could be kept alive or maybe even made to grow a little by fertilizing with the exact balance of necessary nutrients. This is a lot of work, it is easy to over-fertilize, and the plant will always be a RUNT.

Annual plant roots develop and elongate quickly, growing down and out, away from the main taproot. When roots reach the sides of the pot, they grow straight down. I'm sure you have seen soil *contract* and separate from the container wall. When this happens, the root hairs that are responsible for absorbing water and nutrients are left helpless to dry out and die. One way

 Have at least two half-inch or four quarter-inch holes per square foot of bottom. When using a tray under pot, do not let excess water sit in the tray longer than three days. This stagnant water could cause root rot and fungus.

Note the different containers in this grow room.

to help solve this *contraction* problem is to run your finger around the inside lip of the pot, cultivating the soil, filling the crack between the pot and soil. Check this every few days. Also, maintaining evenly moist soil will help keep root hairs on the soil perimeter from drying out.

It is important to transplant before the plant is pot-bound and stunted. Once a plant is stunted, it will take several weeks to grow enough new roots and root hairs to resume normal growth.

MINIMUM CONTAINER SIZE

PLANT AGE IN MONTHS	CONTAINER SIZE
0-1	4″
1-2	1 gallon
2-3	2 gallon
3-4	3 gallon
4-5	5 gallon
4-6	10 gallon

This chart shows the approximate size container a plant should be in at various ages.

The best way to solve the pot-bound problem is to plant annual seedlings or cuttings directly into a five or six gallon pot. This method requires fewer containers and less work, and is less stressful to both plants and transplanter.

Pots are the most common containers for indoor use. They are inexpensive and readily available. Complete individual water and nutrient control may be exercised with pots. An individual plant may be quarantined from the rest of the garden or dipped in a medicinal solution. When plants are small, they may be huddled tightly together under the HID lamp and moved farther apart as needed.

 Allow one gallon of soil for every month the annual will spend in the container. A three-to-six-gallon pot will support a seedling or cutting for three to six months.

Raised beds can be installed right on the earthen floor of a garage or basement. If drainage is poor, a layer of gravel or a *dry well* is laid under 12 to 24 inches of soil, with a 2-by-12-inch board border for the raised bed. If the bed is subterranean, it may be very close to the water table. When it rains, the water may collect underneath. The garden seldom needs watering. Plants are kept a little bit too wet and there may be a buildup of salts (nutrients) in the soil, since it cannot be leached effectively.

If drainage does not present a problem and you are able to grow in a raised bed, by all means do so. The large soil mass gives a chance to build up a good organic base after several crops. There will need to be organic activity within the soil. Your job is to make sure it is the good, not the bad, micro-organisms that live in the bed. When mixing soil or adding amendments, use the best possible organic components and follow organic principles. There should be good drainage and the soil should be as deep (12 to 24 inches) as possible. The more organic matter present, the more fertile the soil will be.

A good deal of heat may be generated by the organic activity. This not only speeds nutrient uptake, but helps heat the room as well. Ventilation is necessary to lower heat and humidity and keep the room free of fungus and bad bugs. The organic garden

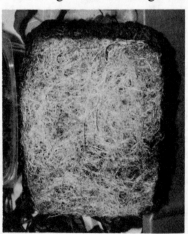

This plant needs to be repotted. The soil can hardly be seen.

may sound great, but it is a lot of work to replicate the great outdoors. Another drawback to the raised bed is that the crop will take a few days to a couple of weeks longer to mature than if it were grown in containers. However, this longer wait is offset by a larger harvest. When plants are grown in a container, with roots restricted from growing, they generally mature and flower faster.

Large planters may be placed on the ground or set up on blocks or casters to allow air circulation underneath. This lessens the chance of fungus growth and keeps the soil warmer than if it were sitting on a cold floor. The planters range in size from 2 feet by 2 feet by 12 inches to 10 feet by 10 feet by 24 inches. The roots have two to three times as much soil to grow in and much less side surface for roots to run into and grow down. Roots are able to intertwine and grow luxuriantly.

Generally plants or cuttings are left in one-gallon pots until they are a month to six weeks old, then transplanted to the large planter box *before* they are root-bound. This allows young plants to be bunched together under the lamp and receive maximum light intensity. As many as 20 plants may be placed in a 2 feet by 2 feet by 12 inch planter, but four to six plants are much more reasonable. Once plants start crowding and shading one another, they may be bent outward and tied down to a trellis that is nailed to the sides of the planter. Large planters work

Large planters on casters are easy to maneuver in the grow room and provide more root space for plants.

very well and are highly recommended because they require less maintenance. Since there is a larger mass of soil, water and nutrients are retained much longer and more evenly.

How to Seed a Pot

In this example we will use a one-gallon plastic pot, which is readily available and reusable.

STEP ONE: Acquire the desired number of clean pots.

STEP TWO: Fill the pot with well-mixed growing medium to about an inch from the top.

STEP THREE: Water with one to two quarts of warm water or until soil is completely saturated and excess water runs out the drain holes. Wait 15 minutes and repeat watering to ensure saturation of the soil.

STEP FOUR: With your finger, make one to 10 small holes one-forth to one-half-inch deep in the surface. Place one to three seeds per hole and cover with soil and pack it down gently, but firmly in place. Place a paper towel over the seeds to keep soil surface moist and to keep soil from washing.

STEP FIVE: Sprinkle water on the surface. Make sure seeds remain at proper depth and do not wash out.

STEP SIX: Keep the soil surface evenly moist until seeds sprout.

STEP SEVEN: Thin to one plant per pot

STEP EIGHT: Grow a strong, healthy plant.

WRITE A POTTING GUIDE THAT HAS SOIL PER POT RATIO

CHAPTER FOUR

Water and Fertilizer

Water and **fertilizer** work hand in hand. The nutrients in fertilizer dissolve in water. Water carries nutrients through the plant. Water is essential to plant growth, making up more than 75 percent of a plant's weight.

The root hairs absorb water, nutrients (fertilizer) and oxygen in the soil and carry them up the stem to the leaves. This flow of water from the soil through the plant is called the *transpiration stream*. A fraction of the water is processed and used in photosynthesis. The water evaporates into the air, carrying waste products along with it, via the stomata in the leaves. This process is called *transpiration*. Some of the water also returns manufactured sugars and starches to the roots.

Unfortunately, common tap water may contain high levels of alkaline salts, sulfur or chlorine, and may have a pH out of the acceptable 6 to 7 range. Water containing sulfur is easily smelled and tasted. Saline water is a little more difficult to detect. Water in coastal areas is generally full of salt, because it washes inland from the ocean. This problem is worst in Southern California and other coastal areas.

Chlorine and salt are added to many household water systems. Chlorine, in small doses, does not seem to affect plant growth, but salt-softened water should be avoided. Enough salt will kill any plant! Chlorine does tend to make soil acidic after repeated use. The best way to get chlorine out of water is to let it sit one or two days in an open container. The chlorine will evaporate as a gas when it comes in contact with the air. An old aquarium pump is excellent for heating the water of a reservoir to maintain it at room temperature. Heating also makes the chlorine dissipate faster. If chlorine alters soil pH noticeably, it may be adjusted with hydrated lime. Salts from saline water or fertilizer residue can build up to toxic levels quickly in container gardens. Excessive salts inhibit seed germination, burn the root hairs and tips or edges of leaves, and stunt the plant. Excess salt built up in the soil can easily be leached out by pouring two gallons of water per gallon of growing medium. Repeat leaching once or twice if burn is severe. This will wash out any toxic buildup of salts. If you use soft or saline water, or have any unwanted substances in the soil, it is a good idea to leach containers every month or two. Hard or well water may be alkaline and usually contains notable amounts of calcium (Ca) and magnesium (Mg). Both of these micronutrients will be put to good use by flowering and fruiting plants. It is doubtful that hard water could contain enough Ca or Mg to toxify the soil. It is still a good idea to leach the soil at least every two months. Generally, water that is OK to drink is OK for plants.

Application

There is no wet and dry rule about how much water to apply or when to apply it.

Large plants use much more water than small plants, but there are many more variables than size that dictate a plant's water consumption. The age of the plant, container size, soil texture, temperature, humidity and ventilation all contribute to water needs. Change any one of these variables and water consumption will change. Good ventilation is essential to promote

 (1) Apply **tepid** (70 to 80° F) water. Plants are able to process tepid or room-temperature water rapidly and it penetrates the soil better. Tepid water does not shock tender root hairs or leaves. Would you rather jump into a warm or a cold swimming pool? What happens to your body when you dive into a cold swimming pool? (2) Water **early in the day** so excess water will evaporate from soil surface and leaves. Keeping foliage and soil wet leads to fungus attack.

transpiration, water consumption and rapid growth. Generally, the healthier a plant, the faster it grows and the more water it consumes.

Many gardeners irrigate on a wet and dry cycle. They water, then let the soil dry out to about 2 inches below the soil surface before the next watering. Other gardeners keep moisture more consistent by irrigating more often. A fertilizer solution is often added with each watering.

Annual flowers and vegetables do not like soggy soil. Soil kept too wet essentially drowns roots, making it impossible for them to breathe. This causes slow growth and possible fungus attack. Tiny root hairs dry up and die if the soil dries out, even in *pockets*. It seems to take forever for the roots to grow new hairs.

These geraniums use as much water under a HID as they would under natural sunlight in the middle of summer.

A **moisture meter** takes most of the guesswork out of watering. They can be purchased for $10 to $30 and are well worth the money. The meter can tell exactly how much water the soil contains at any level or point. Many times, soil will develop dry pockets and/or not hold water evenly. Checking moisture with a finger is, at best, an educated guess and disturbs the root system.

 (1) Irrigate small seedlings and cuttings when the soil surface is dry. For cuttings rooting in sand or vermiculite with good drainage and no humidity tent, the surface is dry almost daily. (2) Irrigate larger plants in the vegetative and flowering stages when soil is dry 2 inches below the surface. Contrary to popular belief, flowering plants use high levels of water to carry on rapid floral formation. Letting a flowering plant wilt between waterings actually stunts flower formation. (3) Line pots up so it is easy to keep track of which ones have been watered.

A water meter makes watering very exact.

A moisture meter will give an exact moisture reading without bothering the roots as much.

The trick is to apply enough water so all of the soil gets wet and not let *too* much run out the drain holes, which will cause a leaching effect, carrying away nutrients. None the less, a little drip (about 10 percent) out the drain holes is beneficial.

Over-watering is a common problem, especially with small plants. Too much water drowns roots by cutting off their supply of oxygen. If you have symptoms of over-watering, *buy a moisture meter!* It will let both you and your garden breathe easier. Sometimes parts of the soil are over-watered and other *soil pockets* remain bone-dry. Cultivating the soil surface, allowing even water penetration and using a *moisture meter* will overcome this problem. One of the main causes of over-watering is poor ventilation. The plant needs to transpire and water needs to evaporate into the air. If there is nowhere for this wet, humid air to go, literally gallons of water may be locked in the grow room. Good ventilation carries the *wet* air away, replacing it with *new* dry air. If using trays to catch runoff water, use a turkey baster (large syringe) or sponge to draw the excess water from the tray. Signs of over watering are: curly, yellow leaves, constant soggy soil, fungus, and slow growth. Over watering may affect a plant and the inexperienced gardener may not see any flagrant symptoms for a long time.

Under-watering is less of a problem. However, it is common if smaller pots are used. Small containers dry out quickly and may need daily watering. If it is forgotten, the poor water-starved plant is stunted. Most gardeners panic when they see their beautiful garden wilted in bone-dry soil.

If the soil is nearly or completely dry, take the following steps: Add a few drops (one drop per pint) of a biodegradable, concentrated liquid soap such as Castile or Ivory concentrate to the

 (1) Large plants transpire more than small ones. (2) Maintain good ventilation. (3) Check the soil of each plant for moisture. This will be a base to work from in developing your watering skill.

water. It will act as a wetting agent, helping the water penetrate
soil more efficiently and guarding against dry soil pockets. Most
soluble fertilizers contain a *wetting agent.* Apply about a fourth
to a half as much water/fertilizer as the plant is expected to
need, wait 10 to 15 minutes for it to totally soak in, then apply
more water/fertilizer until the soil is evenly moist. If trays are
underneath the pots, let excess water remain in the trays a few
hours or even overnight before removing it with a large turkey
baster.

Having a readily accessible water source is very convenient; it
saves time and labor. A 10-by-10-foot garden, containing 24
healthy tomato plants in six-gallon pots, could need 10 to 30
gallons of water per week. Water weighs eight pounds a gallon.
30 gallons × eight pounds = 240 pounds! That's a lot of containers to fill, lift and spill. Carrying water in containers from
the bathroom sink to the garden is all right when plants are

An inexpensive drip watering system makes watering a snap.

small, but when they get large, it is a big, sloppy, regular job. Running a hose into the garden saves much labor and mess. A lightweight half-inch hose is easy to handle and is less prone to damage plants. If the water source has hot and cold water running out the same tap and is equipped with threads, a hose may easily be attached and tepid water used to water the garden. A dishwasher coupling may be used if the faucet has no threads. The hose should have an on/off valve at the outlet, so water flow may be controlled while watering. A rigid watering wand will save many broken branches when you're leaning over to water in tight quarters. The wand may be found at the nursery or constructed from plastic PVC pipe. Do not leave water under pressure in the hose. Garden hose is meant to transport water, not hold it under pressure, which may cause it to rupture.

To make a siphon or gravity-fed watering system, place a barrel at least 4 feet high in the grow room. If humidity is a problem, put a lid on the barrel or move it to another room. The attic is a good place because it warms the water and promotes good pressure. Place a siphon hose in the top of the tank or install a PVC on/off valve near the bottom of the barrel. An inexpensive device that measures the gallons of water added to the barrel may be purchased at most hardware stores. It is easy to walk off and let the barrel overflow. A float valve may also be installed in the barrel so there is a constant supply of water.

Fertilizer

Most flowers and vegetables grow so fast under HID lamps that ordinary potting soil can not supply all necessary nutrients for rapid, healthy growth. Fertilizing is necessary to make extra nutrients available for sustained vigorous growth.

There are about 16 elements known to be necessary for plant life. Carbon, hydrogen and oxygen are absorbed from the air and water. The rest of the elements, called *nutrients*, are absorbed mainly from the soil or fertilizer. The *primary nutrients* (nitrogen (N), phosphorus (P) and potassium (K)) are the elements a plant uses the most. Almost all fertilizers show the N-

P-K percentages in big numbers on the front of the package. They are always listed in the same N-P-K order For example a 23-19-17 fertilizer has 23 percent nitrogen, 19 percent phosphorus and 17 percent potassium.

Calcium (Ca) and magnesium (Mg) are *secondary nutrients* or *elements*[1]. Iron (Fe), sulfur (S), manganese (Mn), boron (B), molybdenum (Mo), zinc (Zn) and copper (Cu) are *micro-nutrients* or *trace elements*. Trace elements are usually found in sufficient quantities in potting soil and in *complete* fertilizers such as Peters and Ecogrow for healthy plant growth and do not need to be added. Unless *fortified*, soilless mixes may be severely lacking in secondary and trace elements. It is still a good idea to use a fertilizer containing trace elements. Secondary and trace elements are usually not listed on fertilizer labels.

Primary Nutrients

Nitrogen (N) is the most important nutrient. It regulates the plant's ability to make proteins, essential to new protoplasm in the cells. N is essential to the production of chlorophyll and is mainly responsible for leaf and stem growth as well as overall size and vigor. Nitrogen is most active in young buds, shoots and leaves. Annuals love N and require high levels during vegetative growth.

Phosphorus (P) is necessary for photosynthesis and provides a mechanism for energy transfer within the plant. P is associated with overall vigor as well as flower and seed production. Plants use highest levels of P during the germination, seedling, and flowering stages of growth.

Potassium (K) is essential to the manufacture and movement of sugars and starches, as well as growth by cell division. K increases chlorophyll in foliage and helps regulate stomata openings so plants make better use of light and air. Potash encourages strong root growth and is associated with disease resistance and water intake. K is necessary during all stages of growth.

---

[1] Ca and Mg are also classified with N-P-K as *macro-nutrients*.

Secondary Nutrients

Magnesium (Mg) is found as a central atom in every chlorophyll molecule and is essential to the absorption of light energy. Mg aids in the utilization of nutrients. It also neutralizes soil acids and toxic compounds produced by the plant.

Calcium (Ca) is fundamental to cell manufacture and growth. Plants must have some calcium at the growing tip of each root.

Trace Elements

Trace elements are essential to chlorophyll formation and must be present in minute amounts, but little is known about the exact amounts that are needed. They function mainly as *catalysts* to plant processes and utilization.

Miracle-Gro is one of the old standard fertilizers.

Eco Grow is both for soil and hydroponics

Peter's General Purpose and Blossom Booster

Fertilizers

The goal of fertilizing is to supply the plant with proper amounts of nutrients for vigorous growth without toxifying the soil by over-fertilizing. A five- or six-gallon container full of rich, fertile potting soil will supply all the necessary nutrients for a month or longer. After the roots have absorbed most of the available N-P-K nutrients, they must be added to the soil to sustain vigorous growth. Unless fortified, soilless mixes require N-P-K fertilization from the start. I like to start fertilizing fortified soilless mixes after the first week or two of growth. Most commercial soilless mixes are fortified with secondary and trace elements. Use an N-P-K fertilizer containing secondary and trace elements in mixes that are not fortified.

A plant has different fertilizer needs as its metabolism changes throughout life. During germination and seedling growth, intake of phosphorus (P) is high. The vegetative growth stage requires high amounts of nitrogen (N) for green leaf growth. P and K are also necessary in substantial levels; a *general-purpose* N-P-K fertilizer is recommended. In the flowering stage, the plant is less concerned with vegetative growth. P intake is highest; N and K are less important. Using a *super bloom* fertilizer, low in N and K, and high in P will promote larger flower growth. However, some gardeners use an N-P-K, general-purpose fertilizer and get acceptable results. A high N content usually promotes greener, leafy growth during flowering. Plants need some N during flowering. Without N, older foliage may yellow and die prematurely.

Fertilizers may be either (water) *soluble* or *gradual release*. Both soluble and gradual release fertilizers can be organic or chemical.

SOLUBLE fertilizers lend themselves to indoor container cultivation and are preferred by commercial nurserypersons as well as many indoor gardeners. Soluble fertilizers dissolve in water and may be added or washed (leached) out of the soil easily. It is easy to control the exact amount of nutrients available to plants in a soluble form. Versatile soluble fertilizer may be applied in a water solution to the soil or misted directly on the leaves. Foliar feeding supplies nutrients directly to the leaves where they are used.

Chemical Soluble Fertilizers

Chemical granular fertilizers can easily be over-applied, creating toxic soil. It is almost impossible to leach them out fast enough to save the plant.

Osmocote™ chemical fertilizers are time-release. They are used by many nurseries because they are easy to apply and require only one application every few months. Using this type of fertilizer may be convenient, but exacting control is lost. They are best suited for ornamental containerized plants when labor costs and uniform growth are the main concerns.

PETERS™ fertilizer has been the choice of professional nurserypersons for many years. Indoor gardeners love it because the salts are pure and easy to work with. It is formulated with chelating agents to prevent settling out of elements, contains necessary secondary and trace elements, and has no chloride carbonates or excess sulfates, preventing buildup of excess salts. It is excellent for use with both soil and soilless mixes. Peters comes in many different N-P-K formulas. Those most commonly used indoors are listed.

The following formulas are mixed from a half-tablespoon to a tablespoon per gallon of water and applied with each watering.

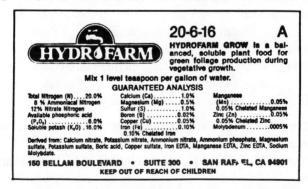

The label from Hydrofarm's vegetative growth fertilizer shows that it contains all of the necessary trace elements.

1. General Purpose (20-20-20) is readily available at most nurseries and used during the seedling and vegetative stages[2].
2. Peat-Lite Special (20-10-20) works very well during vegetative growth in both soil and soilless mixes. Less P helps contain roots. It contains high levels of secondary and trace nutrients[3].
3. Geranium Special (15-15-15), also used during vegetative growth, works very well for low pH situations. Geranium Special has a non-acidic source of N and reduced ammonium toxicity potential[3].
4. Blossom Booster (10-30-20) contains a high level of P, which is necessary during flowering. It increases bud set, count and size[3].
5. Variegated Violet Special (5-50-17) offers an accepted method of holding variegation in a plant's leaves. It reduces nitrogen, greatly increases phosphorus and holds a minimum potassium level. Some gardeners use it as a "super bloom" fertilizer.

Ecogrow® is produced in Seattle by Eco Enterprises. Its various formulas are made with the hydroponic horticulturist in mind, but can be used with soil as well. Ecogrow is a balanced formula that gives plants *all* of the nutrients necessary for strong, healthy growth. All the elements in Ecogrow are derived from *natural* minerals and nothing artificial is added. One of the interesting qualities of Ecogrow is that it does not totally dissolve in the nutrient solution. There *are* enough nutrients in the solution that plants get properly nourished, so do not worry about a little sediment in the solution. The pH is balanced at 6.3 when mixed with neutral tap water.

Ecogrow - secondary and trace element analysis: Ca 6%, S 2.6%, Mg 2.0%, Fe .2%, Mn .1%, Cl .1%, Cu .005%, Zn .05%, B .045%, Mo .002% .001% Co.

1. Standard (10-8-14) - a general-purpose fertilizer formulated for vegetative growth.
2. Monstera (20-6-12) - for plants needing high N intake for

[2] Trace elements: Mg .05%, Fe .05%, Mn .0031%, B .0068%, Zn .0025%, Cu .0036%, Mo .0009%
[3] Trace element content: Mg .15%, Fe .10%, Mn .056%, B .02%, Zn .0162%, Cu .01%, Mo .01%

rapid vegetative growth.

3. Bloom (3-35-10) - blossom-boosting formula low in N and high in P; great for fat, healthy, strong buds.

RA-PID-GRO® is a favorite of some professionals and home gardeners. The Multi-Use (23-19-17) formula will dissolve easily in water, is readily available, and contains a few trace elements, but the manufacturer will not divulge which ones! Supplemental trace element fertilization is necessary. Ra-Pid-Gro is used during the seedling and vegetative growth stages. It may be used during flowering, but supplies high levels of unnecessary N, which could promote undesired green vegetative growth.

MIRACLE-GRO® is the old reliable house plant and vegetable food. It comes in several formulas and may be found at just about any store with a gardening section. Miracle-Gro lists secondary and trace elements on the guaranteed analysis panel: Copper .05%, chelated iron .10%, manganese .05%, and zinc .05%.

1. The tomato formula (18-18-21) also contains magnesium (Mg) .05%. Many vegetables and flowers have very similar nutrient requirements. This formula is great for seedling and vegetative growth.

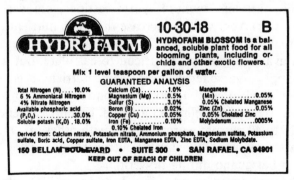

The label from Hydrofarm's flowering growth fertilizer shows that it contains all of the necessary trace elements.

2. The All-Purpose (15-30-15) formula is preferred by gardeners during flowering. The high concentration of phosphorus (P) helps rapid bud formation.

Gradual Release Organic Fertilizers

Organic plants boast a sweeter taste, but implementing an organic indoor garden requires horticultural *know-how*. The limited soil, space and the necessity for sanitation must be considered when growing organically. Outdoors, organic gardening is easy because *all* the forces of nature are there for you to seek out and harness. Indoors, essentially none of the natural phenomena are at play. Remember you are *Mother Nature* and must create everything! The nature of growing indoors does not lend itself to long-term organic gardens, but some organic techniques have been practiced with amazing success.

Most indoor *organic* gardens use potting soil, high in worm castings, peat, sand, manure, leaf mold, compost and fine dolomite lime. In a container, there is really no space to *build* the soil by mixing all kinds of neat composts and organic nutrients to cook down. Even if it were possible to *build* soil in a container, it would take months of valuable growing time and could foster bad bugs, fungi etc. It is easiest and safest to throw old, depleted soil out and start new plants with fresh organic soil.

Organic nutrients, manure, worm castings, blood and bone meal etc. work very well to increase the soil's nutrient content, but nutrients are released and available at different rates. The nutrient availability may be difficult to calculate, but it is hard to over-apply organic fertilizers. Organic nutrients seem to work best when used in combination with one another. This gives a more consistent availability of nutrients. Usually gardeners use a mix of 20 to 40 percent worm castings with other organic agents to get a strong, readily available nitrogen base. They fertilize later with bat guano during flowering.

An indoor garden using *raised beds* (page 126) allows *true* organic methods. The raised bed has enough soil to hold nutrients, promote organic chemical activity and ensure a constant supply of nutrients. It also has enough soil mass to promote heat and all kinds of fundamental organic activity.

The nutrients in organic fertilizers may vary greatly depending upon source, age, erosion, climate etc. The above figures are only approximate. For exact nutrient content, consult the vendor's specifications.

Organic Tea

Five- or 10-gallon pots do not contain enough soil to hold all the organic nutrients a plant will need throughout life. This dilemma is solved by using **organic tea**. The tea is a bit messy,

ORGANIC FERTILIZER	N	P	K	AVAILABILITY
Bat Guano	5	10	2	rapid
Blood Meal	13	1	0	rapid
Bone Meal (steamed)	2	14	0	medium
Cottonseed Meal	6	3	1	slow
Cow manure	2	.5	1.5	medium
Green Sand	0	1.5	4	medium
Kelp	.3	.2	.5	rapid
Sea Guano	15	5	2	rapid
Wood Ash	0	3	5	slow
Worm Castings	3.5	1	1	rapid

NOTE: This list shows only average nutrient yields. The actual yields will vary with the source.

even smelly, but very effective. These tea concoctions may contain just about any organic nutrient diluted in water. Fish emulsion is the most readily available commercial *organic tea*. You can even pour old goldfish water on the plants! *Worm castings*, high in nitrogen, and *bat guano*, high in phosphorus, are the most common ingredients in U-mix organic teas, because their soluble nutrients are immediately available to plants. If bringing bat guano, cow manure or any kind of feces into the home, mixing it with water and pouring it on plants is repulsive to you, do not garden organically!

There are many different mixtures of organic tea, and they are all generally safe to use. Just mix the organic nutrient(s) with water, let it sit overnight, mix it again, then strain out the heavy stuff by pouring the solution through a chesecloth or an old nylon before applying. The tea may be applied as often as each watering.

Bat guano - is highly prized for its high phosphorus content. It also contains many other nutrients. Bat guano is known as the *organic super bloom*. Unlike other organic fertilizers, it holds nutrients that are immediately available to plants. Found sheltered in caves, the guano dries with minimal decomposition. Bat guano can be thousands of years old. If 50 years old or less, it may contain high levels of nitrogen. After that, the nitrogen content dissipates. Bat guano is usually powder-like and can be used as a foliar spray, but it is chunky. Do not breathe the dust when handling; it is full of all kinds of bacteria that could make you sick. It is almost impossible to apply too much guano. An average dosage is one tablespoon per gallon. Bat guano may be difficult to find at retail stores; however, several suppliers listed in this book always have guano on hand.

Fish emulsion - is essentially ground-up fish parts suspended (emulsified) in a liquid. Fish emulsion is high in organic nitrogen and trace elements. This natural fertilizer is difficult to over-apply and is immediately available to plants. Fish emulsion may be used as a foliar spray, but it will clog small nozzles. Even deodorized fish emulsion stinks!

Sea guano - is collected mainly in Peru. This guano is famous for its high nitrogen content as well as other nutrients. The Humboldt Current along the coast of Peru and northern Chile keeps the rain from falling, and decomposition of the guano is minimal. The guano is scraped off the rocks of islands and the shores. Sea guano is very similar to bat guano in its application, and is difficult to find at retail outlets. The average dosage is one tablespoon per gallon of water.

Seaweed - contains all kinds of trace elements in forms that are available to plants. Seaweed is organic and will not burn plants. There are many kinds of seaweed. Each has its own unique structure and nutrient content. Seaweeds come in either powder, liquid or bulk fiber form. Most can be used in a foliar spray.

Worm castings - when pure, look like coarse graphite powder. They are high in available nitrogen as well as many other nutrients. Worm castings are used as an organic fertilizer as part of the soil. Angleworms eat and digest all kinds of decomposing organic matter. The castings are this excreted matter. Some of the qualities of worm castings are that they are heavy and very dense. When mixing with soil, use no more than 30 percent. Because they are so heavy, root growth can be impaired. Worm castings vary in the amount of nitrogen they contain. Most nurseries do not stock worm castings. However, there are many people making their own. Check the newspaper and ask at the nursery for possible sources.

Milorganite - is sewage sludge and is used as an ornamental plant fertilizer. Milorganite is not recommended for growing vegetables indoors because of its origin. It is impossible to tell if the sludge contains harmful heavy metals such as lead or chemicals.

Organics

Chemical fertilizers are highly refined and stripped of all but the precise chemical form listed on the label.

KELP is the "Cadillac of trace minerals" Kelp should be deep green, fresh and smelling like the ocean. Seaweed contains 60 to 70 trace minerals that are already chelated (existing in a form that's water-soluble and mobile in the soil). Greensand and granite dust are the two most common organic potassium sources.

Transplanting, Seedling and Cloning Fertilizers

Ortho **Up-Start**® is recommended for a smooth move of cuttings and transplants, as well as seedling growth. There are many similar products that work just as well as this one. Up-Start is a liquid that will readily dissolve in water. The 3-10-3 nutrient formula provides 10 percent available P, just what young roots need for vigorous growth. **Vitamin B₁** helps ease transplant wilt and shock. The root hormone 1-naphthalene-acetic acid (.015% by weight) stimulates root formation and growth. When cuttings are taken or transplanted, the roots are the first part a plant must develop in order to supply water and nutrients to stems and leaves.

Vitamin B₁, available under many brand names, is an organic vitamin that helps ease transplant shock and wilt. Using vitamin B₁ makes transplanting fast and easy.

It is also used as a fertilizer additive. Along with the first dose of fertilizer, add up to 25 drops per gallon of solution. This (25 drops per gallon) is a one-time-only application. Subsequent dosage is one drop per gallon with each watering.

Trace Element Fertilizers

Compound 111, S.T.E.M. and FTE are all Peters® products. Many other companies, both local and national, produce excellent products that are similar to Peters'. These trace element formulas are used by many indoor gardeners and nurserypeople alike. They work well to alleviate any trace element deficiency except for magnesium (Mg). None of the formulations have any Mg.

Compound 111 is a supplemental formula containing trace elements (Fe 1.5percent, Mn .12 percent, Zn .0754 percent, Cu .11362 percent, B .23242 percent, Mo .10757 percent) chelating agents, penetrating agents and color tracers. This formula is highly recommended if you mix your own fertilizer out of single elements or are using a fertilizer that does not contain trace elements. Compound 111 is the easiest trace element formula to use and the safest. It has less of each element to toxify the soil, and unlike the S.T.E.M. formula, does not contain sulfur. Compound 111 works well to treat any mysterious trace element deficiency. Often there is a suspicion of trace element deficiency, but the exact deficiency is not known for sure. By applying Compound 111, the problem will be solved and you will not have to know the exact nature of the deficiency.

The **S.T.E.M.** (Soluble Trace Element Mix) was developed to furnish trace elements immediately, in large doses. This is the *hottest* or most potent trace element formula around. Be very careful when using it. The S.T.E.M. formula was developed for a one-time application in treating trace element deficiencies. Note the percent concentrations of the trace elements.

The guaranteed analysis of Peters S.T.E.M. formula is: S 15.0%, B 1.45%, Cu 3.20%, Fe 7.5%, Mn 8.15%, Mo .046%, Zn 4.5%.

FTE (Fritted trace elements) are mixed with the soil or soilless mix for a long-lasting, slow-release application of six to 12 months. The elements are encased in a pulverized glass complex that resists heavy leaching. The nutrients are available at a more constant rate throughout life. This is a form of gradual release fertilizer, and is the only one that I recommend. The FTE formula is a safer one to use than the soluble ones, but may be overdone also. Once overdone, FTE may *not* be leached out. Apply only one-third teaspoon per cubic foot of soil.

The guaranteed analysis of Peters FTE is: Mn 5.0%, Fe 14.0%, Cu 1.5%, Zn 5.0%, B 0.8%, Mo 0.07%.

Mixing

To mix, dissolve powder, crystals, or liquid into a little warm (90 to 100° F) water; make sure it is totally dissolved, then add the balance of the tepid water. This will ensure that the fertilizer and water mix evenly.

Containers have very little soil in which to hold nutrients, and toxic salt buildup may become a problem. *Follow dosage instructions to the letter*. Adding too much fertilizer will not make plants grow faster. It may change the chemical balance of the soil and supply too much of a nutrient or lock in other nutrients, making them unavailable to the plant.

Application

The first thing that must be determined is: Do plants need fertilization? This may be determined by visual inspection, making an N-P-K soil test, or experimenting on a test plant(s). No matter which method is used, remember: Plants in small containers use available nutrients quickly and need frequent fertilizing, while plants in large planters have more soil, have more nutrients nutrients and require less frequent fertilizing.

Dissolved Salts (DS) meters, also referred to as Electrical Conductivity (EC) meters, are fundamental to precise control of overall nutrient content in the growing medium.

Visual inspection - If plants are growing well and have deep green, healthy leaves, they are probably getting all necessary nutrients from the soil. The moment growth slows, or leaves begin to turn pale green, it is time to fertilize. Do not confuse yellow leaves caused by a *lack of light* and yellow leaves caused by a nutrient deficiency.

Making an **N-P-K soil test** will reveal exactly how much of each major nutrient is available to the plant. The test kits mix a soil sample with a chemical. After the soil settles, a color reading is taken from the liquid, then matched to a color chart. The appropriate percentage of fertilizer is then added. This method is very exact, but more trouble than it is worth for the hobby gardener.

Many gardeners prefer to **experiment** on two or three test plants. This method yields experience and develops horticultural skills. Cuttings work especially well for this type of experiment. Give the test plants some fertilizer and see if they green up and grow faster.

Now it has been determined that the plants need fertilizer, but how much? The answer is simple. Just mix fertilizer as per instructions and water as normal, or dilute fertilizer and apply more often. If you want to get the most out of fertilization, use a soluble salts meter. Remember, small plants use much less fertilizer than large ones. Fertilize early in the day, so plants have all day to absorb and process the fertilizer.

It is almost impossible to explain how often to apply fertilizer. We know that large plants use more nutrients than small plants. The more often fertilizer is applied, the less concentrated it should be. Frequency of fertilization is one of the most widely disagreed upon subjects in the horticultural industry. Indoor, containerized plants may be *pushed* to incredible lengths; Some of them will absorb amazing amounts of fertilizer and grow well. Many gardeners add as much as one tablespoon per gallon (Peters 20-20-20 or 10-30-20) with each watering! This works best with growing mediums, especially soilless mix, that drain readily and are easy to leach. Other gardeners use only rich organic potting soil with fine dolomite lime added. No supplemental fertilizer is applied until a *super bloom* formula is needed for flowering.

A siphon applicator found at most nurseries will mix soluble fertilizers with water. The applicator is simply attached to the faucet with the siphon submerged in the concentrated fertilizer solution, and the hose attached to the other end. Often applicators are set at a 1:15 ratio. That is, for every unit of liquid concentrate fertilizer, 15 units of water will be mixed with it. Sufficient water *flow* is necessary for the suction to work properly. Misting nozzles restrict this flow. When the water is turned on, the fertilizer is siphoned into the system and flows out the hose. Fertilizer is generally applied with each watering, since a small percentage of fertilizer is metered in.

A garbage can, set 3 to 4 inches off the floor with a garden hose fitting at the bottom, will act as a gravity-flow source for fertilizer solution. The container is filled with water and fertilizer. With this system, the water temperature is easy to keep warm and fertilization is much easier. (see page 113)

I've found that when it comes to fertilization, experience will tell more than anything else. There are hundreds of N-P-K mixes and they all work! When choosing a fertilizer, make sure to read the entire label and know what the fertilizer claims it can do. Do not be afraid to try a few test plants.

Once you have an idea of how often to fertilize, put the garden on a regular feeding schedule of bi-weekly, weekly, bi-monthly, every watering, every other watering or every third watering. A schedule usually works very well, but it must be combined with a vigilant, caring eye that looks for over-fertilization and signs of nutrient deficiency.

Foliar Feeding

Foliar feeding (misting the leaves with fertilizer solution) makes

 Leach soil with one to two gallons of fresh water per gallon of soil every month or two. This is the best form of preventive maintenance against toxic salt buildup in the soil. Leaching too often, say weekly, would essentially wash everything out.

some nutrients available and usable immediately. Food is absorbed directly into the leaves. Foliar feeding is a good way to keep toxic nutrient levels from building up in the soil, but, like soil fertilization, may be overdone. In general, apply all foliar fertilizers at half strength. Daily foliar feeding with a *weak* solution, for example, *leaches* the nutrients from the leaves, just as excessive watering *leaches* nutrients from the soil. A good foliar feeding program would start after the plant's first month of growth. Apply fertilizer solution with a fine spray. See "About Spraying," pages 236-240.

Foliar feeding is more work, but creates almost instantaneous results. Nitrogen-deficient plants have turned from a pale yellow to a lime green in 12 short hours! In the case of nutrient-deficient soil, foliar feeding is a simple quick, cure. The nutrients are supplied directly and used immediately. Soil condi-

Foliar feeding is the quickest way to deliver nutrients to a plant.

tion or pH is not affected, but root absorption may improve. A combination of soil and foliar feeding is common. Good organic foliar fertilizers are fish emulsion and bat guano. Of course, it must be strained through a *tea bag* and the sprayer should not be prone to clogging. There are many chemical foliar fertilizers; Peters, Ra-Pid-Gro and Miracle-Gro. Dilute them the same as for regular fertilization for foliar feeding.

OVER-FERTILIZING can become one of the biggest problems for indoor gardeners. Too much fertilizer causes a buildup of nutrients (salts) to toxic levels and changes soil chemistry. When over-fertilized, growth is rapid and super-lush green, until the toxic levels are reached. When the toxic salt (fertilizer) level is reached, leaf tips burn (turn yellow, then black) and if the problem is severe, the leaves will curl under like a bighorn sheep's horns. Over fertilization is easy to catch in the early stages, two or three weeks before symptoms appear when using a soluble salts meter. page 148.

The chance of over-fertilization is greater in a small amount of soil. It can hold only a small amount of nutrients. While a large pot or planter can hold much more soil and nutrients safely, it will take longer to *flush* if overdone. It is very easy to add too much fertilizer to a small container. Large containers have good nutrient-holding ability.

To treat severely over-fertilized plants, leach soil with two gallons of water per gallon of soil, so as to wash all the excess nutrients out. The plant should start new growth and be looking better in one or two weeks. If the problem is severe, and leaves are curled, the soil may need to be leached several times. After the plant appears to have leveled off to normal growth, start foliar feeding or apply diluted fertilizer solution.

Nutrient Disorders

There are many things which can go wrong indoors that are confused with a lack of fertilizer. The pH of both the growing medium and water is of prime importance. If the pH is not between 6 and 7 (6 to 6.5 for hydroponic units) some nutrients will be locked in the soil, even if the nutrient is in supply. The plant is not able to absorb it chemically because the pH will not let it. For example, a full point movement in pH represents a *tenfold* increase in either alkalinity or acidity. This means that a pH of 5.5 would be *10 times* more acidic than a pH of 6.5. A pH below 6.5 may cause a deficiency in calcium. If this happens, root tips could burn and leaves could get fungus (leaf spot). (see photo, page 235). A pH over 7 could slow down the plant's iron intake, and chlorotic leaves with yellowing veins could result.

Incorrect pH contributes to most serious *nutrient disorders*. It has always amazed me that so many people worry about fertilizer application and do not pay attention to the pH!! See "PH Chart," page 107.

This lime tree is being leached (flushed) with about five gallons of water to wash all the toxic salt from the soil.

Besides the pH problem, there are the basic elements of the environment that must be checked. Since you are Mother Nature indoors, you are responsible for creating a perfect climate or several microclimates for the plants to grow in. Check each of the vital signs and *fine tune* the environment, especially the soluble salts, and *ventilation,* before deciding that plants are nutrient-deficient. See "Checklist," page 256.

Nutrient deficiencies will normally not occur in **fresh** potting soil containing **dolomite lime** or in soilless mix fortified by the gardener and containing all necessary trace elements and dolomite lime. This *fresh* planting mix is coupled with a regular fertilization schedule. There are two basic things that go wrong regarding nutrients: 1) not enough, indicated by lime-green leaves; this is treated by applying a general-purpose fertilizer. N-P-K are all used at similar rates and a single nutrient seldom builds to toxic levels. 2) Too much, indicated by super-dark green leaves and/or burnt tips; treat by leaching the soil of excess nutrients.

Primary Nutrient Disorders **Nitrogen** is the most common nutrient found deficient. Growth slows; lower leaves turn yellow and eventually die. Remedy by fertilizing with N or N-P-K fertilizer. For fast results, foliar feed. An overdose of N will cause soft, weak growth and even delay flower and fruit production if it is allowed to accumulate.

Phosphorus deficiency is less common. Leaves will become deep green and uniformly smaller, and the plant will be stunted. Lower leaves will turn yellow and die. Treat with P or N-P-K fertilizer. Toxic signs of phosphorus will take a long time to surface. Treat toxicity by leaching the soil with fresh water.

Potassium deficiency occurs occasionally. Many times K deficient plants are the tallest and appear healthy. But the lower leaf tips turn yellow, followed by whole leaves that turn dark yellow and die. The K is usually present in the soil, but locked in by high salinity. First, leach the toxic salt out of the soil, then apply foliar N-P-K fertilizer.

Discolored leaf tips (top photo) on this Jeruselum Cherry plant tell the experienced gardener that toxic salt build up is occurring in the soil.

A low pH and lack of fertilizer are responsible for the pale yellow discoloration on the leaves of this geranium (bottom photo).

Secondary Nutrient Disorders

Secondary nutrient deficiencies may easily be avoided by mixing one cup of fine dolomite lime per cubic foot of soil before planting. Dolomite supplies soil with Mg and Ca.

Magnesium (Mg) is the most common secondary nutrient to be found deficient. It is most commonly deficient in soilless mixes, but is also found deficient in soil. Lower leaves yellow, veins remain green, the tips and then the entire leaf turns brown. The leaf tips usually turn upward, then die. The entire plant could discolor and die within a few weeks. Cure by watering as usual, adding one teaspoon *epsom salts* to every two quarts of water. If the deficiency progresses to the top of the plant, turning the growing shoots lime-colored, you will notice the greening-up effect there first. In a few days, it will move down the plant, turning lower leaves progressively greener. Continue a regular watering schedule with Epsom salts added until symptoms totally disappear. In a soilless mix, you may want to use Epsom salts regularly, but it will not be necessary if the fertilizer contains Mg.

Calcium deficiency is uncommon, but when found, it may be too late to do anything. If too much Ca is applied early in life, it stunt growth as well. Signs of deficiency are a yellowing and dying back of leaf edges. Mixing *fine dolomite lime* with the soil before planting is the best way to prevent this ailment. If you must, use a trace element formula containing Ca to treat the deficiency.

Micronutrient Disorders

Sulphur (S) is almost never a problem. Many fertilizers contain some form of sulfur. Deficiency shows when leaves turn pale green and general-purpose N-P-K fertilizer fails to cure the problem. Very seldom is it a problem, but if it is, remedy with trace element fertilizer.

Iron (Fe) deficiency is somewhat common indoors. An iron-deficient (chlorotic) plant is yellowing between the veins, with the veins of the leaves remaining green. Leaves may start to fall if it is severe. Chlorosis (yellowing) is generally caused by a high pH rather than a lack of iron. To remedy, correct pH. If necessary, foliar feed with fertilizer containing soluble chelated iron. I recommend Compound 111.

Other micronutrients - manganese, boron, molybdenum, zinc and copper - are rarely deficient in any soil. By using commercial potting soil, fortified soilless mix, or N-P-K fertilizer with trace elements, you are guaranteed that all necessary trace elements are available. Fertilizers that contain only trace elements are available, but may be very tricky to use. Trace elements are necessary in minute amounts and reach toxic levels easily. I advise NOT using a special trace element fertilizer more than once or twice a crop (once every two months) or unless it is absolutely necessary. If using a trace element mix, Compound 111 is my favorite.

Burned leaf tips on this False Aralia demonstrate severe salt burn. The soil should be leached immediately.

CHAPTER FIVE
Hydroponic Gardening

The roots of *hydroponics* come from two Greek words that were put together: *hydro* meaning "water" and *ponos* meaning "labor." Today hydroponics is the science of growing plants without soil, most often in a soilless mix. With hydroponics, two very important factors may be totally controlled: (1) nutrient intake (2) oxygen intake via roots.

Hydroponic gardening, like HID gardening, is easy and fun, once the concept and principles are understood. There are a few basic rules that must be followed to make a good system be productive. First let's look at how and why hydroponics works.

In hydroponics, the inert soilless medium contains essentially no nutrients of its own. All the nutrients are supplied by the nutrient solution (technically this is aeroponics). This solution passes over the roots or floods around them at regular intervals, later draining off. The oxygen around the roots is able to speed the plants' uptake of nutrients. This is why plants grow so fast hydroponically. They are able to take in food as fast as they are able to utilize it. In soil, as in hydroponics, the roots absorb nutrients and water; even the best soil rarely has as much oxygen in it as a soilless hydroponic medium.

Hydroponics works well for horticulturists who are willing to spend 10 to 20 minutes per day in their garden. The garden requires extra maintenance; plants grow faster, there are more things to check that have the potential to go wrong. In fact, some people do not like hydroponic gardening because it requires too much additional care. I have never seen a hydroponic garden that was less work than a comparable soil or soilless garden.

All too often, people who just started indoor gardening get so excited about it that they go too far too fast. They buy all these *new* little gadgets and have many more projects going than they can properly manage. The biggest problem people have in purchasing hydroponic units, is following the directions to assemble the system. This is important to remember when thinking about constructing and/or inventing your own unit. It will take a month or two to work out most of the bugs in a homemade unit. Do not expect the best results from the garden the first or second time.

Hydroponic gardening is very exacting and not as forgiving as soil gardening. The soil works as a buffer for nutrients and holds them longer than the inert medium of hydroponics. In fact, some very advanced hydroponic systems do not even use a

Dutch greenhouse is completely hydroponic.

soilless mix. The roots are suspended in the air and misted with nutrient solution. The misting chamber is kept dark so algae do not compete with roots.

I have found that plants, properly maintained, grown hydroponically under HID lamps tend to grow a little more lush foliage and at a faster rate than plants grown in soil. The garden calendar is usually moved up one or two weeks. The real benefit with hydroponics is realized later in life. When roots are restricted and growth slows in containerized plants, hydroponically grown plants are still getting the maximum amount of nutrients.

The principles involved in hydroponics are simple and direct, but the application of these principles can become *very* complex. Gravel is the inert medium most commonly used to hold the roots and stabilize the plant while the nutrient solution passes over the roots in one of many ways. The nutrient solution drains away from the roots, so the *oxygen* will have a chance to work with the roots to draw in the nutrients. These are the basic principles of hydroponics; the nutrient solution, its application, and the growing medium are the main variables in hydroponic gardening.

Self-watering containers are very convenient and work best with perennial plants.

Different Systems

The way the nutrient solution is applied distinguishes the various systems. It generally dictates the soilless medium used.

Hydroponic systems may be classified as *active* or *passive*. An *active* system *actively* moves the nutrient solution. Examples of active systems are: (1) fill and drain (2) top feed.

Passive systems rely on capillary action of the wick and the growing medium. The nutrient solution is *passively* absorbed by the wick, medium and roots. The mediums that are normally used in a wick system are vermiculite, sawdust, peat moss etc. For rapid growth, the average wick system keeps the medium too wet; consequently, not enough air is available to the roots. However, the wick system works very well if engineered properly. The soilless medium used, the number of wicks, their gauge and texture are the main variables involved in a wick system. The wick system has no moving parts. There is nothing mechanical to break, replace or malfunction. Wick systems also boast a low initial cost and once set up and functioning properly, they require little work to maintain. One very efficient use of the wick system has been to root cuttings.

Hydroponic systems may be further classified as *recovery* and *non-recovery*. "Non-recovery" means just what it says. Once the nutrient solution is applied to the inert growing medium, it is *not recovered*. These systems use sand, sawdust or some other readily available substance as the medium. No nutrient is recovered; less is applied, promoting less waste, complication and labor. Non-recovery systems are used mainly for commercial applications where the soilless medium is plentiful and the soil is not arable.

The *flood* and *top feed* methods are *active recovery* systems. They *actively* work by moving a volume of nutrient solution into contact with the roots. *Recovery*, because the nutrient solution is recovered after it has drained off and will be used again. These systems tend to use mediums that will drain fairly rapidly and hold lots of air, such as pea gravel, light pumice rock or crushed brick. The flood method is used by most commercial hydroponic operations and many home systems. The Hydropot™ is a (bottom) flood system. This system has proved to be low-maintenance and easy to use.

The top feed method is a little more intricate but used in hydroponic units with excellent results. There are many very efficient top feed systems. The nutrient solution is delivered by a pipe overhead. See photo, page 132.

In a flood system, the water floods into the bed, usually from the bottom, pushing the CO_2-rich, oxygen-poor air out. When the medium drains, it draws the *new* oxygen-rich air into the growing medium. Top feed systems apply the nutrient solution to the base of each plant with a small hose. The solution is aerated as it flows through the air.

The Hydrofarm™ is one of the oldest and most productive hydroponic systems available.

The Growing Medium

The purpose of the growing medium is to harbor oxygen, water and nutrients and support the root system of a plant. As with soil, the *texture* of the soilless medium is of utmost importance. The texture should be one that lets the solution drain rapidly enough for the roots to get a good supply of oxygen. A fast-draining medium, holding little water for a long time, is ideal for active recovery hydroponic systems.

Fibrous materials, such as vermiculite, hold moisture within their cells and water retention is high. This type of medium is desired with a *passive, capillary action,* wick system.

The *size* of the medium is important. As with soil, the smaller the particles, the closer they pack and the slower they drain. The larger the particles, the faster they drain and the more air they hold.

Irregular materials have more surface area and hold more water than round ones, which hold less water. Avoid gravel with sharp edges that could cut a plant's roots if it fell or was jostled around much. Round pea gravel, smooth, washed gravel, crushed brick or some form of lava are the best kinds of mediums for growing flowers and vegetables in an active recovery system. Rock should be of igneous (volcanic) origin. This type of rock tends to have a neutral pH and will not break down under hydroponic growing conditions. Gravel is the most widely used hydroponic growing medium for flowers and vegetables. It holds the exact amount of moisture and nutrients and does not stay too wet. The best kind of gravel to use for growing indoors is a pea gravel one-eighth to three-eights inch in diameter. Ideally, over half of the medium should be about a quarter-inch in diameter.

Applied Hydroponics supplies a new ceramic hydroponic medium that could be better than gravel. In any case, wash rock thoroughly to get out all the dust, which turns to sediment.

The medium should be clean so as not to react to nutrients. For example, gravel from a limestone quarry is full of calcium carbonate and old concrete is full of lime. When mixed with water, calcium carbonate will raise the pH: the concrete kill the garden. Sawdust holds too much water for plant growth and is too acidic. Other mixtures made from pebbles or anything near the ocean could very well be full of ocean salt. If you suspect this, it may be easier to get another load of medium than to try to clean out the salts.

Sterilizing

The medium must be *sterilized* before each new planting. This is much easier than replacing the medium, as advised to do with soil. For apartment dwellers, hydroponics provides an alternative to heavy, messy soil gardening. Instead of toting copious quantities of soil in and out of the building, the soilless medium is sterilized. Soil can become expensive. The reason for sterilization is obvious: to prevent any bad micro-organisms from getting started in the beautiful garden.

Before sterilizing, the roots will have to be removed from the medium. An average tomato plant (four or five inches tall or three or four months old) will have a root mass about the size of a desk telephone. Roots can create a huge mass in larger bed systems. It really does not matter if a few roots are left in the system, but try to get at least 90 to 95 percent. The fewer roots, the less chance the system has of clogging. A clogged system does not fill or drain properly.

The roots will tend to mat up near the bottom of the bed. It is easy to remove them in one large mat. Some of the medium may be embedded in the roots. It is easier to get more medium than trying to pick it from between the roots.

There are many ways to sterilize the garden. The one used by most systems is very easy. First, remove the nutrient solution from the tank, then make up a solution of ordinary laundry bleach such as Clorox or Purex (calcium or sodium hypochlorite) or hydrochloric acid, the kind used in hot tubs and swimming pools.

Apply one cup of bleach per five gallons of water, flood the medium with the sterilizing solution for at least one half-hour, then flush. Use lots of fresh water to leach and flush the entire system: beds, connecting hoses and drains. Make sure all the toxic chemicals are gone by flushing the entire system for at least one hour (two intervals of half an hour each) before replanting.

Rockwool

Rockwool is the neatest invention since the sun! It is an inert, sterile, porous, non-degradable growing medium that provides firm root support. Like all soilless mediums, rockwool acts as a temporary reservoir for nutrients. This affords the grower a tremendous amount of control over plant growth through nutrient uptake.

This revolutionary new growing medium consists of thin strand-like fibers made primarily from limestone, granite or almost any kind of rock. With the appearance of lent collected by a cloths dryer, rockwool does not resemble any other growing media.

Rockwool is the growing medium of choice in Holland. This entire greenhouse is watered automatically.

Rockwool has been used for many years as home and industrial insulation. In fact, the walls in your home may be packed full of rockwool. The rockwool used for insulation is very similar to the horticultural grade except for one thing; it is treated with a fire retarding substance that will kill plants.

Definite advantages are reaped when growing in this soilless substrate. It is economical, consistent and easy to control. But best of all, rockwool's fibrous structure and will hold about 20% air even when it is completely saturated.

If this stuff is so good, why haven't you heard of it yet? Rockwool was just introduced into the U.S. in 1985. The word travels slowly and the American horticultural community has been slow to adapt. Most of growers have not even heard of rockwool yet.

Rockwool has been used in European greenhouses for over 15 years. It was first discovered in Denmark in 1969. Growers began using rockwool as a way around the ban on soil-grown nursery stock imposed by some of the European community. Today, an estimated 50% of all western European greenhouse vegetables are grown exclusively in rockwool.

Other mediums like peat and soils are becoming more expensive to produce and can easily vary in quality. This fact, coupled with the high cost of sterilization, prompted European growers to explore new alternatives.

Rockwool slabs contain pepper plants in neat rows.

European growers switched to rockwool because it is inexpensive and easy to control. But the most important fact is that they not only changed, they continued to use it.

Rockwool is produced from rock alone or a combination of rock, limestone and coke. The rigid components are melted at temperatures exceeding 2,500 F. This molten solution is poured over a spinning cylinder, very similar to the way cotton candy is made with liquified sugar. As the molten solution flies off the cylinder, it elongates and cools to form fibers. These fibers could be likened to cotton candy fibers. The product of these fibers, rockwool, is then pressed into uniform blocks, sheets, cubes or granulated. The blocks are rigid and easy to handle. They may be cut into just about any size desirable. Granulated rockwool is easily placed into growing containers or used like vermiculite or perlite as a soil amendment. The heat used in its production renders rockwool sterile and safe to grow in.

Rockwool can be used in both recovery and non-recovery hydroponic systems. As explained earlier, the nutrient solution in a recovery system is constantly changing. Salts soon build up

Transplanting flowers and vegetables grown in rockwool is simply a matter of setting a four-inch square on a slab of rockwool.

to toxic levels as plants use selected nutrients within the solution. The nutrient solution must be monitored constantly and adjusted to provide the exact concentration of nutrients for optimum growth. However, with a non-recovery system, the excess nutrient solution drains off and is not recovered. The plants get all the nutrients they need and any nutrients that are not used will simply drain off. A fresh nutrient-rich solution is used for the next watering. Apply enough nutrient solution to get a 25% drain or leaching effect. This serves two purposes: 1) it flushes out excess salts from the medium and applies adequate nutrient solution to the medium.

When used with an open ended drip system, rockwool is easily irrigated with a nutrient solution controlled by a timer. The usual procedure in Europe is to apply a small amount of fertilizer two or three times a day. Enough excess solution is applied to obtain a 10-25% leaching effect every day.

Do not let all of this control fool you. Even though rockwool will hold 10-14 times as much water as soil, it does not provide

A plastic covering prevents the growth of algae on rockwool slabs. The convenient square shape makes the slabs easy to stack in the corner.

the buffering action available in soil. The pH of rockwool is about 7.8. An acidic fertilizer solution (about 5.5 on the pH scale) is required to maintain the actual solution at a pH of about 6.5 or lower. Errors made in the nutrient solution mix or with pH level, will be magnified. Be careful to monitor both the pH and nutrient level with a watchful eye.

There are some tricks to handling rockwool. Dry rockwool can be abrasive and act as an irritant to the skin. When handling dry Rockwool, use gloves and goggles. Once the rockwool is thoroughly wet, it is easy and safe to work with; it creates no dust and does not irritate to the skin. Keep out of the reach of children and wash clothes thoroughly after prolonged use around rockwool as a safety precaution.

Rockwool stays so wet that algae grows on surfaces exposed to light. While this green slimy algae is unsightly, it does not compete with plants for nutrition. However, harmless fungus gnats could take up residence. Avoid the unsightly algae by covering the rockwool with plastic.

A spaghetti hose drips nutrient solution to a healthy pepper plant.

The Hydroponic Nutrient Solution

To gain a more complete background on nutrients, etc., read Chapter 4, "Water and Fertilizer." The same principles that apply to soil apply to the hydroponic medium.

Always use the best fertilizer you can find. The fertilizers recommended in this book have worked well for hydroponic gardening. Ecogrow and Dyna Gro lead in popularity because of their *complete* formulas. All hydroponic fertilizers should have *all* of the necessary macro- and micronutrients.

Whether or not a hydroponic garden is organic or chemical is up to you. An organic garden will be more work to maintain than one using prepared *chemical* fertilizers.

Organic teas must be prepared in the tea bag to ensure that the pipes do not plug up from sludge. Cheap fertilizer (not recommended), like organic fertilizers, will contain sludge, which could build up and require more frequent cleaning of the system.

There are numerous brands of hydroponic fertilizer to choose from.

Fertilizers should be chelated, to help nutrient uptake by roots. Chelated nutrients are immediately available to the plant.

Sometimes it is necessary to add trace element mixes, such as Compound 111.

For fast-growing annuals, the nutrient solution should be changed at least every two (at the most three) weeks. It can go longer, but growth could slow and deficiencies result. Changing the solution as often as every week would not hurt anything. Plants absorb nutrients at different rates and some of the elements run out before others. The best form of preventive maintenance is to change the solution often. Fertilizer is probably the least expensive necessity in a garden If you skimp on fertilizer or try to save it, the garden may be stunted so badly it will not recover in time to produce a good crop. The pH is also continually changing, due to its reaction to the nutrient uptake, providing another reason to change the nutrient solution frequently. The nutrients being used at different rates could create a salt (unused fertilizer) buildup. This problem is usually averted by using pure nutrients and flushing the soilless medium thoroughly with fresh, tepid water between nutrient solutions.

Hydroponics gives the means to supply the maximum nutrients a plant needs, but it can also starve them to death or over-feed them rapidly. Remember this is a *hot* or fast *high-performance* system. If one thing malfunctions, say the electricity goes off, the pump breaks, the drain gets clogged with roots, or there is a rapid fluctuation in the pH, each of these things could cause severe problems with the garden. A mistake could kill or stunt plants so badly that they never fully recover.

PH

Most flowers and vegetables grow hydroponically within a pH range of 5.8 to 6.8, 6.3 is ideal. The pH in hydroponic gardens requires an extremely vigilant eye by the gardener. All of the nutrients are in solution. The pH of the nutrient solution

Change the nutrient solution every two weeks.

changes easily. The roots use nutrients at different rates. The changes in the amounts of nutrients in the solution will change the pH. If the pH is not within the *acceptable hydroponic range* (6 to 6.5), nutrients may not be absorbed as fast as possible.

Do not use sodium hydroxide to raise pH. It is very caustic and difficult to work with. Potassium hydroxide is much easier to use.

 Check the pH of the nutrient solution every day and keep the pH at 6.3.

The reservoir for the Hydrofarm can also serve as a plant stand.

The Reservoir

The reservoir should be as large as possible. Be prepared! Forgetting to replenish the water supply and/or nutrient solution could easily result in crop failure! Plants use much more water than nutrients, and water also evaporates from the system. An approximate water loss of 5 to 25 percent per day, depending on climate conditions (mainly humidity and temperature) and the size of plants, can be expected. This amounts to many, many gallons of solution per week. Less evaporation occurs when there is a top on the reservoir. When the water is used, the concentration of elements in the solution increases; there is less water in the solution and nearly the same amount of nutrients. More sophisticated systems have a valve (usually a float valve like the kind found in a toilet) that adds more water as it is used from the reservoir. Most systems have a *full* line on the inside of the reservoir tank to show when the solution is low. Water should be added as soon as the solution level lowers, which could be as often as every day! The reservoir should contain *at least* 20 percent more nutrient solution than it takes to fill the beds, to compensate for evaporation. The larger the volume of liquid, the more forgiving it is and the easier it is to control.

It is a big job to empty and refill a hydroponic unit with 20 to 60 gallons of water. To make it easier, the system should be able to pump the solution out of the reservoir. If the water must sit for a couple of days to let chlorine dissipate or to alter the pH before putting it into the tank, the system should pump water back into the reservoir. This will greatly ease your task as a hydroponic horticulturist. The *used* nutrient solution may be pumped into the vegetable garden or down the nearest drain but not into a septic tank. Do not try to use this *used* nutrient solution on other indoor plants.

 Check the level of the reservoir daily and replenish if necessary.

If the system is unable to pump the *used* nutrient solution out of the bed, place the unit at such an altitude that it may be siphoned or flow by gravity into a drain or outdoor garden.

The Irrigation Cycle

The irrigation or watering cycle depends on the same things as does the soil: plant size, climate conditions and the type of medium used. If the particles are large, round and smooth, and drain rapidly like pea gravel, the cycle will be often: two to four times daily. Fibrous mediums with irregular surfaces, such as vermiculite or rockwool drain slowly. These mediums are watered less often or utilize a capillary wick system.

Flood systems with pea gravel are generally flooded two or three times daily for 30 minutes. The water comes to within half an inch of the top of the gravel and should completely drain out of the medium at each watering. Top feed systems are usually cycled for about 30 minutes and should be watered two to four times daily.

During and soon after irrigation, the nutrient content of the bed and the reservoir are the same concentration. As the time passes between irrigations, the nutrient concentration and the pH gradually change. If enough time passes between waterings, the nutrient concentration may change so much that the plant is not able to absorb properly.

There are many variations on frequency of watering. As with soil, experimentation will probably tell you more than anything else. One gardener explained to me, "After a while you kind of get the feel for it." It took this hydroponic horticulturist two years to make it work right. If possible try experiments on one or two plants at a time, instead of subjecting an entire bed or garden to an experiment.

The temperature of the nutrient solution should stay somewhere in the range of 65 to 75° F. If there is a problem with keeping the room warm in winter, the nutrient solution may be heated instead of the room Submerge a grounded aquarium heater or grounded heat cables to heat the nutrient solution. It may take a few days for the cables or heater to heat a large volume of solution. Never place the heat cable in the soilless hydroponic medium. The heat from the cable could fry the roots when the medium dries out.

When air is cooler than water, the water evaporates into the air rapidly. The greater the temperature differential, the more humid the air! Remember to weigh the costs when using this technique: temperature vs. humidity vs. cost.

The nutrient solution should be replaced with water that is at least 60° F. Cold water will shock the plants. It could take a few days to warm up, thus stunting all the plants!

Never let the water temperature get higher than 85° F. If roots get too hot, they could be damaged. Submersible heaters of any kind must be *grounded* and constructed of materials (usually plastic) that give off no harmful residues; the most common one is lead.

Hydroponic Nutrient Disorders

When the hydroponic garden is on a regular maintenance schedule, nutrient problems are usually averted. Change the nutrient solution if the cause of the nutrient disorder is not known for sure. This method is the easiest and the most secure. If you can determine the exact cause of the disorder, add 10 to 20 percent more of the deficient ingredient for two weeks or until the disorder has disappeared.

Read "Nutrient Disorders," pages 152-157. Hydroponic gardens must be watched more closely than a soil garden. If the pH is off and there is a nutrient deficiency, this could severely affect the garden, and the novice gardener may not notice the problem until it is in its advanced stages. Treatment must be rapid and certain, but it will take a few days for the plant to respond to the remedies. Foliar feed the sick plants for fast results. What if two or more elements are deficient at the same time? This may give plants the appearance of having no specific cause, just symptoms! What do you do when the garden enters the

If the garden has a nutrient disorder, change the nutrient solution and adjust the pH.

unknown nutrient deficiency syndrome? When this sort of mind-bending problem occurs, *change the nutrient solution immediately!* This will supply the missing elements. The plants do not have to be diagnosed, just treated.

Over-fertilization (page 152), once diagnosed, is easy to deal with. Drain the nutrient solution, then flush with *fresh* tepid water. The number of times the system is flushed depends on the severity of the problem. Flush at least twice. Replace with properly mixed solution.

Nutrient disorders will occur to all the plants at the same time if they are receiving the same solution. Climatic disorders - windburn, lack of light, temperature stress, fungi and insect damage - usually show up on the plants that are most affected. For example, plants that are next to a heat vent may show signs of heat scorch, while the rest of the garden looks healthy. Or a plant on the edge of the garden may be small or leggy, since it receives less light.

Building Your Own Hydroponic System

One option is to build your own hydroponic unit. This is easy, but there are certain things that must be looked after for the system to work properly. Sealing up all joints and using few or no seams are two basic codes of hydroponic unit construction. Seal seams with waterproof caulk or use fiberglass resin and material for no-leak construction. You don't want to go on vacation for a few days, only to find on your return that the hydroponic system flooded out the upstairs bedroom the afternoon you left. Drain holes or pipe connections must be sure fit, with no leakage. Teflon tape is a good companion for threaded connections.

Many hydroponic systems using the fill-and-drain method must have elevated beds so the solution may drain back into the reservoir. Consider this when building and installing hydroponic units in rooms with limited ceiling space. The reservoir can be placed in a hole in the floor if ceiling space is limiting. Some gardeners use a sump pump in a concrete basement hole.

A large, covered reservoir is very important. Remember, the larger the reservoir, the more forgiving. The larger the container, the more solution. The more solution there is, the longer it will take for it to become depleted; the pH will fluctuate less and it will generally be more stable.

The size of the hydroponic container is important. The roots have to grow big enough to support a plant. In large bed systems, the roots glob up at the bottom of the tank. In fact, they get so big they look like a large mat or mattress of roots. In smaller beds, one to three gallons, roots could fill the container and grow out the bottom in two to six weeks. As with soil, the size of the hydroponic container dictates its buffing or forgiving effect.

Roots may clog the drain. Place a small mesh (quarter-inch or less) screen made from a non-corrosive material, such as plastic over the drain. The screen should be easy to remove and clean.

The frequency of watering depends on the kind of soilless medium used. A fast-draining medium such as pea gravel requires watering two to four times daily, while slow-draining vermiculite requires watering only once a day or less. Fill the bed so it is evenly moist; drain it completely and rapidly so oxygen will be available to roots as soon as possible.

A *flood* system could be as simple as using a five-gallon plastic bucket filled with washed gravel and a drain hole in the bottom. The hole is plugged with a cork, then nutrient solution, kept in another five-gallon bucket, is poured in. After 20 to 30 minutes, the cork is removed, and the nutrient solution is drained back into the other bucket for application later that day or the next day. This method is a little sloppy since the liquid is poured through the air (which also aerates it). This system provides an easy, inexpensive way for *soil* gardeners to get a look at hydroponic gardening. It is not the most efficient nor the most productive system, but it will get your feet wet!

Another *manual, gravity-flow* system attaches a reservoir bucket to a soilless medium or bed bucket with a flexible hose.

The reservoir bucket is then raised above the pot so the nutrient solution flows into it. After a couple of hours, the bucket is lowered to let the solution flow back into the reservoir bucket. This system could take a couple of hours to set up and may require a trip to the hardware store for some plastic fittings. Once set up, the system is no mess and no fuss. Just be there daily to lift and lower the bucket and pay attention to the evaporation of the nutrient solution!

The next kind of *active, recovery* hydroponic unit uses an aquarium pump and works on the bottom *flood* method as well. It pumps air into a sealed container full of nutrient solution. The pressure from the pump makes the solution pump up into the hydroponic bed. The pump actually pumps air into the nutrient solution! After the solution is in the bed, the pump continues forcing air through the solution. It aerates the nutrient solution while in contact with the roots. This system is easily automated. An inexpensive timer may be attached to the pump so the unit will operate automatically, keeping the solution in the bed for about two hours. This method is good for people who will not be there every day to cycle the nutrients manually. If you automate, be careful not to run the pump dry.

A basic hydroponic system is manufactured with a simple hose and a mobile bucket.

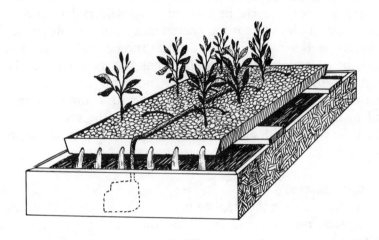

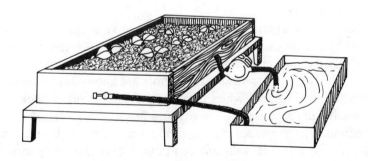

The hydroponic system above moves the nutrient solution with a submergible pump. An external pump transfers the nutrient solution from the growing bed to the nutrient solution reservoir in the bottom system.

Another kind of *active, recovery, bottom flood* system uses a submergible pump, which is a little more expensive. This type of system is able to recycle the nutrients several times daily at 20- to 30-minute cycles. This is the system many home gardeners and professionals use. It is one of the most successful, because of its ease of operation and the control that may be exercised. The nutrient solution is cycled several times per day; maximum nutrient application and uptake are achieved. A timer is attached to the irrigation cycle, which automates the system. Make sure the system is designed to keep the pump submerged to prevent air lock. Also, watch out for unwanted siphoning.

Getting Started

Starting seeds in the medium may not be very easy. Tiny seeds easily wash away, get too deep or dry out. Many people prefer to plant seeds or cuttings in a peat pot or root cube. The pot or cube is transplanted into the medium after the plant is two or three weeks old. Cuttings transplant best into a hydroponic garden using a root cube or peat pot. This way, when cuttings are placed into the hydroponic medium, the root cube will be able to hold the extra moisture it needs for the dry times in between waterings.

Read "Transplanting," pages 259-261. Transplanting is easy with hydroponics; simply remove the plant from the medium, and place it in another place in the medium. The younger the plant the better this works. If the roots are allowed to grow very long, they will break when moved in transplanting. Shock will result if the roots are broken off and not gently returned to the medium. After transplanting, scoop up some of the nutrient solution or mix a B_1 solution and pour it over the newly moved transplant, then cycle the nutrient solution through the system so it gets adequate moisture to let roots settle in.

It is OK to water a bed four to six times per day if necessary. Make sure the nutrient solution drains completely out each time and there is no water that is still soaking roots, keeping them too wet. The maximum watering cycle should be no longer than 30 minutes.

CHAPTER SIX

Air

Fresh air is at the heart of all successful indoor gardens. Think about your role as *Mother Nature*. In the great outdoors, air is abundant and almost always fresh. The level of CO_2 in the air over a field of rapidly growing vegetation could be only one-third of normal on a very still day. Soon the wind blows in *fresh new* air. Rains cleanse the air and plants of dust and pollutants. All of this happens in the atmosphere, a very large place. When plants are growing in a small room, Mother Nature really has to be on her toes to replicate the air of the great outdoors. Since there are none of the natural elements to *make* CO_2-rich, *fresh* air, you, *Mother Nature*, must take on the task!

Air is also used by the roots. Oxygen must be present along with water and nutrients for the roots to feed properly. If the soil is compacted or water-saturated, the roots have no air, and suffocate.

Fresh air is easy to come by and inexpensive to maintain. The main tool used to maintain fresh air is an *exhaust fan placed near the ceiling of the room.*

Air provides essential elements for plant growth. A plant uses carbon dioxide (CO_2 and oxygen (O_2) from the air. Oxygen is used for respiration, burning carbohydrates and other foods, which produces energy. Carbon dioxide must be present during photosynthesis. Without CO_2 a plant will die! CO_2 uses light energy to combine with water, producing sugar. These sugars are used to fuel the growth and metabolism of the plant. With reduced levels of CO_2, growth slows rapidly. Oxygen is given off as a by-product of this process. A plant will release more O than is used and use much more CO_2 than it releases, except during darkness, when more oxygen is used.

Plants and animals (remember people are animals too) complement one another. Plants give off oxygen as a by-product, making it available to people. People give off CO_2 as a by-product, making it available to plants. Without plants, animals could not live, and without animals, plants could not live as we know life today. Animals inhale air, using O_2 to carry on life processes, and exhale CO_2 as a by-product.

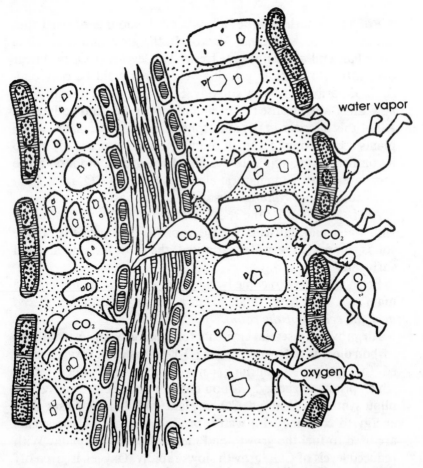

Close up of the stomata shows the exchange of oxygen and CO_2.

Air Movement

In order to have a good flow of air through the stomata, adequate air *circulation* and *ventilation* are necessary. *Indoors, fresh air is one of the most commonly overlooked factors contributing to a bountiful harvest. Fresh* air is the least expensive element that can be made available to a plant. Experienced gardeners really understand the importance of *fresh* air, and take the time to set up a *vent fan*. Three factors affect air movement: (1) stomata (2) ventilation and (3) circulation.

STOMATA are microscopic pores on the leaf's underside, similar to an animal's nostrils. Animals regulate the amount of O_2 inhaled and CO_2 exhaled through the nostrils via the lungs.

 Plants should be washed with clean, tepid water on both sides of the leaves at least once a month. See: "About Spraying," pages 236-240.

Vent fan is set in lower half of open window.

In a plant, O_2 and CO_2 flows are regulated by the stomata. The larger the plant, the more stomata it has to take in CO_2 and release O_2. The greater the volume of plants, the more CO_2-rich air they need to keep them growing fast. Dirty, clogged stomata restrict the air flow. Stomata are easily clogged by dirt, polluted air or sprays that leave a filmy residue. Dirty, clogged stomata are sealed off and unable to function. In nature, stomata are cleaned by rain and wind. Indoors, the horticulturist must *make* rain with a sprayer and wind with a fan.

CIRCULATION - If the air is totally still, plants tend to use all of the CO_2 next to the leaf. When this air is *used* and no *new* CO_2-rich air is forced into its place, a dead air space forms around the leaf, stifling the stomata and slowing growth. Air also tends to stratify. The warm air stays near the ceiling and cooler air, close to the floor. All of these potential problems are avoided by opening a door or window and/or installing an oscillating fan or Casablanca-type ceiling fan. Air circulation is also important for insect and fungus prevention programs. Mold spores may be present in a room, but kept from landing and growing when the air is stirred up by a fan.

A Oscillating circulation fan will keep the air from stratifying in the grow room.

VENTILATION - An average 10-by-10-foot vegetable garden will use from 10 to 30 gallons or more of water per week. *Where does all that water go?* It is transpired, or evaporated into the air. Therefore, *gallons of water* will be held in the air every week. If this moisture is left in the small room, the leaves will get limp, transpiration will slow and the stomata will be stifled. This moisture must be replaced with dry air that lets the stomata function properly. *A vent fan that pulls air out* of the grow room will do the trick!

Successful indoor gardeners know that a vent fan is as important as water, light, heat and fertilizer. In some cases *fresh* air is even more important. All greenhouses have large ventilation fans. Grow rooms are very similar to greenhouses, and their example should be followed. In most grow rooms there is a window or some easy-to-use opening in which to mount a fan. If no vent opening is available, one will have to be made.

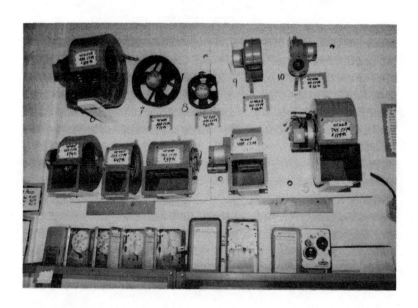

Many different vent fans and timers are available to the indoor grower.

The main concerns when installing a vent fan are to allow for an adequate exchange of air but to allow no cold backdrafts.

Use a dryer vent opening with a flap to prevent backdrafts. Use a four-inch flexible dryer hose for smaller grow rooms and eight-inch galvanized heat duct pipe for large installations. Place one end of the hose outdoors. One of the best vents is the chimney. The other end of the hose is attached to the vent fan. The vent fan is placed near the ceiling so it vents hot, humid air. Check for leaks. Set up the fan. See: "Setting Up the Vent Fan," page 208-210.

Greenhouse fans are equipped with baffles or flaps to prevent backdrafts. In cold or hot weather backdrafts could change the room temperature and stifle the garden or encourage a menagerie of bad bugs and fungi. Vent flaps avoid this problem.

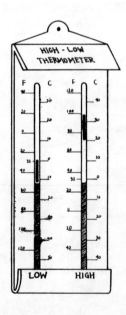

A maximum/minimum thermometer will measure the present temperature and tell you how cold it was last night.

Why use a vent fan? The reason is simple: *efficiency*. A vent fan is able to *pull* air out of a room many times more efficiently than a fan is able to *push* it out. Vent fans are rated by the number of cubic feet of air per minute (CFM) they can replace or move. Buy a fan that will replace the volume (cubic feet) of the grow room in about five minutes. The air *pulled* out is immediately replaced by *fresh* air that is *drawn* in through the numerous tiny cracks or openings in the room. If the grow room is sealed tightly and has few cracks, an open window or air intake vent may be necessary to allow for enough inflow of air.

A fan in the middle of a room that pushes the air out of a room is up against a tough physical principle. It is all a matter of pressure. The fan pushes air, increasing the air pressure in the room. This pressure must increase substantially in order for a rapid exchange of air to take place. The vent fan, on the other hand, is able to change the pressure rapidly. It is much easier to lower the air pressure, causing new fresh air to rush in to fill the vacuum.

The vent fan is used to cure almost all problems of *air* deficiency.

TEMPERATURE

Every grow room should be equipped with an accurate thermometer to measure the temperature. The mercury or liquid type is usually more accurate than the spring or dial type. Thermometers are inexpensive and easy to acquire. They supply much important information so make sure to get one. The ideal thermometer is a day-night or maximum-minimum type. Using this thermometer, the horticulturist is able to see how *low* the temperature drops at night and how high it reaches during the day. This is very important for many reasons that are explained below.

Under normal conditions, the ideal temperature range for indoor plant growth is 72 to 76° F. To get a better idea of what the temperature range for each plant, see the individual plant requirements, pages 277-283. At night, the temperature can usually drop 10 to 15° with no effect   The temperature should not drop more than 20° F, or excessive humidity and mold may become a problem. Daytime temperatures over 100° F and below 60° F seem to slow down growth in most plants. Maintaining the proper, constant temperature in the grow room promotes strong, even, healthy growth. Make sure plants are not too close to a heat source, such as a ballast or heat vent, or they may dry out, maybe even get heat scorch!

Temperatures above 90° F are not recommended. Since the increase in temperature makes the chemical activity faster, everything else must be increased, mainly ventilation. As explained in the following section on humidity, the warmer it is, the more water the air is able to hold. This moist air stifles the stomata and slows rather than speeds growth. Many other problems could result as well from the excess moisture, including: fungi and moisture condensation when the temperature drops at night.

Heat buildup indoors can become a problem in warm or hot weather. The ideal grow room is located underground, in a basement, with the insulating qualities of the earth. With the added heat of the HID, and 100° temperatures outdoors, a room can heat up really fast. Several gardeners have lost their gardens to heatstroke during the Fourth of July weekend. This is the first big summer holiday and everybody in the city wants to get away to enjoy it. There are always some gardeners who forget to maintain good ventilation in the grow room while on vacation. In a grow room that is improperly set up, with no vent fan and no insulating walls, the summer temperatures may climb to 120°″ ″. There is no way a plant can live in this climate without incredible amounts of water and ventilation. *Mother Nature* would never let her climate change to this lethal level; would you?

The cold of winter is the other extreme. Several years ago, the Oregon winter was colder than normal. In Portland, electricity went out, heat went off and pipes froze. Residents were driven from their homes until the electricity was restored a few days later. Several gardeners returned and found their lovely garden wilted, with the deepest, most disgusting green only a freeze can bring, and broken pipes spewing water everywhere. It is very important to keep the grow room above 30° F. If it drops far below this level, the freeze will destroy the cells of warm-weather plants, and foliage will die or not be able to grow very fast. Growth generally slows when the temperature is below 50° F, so try to keep the grow room warm. If you want to stress your plants by a freeze test, do so at your own risk!

A **thermostat** regulates the temperature in a room. It measures the temperature, then turns a heat or cooling source *on* or *off* so the temperature stays within a specified range. A thermostat may be attached to an electric or combustion heater. In fact, many homes are already set up with electric baseboard heat and have a thermostat in each room.

The thermostat is attached to a vent fan in all but the coldest grow rooms. When it gets too hot, the thermostat turns the vent fan *on*, forcing the hot, stale air out of the room. The vent fan remains *on* until the desired temperature is reached, then the thermostat turns off the fan. The vent fan should be all the temperature control necessary. A refrigerated air conditioner can be installed if heat and humidity are a big problem. If excessive heat is a problem, but humidity is not a concern, a swamp cooler will work well.

There are two types of thermostats: single-stage and two-stage. The single-stage costs $20 to 30 and is able to keep the temperature the same both day and night. The two-stage thermostat is more expensive, about $50, but can maintain different day and night temperatures. This is very convenient and can save you quite a bit of money, since the room temperature may drop 10 to 15° F at night with no effect on growth.

Uninsulated grow rooms and greenhouses with a wide change in temperature require special considerations. First, it would probably be easiest to grow somewhere else, but if you have to use an attic or hot spot, get lots of ventilation. Make sure to enclose the room so heating and cooling are easier and less expensive.

When CO_2 is enriched to .12 to .15%, a temperature range from 75 to 85° F promotes more rapid exchange of gases.

Photosynthesis and chlorophyll synthesis are able to take place at a more rapid rate and plants grow faster. Remember, this extra 10 to 15° increases water, nutrient and space consumption, so be prepared!

Seeds germinate faster and cuttings root quicker when the temperature range is from 75 to 85° F. Two easy ways to increase temperature when cloning are: (1) use soil heating tape (2) build a (plastic) tent to cover young germinating seeds or cuttings. This increases not only temperature, but humidity as well. Remove the tent cover as soon as the seeds sprout above the soil, to allow for circulation. Cuttings, however, should remain covered throughout the entire rooting process. Always watch for signs of mold or rot when using a humidity tent with cuttings. Allowing a bit of air circulation and ventilating cuttings under the tent helps prevent fungus. An alternative to a humidity tent would be to mist the cuttings several times daily with a spray bottle.

The temperature in the grow room tends to stay the same, top to bottom, when the air is circulated with an oscillating fan. Normally, in an enclosed grow room, a 1000-watt HID lamp and ballast will provide enough heat. A remote ballast, placed on a shelf or a stand near the the floor, also helps break up air stratification by radiating heat upward. Cooler climates have enough heat during the day when the outdoor temperature rises, but not enough when lower temperatures set in at night. The lamp is adjusted to be *on* during the cool nights. This will warm the room to an acceptable level both night and day.

Sometimes it is just too cold for the lamp and ballast to maintain adequate room temperatures. Many grow rooms are equipped with a central heating and/or air conditioning vent. This vent is usually controlled by a central thermostat that regulates the entire home's heat. By adjusting the thermostat to 72° F and opening all the internal doors in the home, the grow room can stay a cozy 72°. For most gardeners, this is too expensive and very wasteful. Usually, keeping the thermostat between 60 and 65°, coupled with the heat from the HID system, is enough to sustain the desired temperature range. Other supplemental heat sources may work better than the above. Incandescent light bulbs and electric heaters are expensive, but provide instant heat. Incandescent bulbs even increase light intensity and add to the spectrum. Propane and natural gas heaters not only heat the air, but burn oxygen from the air, creating CO_2 as a by-product. This dual advantage makes their use even more economical.

There are several new kerosene heaters on the market today that work well for heating and CO_2 generation. Look for a heater that burns its fuel completely and leaves no telltale odor in the room. Watch out for old kerosene heaters or inefficient fuel oil heaters of any type. They could be dangerous! Diesel oil is a common type of indoor heat. Many furnaces use this dirty and polluting heat source. Wood heat is not the cleanest, but works well as a heat source. A vent fan is extremely important to bring new fresh air into a room heated by a polluting furnace.

Insect populations and fungi are also affected by temperature. In general, the cooler it is, the slower the bugs and fungus reproduce and develop. Temperature control is integrated into many insect and fungus control programs.

Relative humidity increases when the temperature drops at night. The more temperature variation, the greater the relative humidity variation. Supplemental heat or extra ventilation may be necessary at night if temperatures fluctuate more than 15° F.

Humidity

Relative humidity is the ratio between the amount of moisture in the air and the greatest amount of moisture the air could hold at the same temperature. The hotter it is, the *more* moisture the air can hold; the cooler it is, the *less* moisture the air can hold. When the temperature in a grow room drops, the humidity climbs and moisture condenses. For example, a 1000-cubic foot (10-by-10-by-10-foot) grow room will hold a maximum of about 17.5 ounces of water when the temperature is 70° and relative

The moisture-holding capacity of air doubles with ever 20°F increase in temperature.

humidity is at 100 percent. When the temperature is increased to 100° the same room will hold about 45 ounces of moisture at 100 percent relative humidity. That's 2 ½ times as much moisture. Where does this water go when the temperature drops?

Most vegetables grow best when the relative humidity range is from 40 to 60 percent. As with temperature, more or less constant humidity promotes healthy, even growth. Humidity affects the transpiration rate of the stomata. When high humidity ex-

A 10-by-10-by-8-foot (800-cubic-foot)
grow room can hold:

4 oz. of water at 32°
7 oz. of water at 50°
14 oz. of water at 70°
18 oz. of water at 80°
28 oz. of water at 90°
56 oz. of water at 100°

ists, water evaporates slowly. The stomata close, transpiration slows, and so does plant growth. Water evaporates quickly into drier air-causing stomata to open, increasing transpiration and growth.

The proper relative humidity level is essential for healthy tropical and subtropical plants. Most flowering indoor plants require at least 50 percent relative humidity. Vegetables are just the opposite, they thrive in 50 percent or *less*, while indoor tropical gardens thrive in a relative humidity range of 65 to 70 percent.

Transpiration in arid conditions will be rapid only if there is ugh water available for roots. If water is inadequate, ata will close to protect the plant from dehydration, caus-wth to slow.

ve humidity control is an integral part of bug and evention and control. High humidity (80 percent plus) ungus and stem rot. Maintaining low (50 percent or v greatly reduces the chances of fungus formation.

Some bugs like humid conditions, others do not. Spider mites take much longer to reproduce in a humid room.

Relative humidity is measured with a **hygrometer**. This extremely important instrument could save you and your plants much frustration and fungus. If you know the exact moisture content in the air, the humidity may be adjusted to a *safe* 50 percent level that encourages transpiration and discourages fungus growth.

There are two common types of hygrometers: the spring type, which is inexpensive (less than $10) and accurate to 5 to 10 percent. This hygrometer is just fine for most grow rooms, since the main concern is to keep the humidity *near* 50 percent. The other type of hygrometer, actually called a psychrometer, is a little more expensive ($30 to 50) but is *very* accurate (page 194). This hygrometer (psychrometer) uses the wet and dry bulb principle. It is recommended if you are using several lamps and/or extreme accuracy is important.

A **humidistat** is similar to a thermostat, but regulates *humidity* instead of temperature. Humidistats are wonderful! They make playing Mother Nature a snap! Humidistats cost $30 to 50 and are worth their weight in flower blossoms. The more expensive models are more accurate. The humidistat is wired *in line* with the thermostat (See page 194) to the vent fan. Each can operate the fan independently. As soon as the humidity (or temperature) gets out of the acceptable range, the fan turns on to vent the humid (or hot) air outdoors.

The HID lamp and ballast radiate dry heat, which lowers humidity. Dry heat from the HID system and a vent fan are usually all the humidity control necessary. Other dry heat sources, such as a heat vent from the furnace or wood stove, work well to lower humidity. If using forced air from a furnace to lower humidity, make sure warm, dry air does not blow directly on plants. This dry air will dehydrate plants rapidly.

A vent fan offers the best humidity control possible in most gardens.

One gardener swears by silicon packets to absorb excess moisture in the small grow room.

Humidity is easily increased by misting the air with water or setting a bucket of water out to evaporate into the air. Draping a

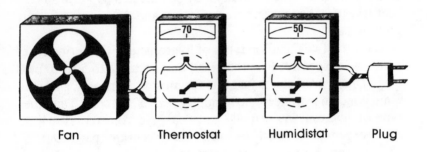

Fan   Thermostat   Humidistat   Plug

The simple diagram above shows how to wire a vent fan to a thermostat and a humidistat so that the fan will vent the room when either the humidistat or thermostat activate. The drawing shows a very accurate hygrometer that measures relative humidity to within one percentage point.

cheesecloth over grill of a fan will buffer the breeze of a circulation fan over tender plants. This same principle can be used to make a simple but effective humidifier. Simply place a wick between the cheesecloth and a container of water. The cloth wick will draw water up onto the cheesecloth and the fan will blow the moist water into the air. A humidifier may be purchased for $100 to $150. It is essentially a fan over a bucket of water controlled by a humidistat. The fan evaporates water vapor into the air. A humidifier is usually not necessary unless there is an *extreme* problem with the grow room drying out. A *de*humidifier removes moisture in a room. These units are a bit more complex, since the water must be *condensed* from the air. A dehumidifier can be used anytime to help guard against fungus. Just set the dial at the desired percent humidity and presto, perfect humidity. They cost from $150 to $200, but are worth the money to gardeners with *extreme* humidity problems that a vent fan has not yet cured. The best price on dehumidifiers has been found at Montgomery Ward and Sears. Dehumidifiers may also be rented if needed for only a month or so.

Young seedlings and rooting cuttings do better when the humidity is between 70 and 80 percent. Under arid conditions, the underdeveloped root system is not able to supply water fast enough. High humidity prevents dehydration.

CO_2 Enrichment

Carbon dioxide (CO_2) is a colorless, odorless, non-flammable, non-toxic gas. The air we breathe contains .03 to .04 percent CO_2. Plants use all of the available CO_2 in an enclosed grow room rapidly. Photosynthesis and growth slow to a crawl when the CO_2 level falls below .02 percent.

CO_2 enrichment has been used in commercial greenhouses for many years. It makes more CO_2 available to plants, thus stimulating growth. Indoor cultivation is similar to conditions in a greenhouse, and the same principles may be applied to the indoor garden. Plants are able to use more CO_2 than the .03 to .04 percent that naturally occurs in the air. By increasing the amount of CO_2 to .10 to -.15 percent (1200 to 1500 parts per million (ppm)), the optimum amount widely agreed upon by professional gardeners, plants may grow two to three times as fast, *providing that light, water, and nutrients are not limiting.* CO_2 enrichment has little or no effect on plants grown under fluorescent lights. The tubes do not supply enough light for the plant to process the *extra* available CO_2. On the other hand, HID lamps supply ample light to process the enriched CO_2 air. In a grow room using an HID light source, CO_2-enriched air, adequate water and nutrients, mind boggling results may be achieved. In fact, with this basic combination, plants grow much faster and more efficiently than outdoors under ideal conditions.

CO_2 enrichment produces more foliage in a shorter period of time.

The demands of CO_2-enriched plants are much greater than normal, and plants *must have increased maintenance.* They will use nutrients, water and space about twice as fast as normal. A higher temperature range, from 75 to 85° F, will help stimulate more rapid chemical processes within the *super* plants. Properly maintained, they will grow so fast and take up so much space that flowering will have to be induced sooner than normal.

In fact, some people get frustrated using CO_2. It causes plants to grow so fast, that unsuspecting gardeners are unable to keep up with them. With CO_2-enriched air, plants that do not have the support of the other critical elements for life will not benefit *at all* and the CO_2 is wasted. The plant can be limited by just one of the critical factors. For example, the plants use water and nutrients much faster and if these are not supplied, they will not grow. They may even be stunted or, if plants need a larger pot but do not get it soon enough, they will be runts.

Increasing light intensity by adding another HID lamp helps speed growth, but may not be necessary. The extra lamp may make the garden grow so fast that it is impossible to keep up

 CO_2 enrichment means more time in the garden and moving up the garden calendar one to four weeks.

with. More CO_2 does not mean more hours of light per day. The photoperiod must remain the same as under normal conditions for healthy growth and flowering.

Check with the light meter to see if plants really need more light.

To be most effective, the CO_2 level must be kept near .10 to .15 percent *everywhere* in the room. To accomplish this, the grow room must be completely enclosed. Cracks in and around the walls over one-eighth-inch should be sealed off to prevent CO_2 from escaping. Enclosing the room makes it easier to control the CO_2 content of the air within. The room must also have a vent fan with flaps or a baffle. The vent fan will remove the *stale* air that will be replaced with CO_2-enriched air. The flaps or baffle will help contain the CO_2 in the enclosed grow room. Venting requirements will change with each type of CO_2 enrichment system. Venting is discussed in detail in the "CO_2 Generator" and "Compressed CO_2 Gas" sections.

Some of the problems associated with keeping the amount of CO_2 constant in the air are the amount of plants in the room and the rate at which these plants are growing. If the plants are growing rapidly and are tightly packed into a leaky room, the CO_2 level will be difficult to maintain using the information provided by measuring the amount of CO_2 produced. If the temperature climbs to 80 to 90° F, the CO_2 is diluted in the air and must be increased. A room that is not tightly sealed could use as much as 50 percent more CO_2.

Producing CO_2

There are many ways to raise the CO_2 content of an enclosed grow room. CO_2 is one of the by-products of combustion. Any hydrocarbon fuel can be burned to produce CO_2, except for those containing sulfur dioxide and ethylene, which can be harmful to plants. See "CO_2 Generators" below. A by-product of fermentation and organic decomposition is CO_2 gas. The CO_2 level near the ground of a rain forest covered with decaying organic matter could be two to three times as high as normal. But bringing a compost pile inside to cook down is disgusting!

Dry ice is made from frozen CO_2. The CO_2 is released when it comes in contact with the atmosphere. It can get expensive and be a lot of trouble keeping a large room replenished with dry ice.

There are lots of spin-offs to all of these principles and they all work in varying degrees. It is difficult to calculate how much CO_2 is released into the air by fermentation, decomposition or dry ice, without using very expensive equipment to measure it. Dry ice gets very expensive in prolonged use. Two pounds of dry ice will raise the CO_2 level in 10-by-10-foot grow room to about 2000 ppm. for 24 hours. One chagrined gardener remarked: "I can't believe that stuff melts so fast." A filthy, decaying compost pile is out of the question indoors! Besides, a new compost pile would have to be moved twice a day to release enough CO_2.

Fermentation is an acceptable way to produce CO_2, but it is difficult to tell how much is produced. Here is a recipe for brewing CO_2. A one-gallon plastic milk jug works best, but any container will do. Mix one cup of sugar and a packet of brewers yeast with about three quarts of warm water. The concoction smells horrid, but produces a fairly decent burst of CO_2. This method is one of the least expensive ways of producing CO_2, but it works best when used in a small growth chamber. Seedlings that get started with CO_2 seem to get a head start that is maintained throughout life. The CO_2 produced by the fermentation is soon released in the enclosed chamber. The concoction is changed one to four times daily. Half of the solution is poured out, then 1½ quarts of water and another cup of sugar are added. The yeast may not continue to grow during the fermentation process. After the first packet of yeast, more yeast may need to be added. This CO_2 mix is like a sourdough starter mix. Try to keep it from dying. As long as the yeast continues to ferment, the mix may be used indefinitely to generate CO_2. In fact, if a gardener were really into it, there could be several gallons and one would be changed every couple of hours. But smell would soon gag a maggot!

CO_2 Generators

Commercial nurseries produce CO_2 with large generators. These generators produce CO_2 by using propane, butane or natural gas to burn oxygen out of the air in a chamber. The CO_2-rich air is then circulated among the plants. *Heat, CO_2* and *water* are by-products of combustion. Each pound of fuel burned = three pounds of CO_2, 1½ pounds of water and approximately 22,000 BTU (British Thermal Units) of heat. Small, one lamp grow rooms can burn ethyl or methyl alcohol in a kerosine lamp. In a 10-by-10-foot grow room, three ounces of fuel will produce about 2000 ppm of CO_2 in 24 hours.

A CO_2 generator will heat as well as produce carbon dioxide for the grow room.

Heat buildup makes large CO_2 generators impossible to use in the heat of summer. The CO_2 generators used in greenhouses are too large to be practical for the average grow room. Several Northwest companies manufacture small-scale CO_2 generators that are similar to the large commercial ones. These smaller CO_2 generators were designed for grow rooms of 1500 to 4000 cubic feet.

These CO_2 generators work very well for larger or cool grow rooms. The generators can create quite a bit of heat. Remember, each pound of gas burned will create about 22,000 BTU and 1½ pounds of water. In a small grow room, the heat and moisture produced could make it impractical to use.

The CO_2 generators that I have seen are of two basic designs. The first, pictured on page 157, is hung from the ceiling. CO_2-rich air is produced and cascades over the plants. This model uses a pilot light with a flow meter and burner. This unit looks like a gas stove burner and pilot light in a protective housing. For safety's sake, *the generator must have a top covering the open flame at all times*. The unit is equipped with a *safety valve* and a pilot light. It may be operated manually or placed on the same timer as the lamp via the solenoid switch. An

NOTE: CO_2 is used by humans at low levels. Levels above .4% (4000 ppm) could be hazardous if inhaled for long. The CO_2 level is easy to control with the proper metering system. Besides being hazardous to people at high concentrations. CO_2 can become toxic to plants at levels above .2% (2000 ppm).

A relatively small flame will alter the CO_2 level in an enclosed grow room. With the help of a vent fan, there is little chance of any CO_2 gas buildup. Apply a solution of 50 percent water and 50 percent concentrated dish soap to all connections to check for leaks. When the bubbles appear, gas is escaping. **Never use a leaky system!**

oscillating fan is placed near the floor to keep the CO_2-rich air stirred up. This model is designed for a room of 1500 to 4000 cubic feet.

The second model is placed on the floor and has a fan on the side of the burner housing. The fan circulates the warm CO_2-rich air among the plants. The unit has an electronic pilot light with a safety timer that is electronically controlled to relight safely if the flame blows out for any reason. This unit easily adapts to a timer and is designed for a room of 500 to 1500 cubic feet.

LP gas is readily available at gas stations; the tanks are easy to move when full and very light when empty.

Propane tanks are easy to acquire and easy to fill, unlike the heavy, awkward, compressed CO_2 tanks discussed below. Propane is readily available.

Some new propane tanks are filled with an inert gas to protect them from rust. Empty the inert gas out before filling a new tank for the first time. The inert gas does not mix well with propane, nor will it burn.

NOTE: Never over-fill the tank! The gas will expand and contract with temperature change.

Many people prefer to manufacture their own CO_2 generator. To make a CO_2 generator, find a heater that burns clean and has a knob to control the *exact* flame produced. A blue flame is produced by propane or natural gas that is burning clean. A yellow flame has unburned gas (creating lethal carbon monoxide) and needs more oxygen to burn clean. Good examples of homemade CO_2 generators are propane heaters, stoves or lamps. In fact, even a Coleman lantern works quite well, but it must be started and stopped manually. One gardener uses unleaded (white) gas rather than expensive Coleman fuel. Follow the formulas given below for CO_2 generators. Examples are given to find out how much CO_2 to generate in a room. First, the *TOTAL VOLUME* of the room is found, then the amount of fuel burned to produce the desired amount of CO_2 is calculated.

Unless your grow room is huge, you do not need to allow for CO_2 to be present in the air. This excess CO_2 will be compensated for by the CO_2 that leaks out the cracks in the walls and through open doors.

To find out how much CO_2 it will take to bring the grow room up to the optimum level, find the *total volume* of the grow room, then divide by the *optimum level* of CO_2.

Example:

TOTAL VOLUME = L × W × H

TOTAL VOLUME = 10′ × 8′ × 10′

TOTAL VOLUME = 800 cubic feet

OPTIMUM LEVEL = .0015

.0015 × 800 cubic feet = 1.2 cubic feet

It will take 1.2 cubic feet of CO_2 to bring the 800 cubic feet grow room up to the optimum level.

Each pound of fuel (kerosene, propane or natural gas) burned produces approximately three pounds of CO_2. One-third of a pound (5.3 ounce), produces about one pound of CO_2. At 68°, one pound of CO_2 displaces 8.7 cubic feet.

Total amount of CO_2 needed ÷ 8.7 × .33 = pounds of fuel needed

1.2 ÷ 8.7 × .33 = .045 pounds of fuel needed

.045 × 16 = .72 ounce of fuel

To measure the amount of fuel used, weigh the tank before it is turned on, use it for an hour, then weigh it again. The difference in weight is the amount of gas or fuel used.

It is easier to measure the amount of CO_2 produced rather than measuring the amount of CO_2 in the atmosphere of the grow room. Measuring the content of CO_2 is not very common among indoor gardeners. There are no inexpensive measuring kits on the market The least expensive kit costs about $250 and each test requires chemicals within a glass tube and costs about $5. These kits may be purchased from National Dragger, Inc., P.O. Box 120, Pittsburgh PA, 15275. There are several people working on less expensive kits to measure CO_2, but to date none are on the market.

Exact venting requirements are difficult with CO_2 generators. Since it is difficult to measure the exact amount of CO_2 present in the room, it is difficult to detect exactly how much to vent the room. One experienced gardener says he is able to sense the level of CO_2 in the air. The best way to figure out how much to vent a grow room would be to measure the amount of CO_2 present in the air, then vent the room accordingly. However, this practice is too expensive for most people. To vent a room using a CO_2 generator, wire a vent fan *in line* to a humidistat and thermostat (page 194). Set the humidistat at 50 percent relative humidity and the thermostat at 90° F. This will maintain the CO_2 close to the perfect level. If the vent fan is on all the time, something must be wrong! The fan should not come on more than once an hour for the CO_2 level to remain near the perfect level.

Compressed CO_2 gas generally works best in grow rooms smaller than 200 to 300 square feet. Generators are designed for rooms 500 to 1500 cubic feet or larger where heat buildup is usually a problem. The CO_2 is injected into the room from the compressed tank. It creates no heat and is able to meter out the exact amount of CO_2 desired. This means that a room could be virtually any size and the exact amount of CO_2 could be metered in. CO_2 tanks reach a point of diminishing returns. That is, rooms over 1500 to 4000 cubic feet have more room for the heat produced by the CO_2 generator to dissipate. The CO_2 generator is also more cost-effective for larger rooms than compressed CO_2. Some people do not want any kind of an unattended flame burning in their home. Use the CO_2 burner only if you feel comfortable with it.

Place the CO_2 emitter over the lamp so the heavier-than-air CO_2 can cascade over the plants to be more useful.

When venting a CO_2-enriched room, use a fan placed high in the room. CO_2 is heavy; this way it will not escape!

Compressed CO_2

Compressed CO_2 gas is very safe, versatile and easy to control. For use with many HID systems, compressed CO_2 is an excellent choice.

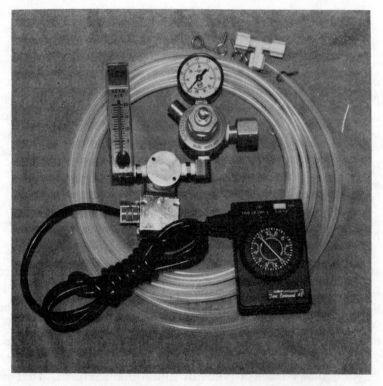

High tech CO_2 emitter developed by Applied Hydroponics delivers a constant level of carbon dioxide to the grow room.

Compressed CO_2 enrichment systems contain a combination regulator/flow meter, solenoid valve, short-range timer and tank of compressed CO_2 gas. There is a very good book on CO_2 systems, explaining in detail how each component of the system works. It is a *Manual on the Use of CO_2 With Metal Halide Grow-Lights* and is available through INTERPORT @ $3.50 (see order blank in the back of this book). This book also gives step-by-step instructions on how to build and set up your own CO_2 enrichment system.

Compressed CO_2 is stored in metal cylinders or tanks under high pressure. Small cylinders contain 20 pounds and larger ones contain 50 pounds. The gas is kept between 1,600 and 2,200 pounds of pressure (PSI). The CO_2 gas passes out of the tank into the flow meter/regulator where the pressure is reduced to a more reasonable 10 to 200 PSI. The solenoid valve opens and closes to let the CO_2 into the room. Most flow meter/regulators emit 10 to 50 cubic feet of CO_2 per hour. If the flow meter/regulator were set at 10 cubic feet per hour and left on for half an hour five cubic feet of CO_2 would enter the room. The *total amount of CO_2 needed* to bring the level up to 1500 ppm for a 10-by-8-by-10-foot grow room is 1.2 cubic feet. By altering the flow rate and time, the exact amount of CO_2 can be injected into the grow room.

For example:

Total amount of CO_2 needed ÷ flow rate = time

1.2 ÷ flow rate = time

1.2 ÷ 10 = .12 hour

.12 hour × 60 minutes = 7.2 minutes

If the flow meter is set at 10 cubic feet per hour, the timer will need to be *on* 7.2 minutes to bring the CO_2 level up to the optimum 1500 ppm.

A short-range timer measures short periods of time accurately. The regular 24-hour timer will not measure increments of time less than one hour accurately. If the short-range timer is set to be *on* for 7.2 minutes every few hours, the CO_2 level of the room will go up to the optimum level, then taper off until the next burst of CO_2 is injected. It is a good idea to split the 7.2 minutes down into smaller increments so there is a regular supply of CO_2 in the room.

Vent the room using a CO_2 tank about 10 minutes before the CO_2 is injected into the room. Make sure the vent fan is not *on* while the CO_2 is being injected into the room, and for at least an hour afterward.

To vent the room with a ventilation fan, the CO_2-enriched room should have the vent high in the room. Vent gives *fresh* cool air without *stealing* heavy CO_2.

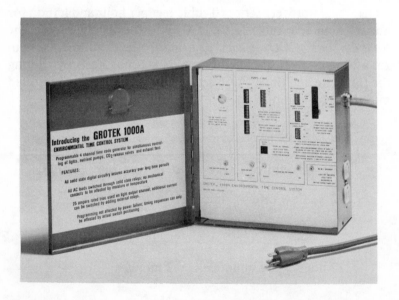

The Groteck is one of the most sophisticated timers available to the indoor gardener. It integrates all timing lights, fans, CO_2, etc., functions into the same electronically controlled system.

Negative Ions

A deionizer or negative ion generator makes negative ions, which purify the air and also remove odors. They produce a negative electrical charge or negative ions. The negative ions pour out into the air. They seek out and attach themselves to particles (pollutants, fungus spores etc.) in the air and neutralize them.

Plants grown in such an environment are generally *very* healthy. The generator uses very little electricity and plugs into a regular 110-volt current. Visually check the filter every few days and make sure to keep it clean.

Exhaust fans are rated in the amount of square feet of air they can displace, or move, in a minute.

 Use a vent fan that is able to replace all of the air in the grow room within five minutes or less.

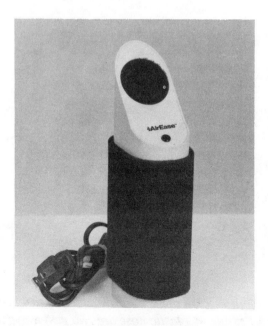

A negative ion generator will keep grow rooms smelling fresh.

Setting Up the Vent Fan

STEP ONE: Figure out the total volume of the grow room. Length × width × height = total volume. A grow room 10-by-10-by-8-feet has a total volume of 800 cubic feet (10′ × 10′ × 8′ = 800 cubic feet)

STEP TWO: Find a VENT fan that will remove the *total volume* of air in five minutes or less. Buy a fan that can easily be mounted to the wall (8-inch fans are my favorite for larger rooms) or attached to the *flexible* 4-inch dryer hose. A high-speed squirrel-cage fan will be necessary to maintain enough air flow through 4-inch flexible duct.

STEP THREE: Place the fan high on a wall or near the ceiling of the grow room so it vents off hot, humid air.

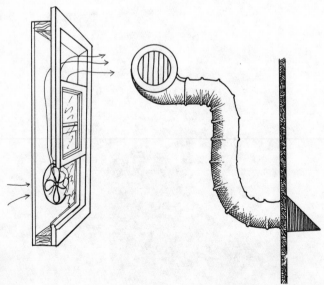

A wall fan built into an open window and a squirrel cage fan attached to a flexible 4″ plastic hose are two easy ways to vent the grow room.

STEP FOUR: If possible, cut a hole in the wall and secure the fan in place over the hole. Do not worry about the hole, it can be patched, and the garden will love you for the breath of fresh air. However most locations require special installation. See 5-9 below.

STEP FIVE: Placing a fan in a window helps prevent backdrafts. Cut a quarter-inch piece of plywood to fit the window sill. Cover window with a light-proof black paint or similar covering. Mount the fan in the top of the plywood, venting out. Secure the plywood and fan in the window sill and open the window from the bottom.

STEP SIX: Another option for a fan with minimum backdraft is to use a 4-inch flex dryer hose. Vent the hose outdoors and attach a small squirrel-cage fan to the other end of the hose. Make sure there is a tight connection between the fan and the hose by using a large hose clamp. A dryer hose wall outlet with a flap will help decrease backdrafts.

STEP SEVEN: Another option is to vent the air up the chimney. If using the chimney for a vent, first clean the excess ash and creosote from the inside. Tie a chain to a rope. Lower the chain down the chimney, banging and knocking all debris inside to the bottom. There should be a door at the bottom for removing the debris. This door is also used as the vent.

STEP EIGHT: The fan may be attached to a thermostat and humidistat to vent hot, humid air outside when necessary. Instructions are available with the thermostat for wiring to the vent fan. The diagram on page 194 shows how to wire a thermostat and humidistat to the same fan.

STEP NINE: Attach the vent fan to a timer and run for a specific length of time. This method is generally used with CO_2 enrichment. The fan is set to turn on and vent out *used* air just before *new* CO_2-rich air is injected.

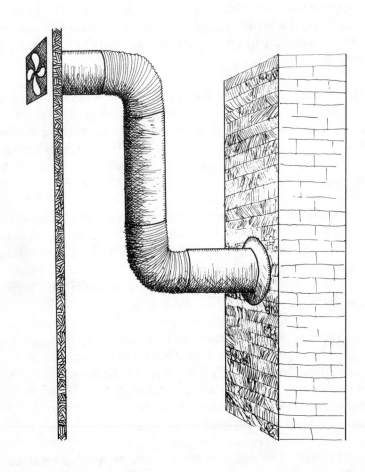

A vent fan is easily vented out the chimney of a basement using 8-inch stove pipe.

CHAPTER SEVEN
Bugs and Fungi

Bugs will creep into your garden, eat, reproduce and be merry. Bugs live everywhere outdoors. Indoors, bugs will live just about anywhere that you (*Mother Nature*) let them. Fungus is present in the air at all times. It may be introduced by an infected plant or from air containing fungus spores. Fungus will settle down and grow if climatic conditions are right. Both fungus and bugs can be prevented, but once an infestation has started, severe methods of control may be necessary to eradicate them.

Prevention

Cleanliness is the key to bug and fungus prevention. The grow room should be totally enclosed, so the environment may be easily controlled. Keep the floor clean. Keep all debris off soil surface. Do not use mulch. Bugs and fungus like nice hideaway places, dirty corners, old damp leaves and mulch. You, the horticulturist, and your tools could be the transporters of many microscopic bugs and fungi that may be fatal to the garden. Thoroughly wash and disinfect all new plants that will move into the grow room. These plants are the potential silent carriers of devastating disease. This does not mean you and your tools have to be hospital-clean every time you enter the grow room, even though that would be nice. It does mean that normal and regular sanitary precautions do need to be taken. Wear clean clothes and use clean tools. Have a separate indoor set of tools to be used only in the grow room. Disinfect tools by dipping them in rubbing alcohol, or wash with soap and water after using them on a diseased plant. Bugs and fungus love to ride from plant to plant on dirty tools.

Personal cleanliness is very important for bug and fungus prevention. Wash your hands before handling plants and after handling diseased plants. Do not walk around your buggy outdoor garden, then visit your indoor garden; do it vice versa. Think before entering the indoor garden and possibly contaminating it. Did you walk across a lawn covered with rust (rust is a rust-colored fungus) or pet the dog that just came in from the garden outside? Did you just fondle your spider-mite-infested split-leaf philodendron in the living room?

Once you have grown an annual crop in a potting soil or soilless mix, *throw it out*. Some gardeners have used the same OLD potting soil over and over with acceptable results. They place charcoal in the bottom of containers to absorb excess salts and maintain *sweet soil*. Used soil makes excellent outdoor garden soil. Used soil may harbor harmful bugs and fungi that have developed an immunity to sprays. Starting a new crop in *new* potting soil will cost more initially, but will eliminate many potential problems.

Most important, once potting soil is used it loses a good deal of the *fluff* of its texture. Compaction becomes a problem. Roots have trouble penetrating compacted soil and there is little room for oxygen, so roots do not breathe. Used potting soil is depleted of valuable N-P-K nutrients as well as secondary and trace elements. A plant with a slow start in poor soil is a perfect target for disease.

Companion planting works well to discourage bugs. Bugs, except for thrips, hate garlic. Since garlic cloves are readily available, take up little room, transplant well and discourage bugs, they are by far the best companion plant for indoor vegetables or flowers. When sowing seeds or transplanting, just plant a few cloves of garlic about a half-inch deep with them. The cuttings will sprout and grow in a week or two, driving insects away. Garlic will grow straight up, creating very little shade, and has a compact root system attached to the bulb below the soil. When transplanting, just move garlic along with the vegetable or flower. Garlic is very resilient and can take more *shock* during transplanting than most vegetables or flowers. Vegetables are usually harvested before garlic is mature. These garlic plants may be transplanted to become companions to other young plants through life. It is still a good idea to dip the garlic transplant into an insecticide/fungicide solution to prevent transferal of disease.

Marigolds also discourage bugs, but not as well as garlic. Marigolds are much prettier than garlic, but they must be blooming to effectively discourage bugs.

Plant insect- and fungus-resistant strains of flowers and vegetables. Most seed houses supply seed that is resistant to bug and fungus attacks. When choosing your mother plants for vegetative propagation, inspect them regularly and compare them to one another for bug and fungus resistance. It is incredible how some plants attract disease and may be infested, while others growing nearby have little or no problem at all.

Keep plants healthy and growing fast at all times. Disease attacks sickly plants first. Strong plants tend to grow faster than bugs can eat or fungus can spread. With strong, healthy, fast-growing plants, a few bugs or a little fungus could not do much damage.

Forced-air circulation makes life miserable for bugs and fungus. Bugs hate wind; they cannot hold on to the the plants or fly very well in a windy environment. Fungus has little time to settle in a breeze and does not grow well on wind-dried soil, stems and leaves.

Ventilation will change the humidity of a room quickly. In fact, a vent fan attached to a humidistat is the most foolproof form of humidity control. Mold was a big problem in a grow room that did not have a *vent fan*. It was terrible! Upon entering the enclosed grow room, with the humidity near 100 percent, eyeglasses would steam up immediately. If fact, the room was so humid that roots were growing from the stems of plants. The gardener installed a *vent* fan, which drew the moist, stale air from the grow room, venting it outdoors, and the mold problem disappeared.

Every indoor gardener should practice *all* of these preventative measures. It is much easier to prevent a disease from getting started than it is to wipe out an infestation. If bugs or
fungus multiply and are left unchecked, the entire garden could
be devastated in a few weeks.

Insect and Fungus Control

Sometimes, even with all preventive measures taken, bugs and
fungus still creep in and set up housekeeping. First they will
establish themselves on a weak, susceptible plant, then launch
an all-out assault on the rest of the garden. They will move out
in all directions from the infested base, taking over more and
more space, until they have conquered the entire garden. This
can happen in a matter of days. Bugs can lay thousands of eggs
that grow into mature adults within a few weeks. For example,
say you failed to take preventive measures or closely examine
plants for disease, and 100 microscopic munchers each laid 1000
eggs, which grew into adults two weeks later. By the end of the
month, there would be millions of insects attacking the infested
garden.

Sprays essentially kill adults and, all too often, only some of
them. Sprays should be applied soon after eggs hatch so young
adult bugs are caught in their weakest stage of life. Horticultural
oil spray works well alone or as an additive to help kill larvae.

The availability of sprays can be seasonal. Garden sections of
stores are changed for the winter. The stock is sometimes kept in
the storage room, but usually it is sold in a season-end sale. Excellent bargains on sprays are available for the winter growing
season at these season-end sales.

The products recommended have worked before and are
readily available. This does not mean they are the best or the only products to use. There are many local products that are just as
good as national or Northwest brands. Always follow the directions on the label.

Follow the logical progression for bug and fungi control.

Bugs

The indoor gardener has many options open for bug and fungi control. As we have seen, prevention and cleanliness are at the top of the list. There is a *logical progression* to bug and fungus control that is outlined in the chart below. Notice that it starts with cleanliness and progresses through the most basic elements.

Manual removal is just what the name implies: smashing all bugs in sight between the thumb and forefinger or between two sponges. Make sure not to infect other plants with filthy hands or sponges. This method is best for just a few mites. It takes forever.

If you must use a spray, always use a natural one. Harsh chemicals are only a last resort. With the development of an environmental consciousness and technology, several new natural-based sprays have been developed. They offer unique qualities unknown to harsh chemical sprays. As with any spray, it always seems to slow plants down a little, even if it is natural. The plant is covered with the filmy residue of the spray for some time. The stomata are clogged until the spray wears off or is washed off. It is a good idea to spray the plants as little as possible and not

LOGICAL PROGRESSION OF BUG CONTROL

1. Prevention

_____a. cleanliness
_____b. use "new" soil
_____c. one "indoor" set of tools   **3. Organic Sprays**
_____d. disease resistant plants
_____e. healthy plants
_____f. companion planting
_____g. climate control   **4. Natural Predators**
_____h. no animals

2. Manual Removal   **5. Chemicals**

_____a. fingers
_____b. sponges

spray at all for two weeks before harvesting edible fruit or cut flowers. Please read "About Spraying" (pages 236-240) at the end of this chapter. Read thoroughly *ALL* the labels of all sprays before you use them. Use only *contact* sprays for *edible* plants. Systemic sprays can be used for ornamental plants. Do not use any sprays at all on young seedlings or tender cuttings. The spray could burn the tender little plant.

Homemade sprays are made from a few drops (approximately one-percent 1% solution: one tablespoon of soap per quart of water) of a biodegradable soap concentrate such as Castile or Ivory liquid. Use a soap with no sulfates or harsh agents that will cause leaf spot. The soap is mixed with a quart of water and the juice from a freshly squeezed garlic, chili powder, rubbing alcohol or ground-up bugs. The mix is then shaken up vigorously. Natural, homemade sprays are so effective that some gardeners will not use anything else. If the homemade mixes do not work after one or two applications, try a stronger spray.

Safer's Insecticidal Soap is the first choice of many horticulturists for an *all-round* organic bug spray. Safer's is made from potassium fatty acid salts and a little alcohol. Exactly how it kills the little pests is not completely known. It is believed to penetrate their bodies, paralyze the nervous system, cause the body fluids to flow away, suffocate by blocking breathing pores, and desiccate the bodies. Once an insect is covered with Safer's, it will take about an hour for death to occur.

Safer's has no residual effect. That is, if you spray a plant at 8 a.m., a bug that lands on the same plant at noon will not be affected by the spray. This is good and bad. It means the foliage may be ingested soon after spraying, but it could take multiple applications to make sure you get all the bugs.

There is a trick to using Safer's. It is very simple: *Apply it heavily. Drench* the garden. Since it works by suffocation and penetration upon contact, it is necessary to get a good big dose to completely cover the bugs. However, this does not mean to mix it any heavier than the recommended 1 to 40 ratio. Safer's may be applied as often as every two days.

Another neat feature about Safer's is that you can use it with no fear of becoming sick. Fatty acids are produced by humans. They are one of our defenses against disease-causing fungi.

Pyrethrum in a *fogger/aerosol* can is a relatively new product manufactured and distributed by *Raid* (Johnson Wax) and several other new manufacturers. *This is the best natural product I have seen for killing spider mites and just about any other insect except bees.* The natural *pyrethrum* comes from the pyrethrum flower found in southern Africa. The daisy-like flower is a member of the chrysanthemum family. This natural, contact insecticide is very toxic to insects, especially spider mites, but decomposes rapidly when exposed to air and sunlight.

Pyrethrum is easy to spot at the store; it comes in a green can, while the other bug sprays come in red cans. In the Pacific Northwest, Raid's Pyrethrum is the fastest-selling insecticide on the market! Most RAID products only are sold in grocery stores. Pyrethrum also comes in pump type applicator bottles. They do not work very well because the method does not saturate the air.

It is almost impossible to apply the aerosol/fogger incorrectly, except for standing too close. Even the novice gardener using it the first time gets excellent results. The secret is in the *fogger*

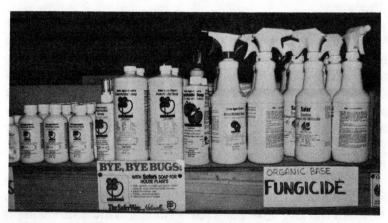

Safer's Insecticidal Soap is one of the sprays for all grow room insects.

method of application. The pyrethrum is shot out in a *fog* that permeates the grow room. The spray goes everywhere, even bottoms of the leaves, anywhere bugs can hide. Care must be taken to be far enough away from the plants when spraying. When the fog comes out of the nozzle, it is ice-cold. If this ice-cold spray is applied too close, foliar damage may result. To apply, follow the directions on the can.

Wear a respirator or a protective mask with this insecticide. The misty fog permeates the air, making it easy to inhale. Pyrethrins can be toxic to humans.

Do not use synthetic pyrethroids. Synthetic pyrethroids are toxic to honeybees. Always purchase *natural* pyrethrum.

KXL is a combination, year-round spray manufactured by Agro. It has natural ingredients that wipe out both insects and fungi. KXL contains vegetable oils, copper oleate, pyrethrins, rotenone, cube resins, xylene range solvents and iron, manganese and zinc. The copper works well on foliage fungus as well as mold on the soil surface. The pyrethrins and rotenone control the bugs. KXL works OK for spider mites, especially if they are not very well established. KXL is an excellent all round spray for all other garden pests.

Predators

A predator may be a small parasite that affixes itself to the host's body, taking many days to consume it, or it may be a huge bug that can devour many victims daily. The rate at which the predators keep the infestation in check is directly proportionate to the amount of predators. The more predators, the sooner they will take care of any infestations. Predators work by out breeding their victim, producing more predators than the victim is able to keep up with. *The predators are the crusading warriors in the never-ending battle of pest-free horticulture.*

One of the best places in the country to buy predatory insects is from *Natures Control,* Medford, Oregon. This supplier (Don Jackson) will give advice and sends along specific instructions as well as a brochure about all the predators he offers. Another supplier: the *Alternative* 3439 E. 86th St., Suite 259-S, Indianapolis Indiana 46240. Predators are shipped special delivery and may arrive *after* the daily mail delivery. The inside of a mailbox in the hot sun easily reaches 120°″ " or below freezing in winter. Check the mailbox regularly if ordering predators.

When any predator is introduced into the garden, there must be special precautions taken to ensure the little killer's well-being. Stop spraying all toxic chemicals - malathion, kelthane, diazinon etc. - at least two weeks before introducing the predators. Pyrethrum and Safer's Insecticidal Soap can be applied up to a few days before, providing any residue is washed off. Do not spray for 30 days after releasing predators.

Most of the predators that do well in the HID garden cannot fly. Bugs that can fly usually go straight for the lamp. The ladybug is a good example. Say 500 of them are released on Monday, by Friday, only a few die-hards will be left; the rest will have popped off the lamp. If using flying predators, release them when it is dark. They will last longer.

Predators are usually very small and must be introduced to each plant separately. This could take a little time and patience, so budget time for it. Predators also have specific climatic requirements. For best results, *pay attention; note the predator's needs and maintain them.*

Kelthane is one of the strongest miticides on the market. Use only as a last resort! Kelthane is a chemical miticide developed specially to exterminate spider mites. It has a two-day *toxic* life, but when it is used indoors, wash plants thoroughly, then wait at least a week before harvesting. It is the strongest and most effective miticide on the market; it is also a strong chemical. Kelthane is the most common miticide used in greenhouses.

Oil sprays are widely used in greenhouses. They are not the same kinds of oils used in the car or sold at the hardware store. Do not use *3-in-1* oil or anything similar in place of horticultural petroleum oil. Horticultural oil is refined by removing most of the portion that is toxic to plants. This oil works well to smother bugs and eggs, as well as generally impair the life cycle of the insect. If using the oil alone or as an additive with Kelthane, make sure it is a lightweight horticultural oil with a viscosity of 60 to

70. The lighter the oil, the less toxic it is to plants. I prefer to use oil sprays only during vegetative growth. This way, the residue has ample time to dissipate before harvest.

Mix two drops of oil spray (no more than a one-percent solution) per quart of diluted Kelthane solution. More than a few drops could burn tender growing shoots and clog stomata. Repeat applications as needed, usually three applications, one every five to 10 days will do it. The first application will get most of the adults and many eggs. Eggs hatch in about 10 days. The second spraying will kill the newly hatched eggs and the remaining adults. The third application will finish off any survivors.

Malathion is not the safest spray to use, and is not very effective against spider mites. It comes in a wettable powder or liquid concentrate. Malathion is used to control a wide variety of insects, including aphids, whiteflies, mealy bugs, scale and thrips. One of the bad and good things about Malathion is that it remains **live** or **toxic** for a week or more after application. This is bad, because this *toxic* residue remains and the gardener is not truly sure·when it is gone. The good part is, if human do not know when it is gone, neither do the bugs! According to the EPA (Environmental Protection Agency), malathion is toxic to humans, and bugs can rapidly build up an immunity to it.

Diazinon is a strong spray very similar to malathion. It is effective against aphids, whiteflies, mealybugs, scale and thrips. Its characteristics are very similar to most of malathion's. In most cases, when malathion is no longer effective, diazinon is used in its place.

Bug bombs are very strong insecticides that essentially exterminate everything living in the room They were developed to kill fleas and roaches. Bug bombs are used *between crops* to rid the grow room of all bugs before introducing the next crop. Many manufacturers produce bug bombs under various brand names containing a wide variety of toxic chemicals.

Place the bug bomb in the *empty* room. Turn it on. Then leave the room. The chemicals are very toxic! Follow directions to the letter!

Shell Vapona Strips can be hung in the garden to deter most

of the flying, sucking insects. Change the strips every three months for maximum efficiency. Keep the strips out of living areas.

Spider Mites

The spider mite is the most common insect found on flowers and vegetables indoors. (Actually, it is not really an insect, it is a spider. Insects have six legs and spiders have eight.) These microscopic mites are found on the leaf's undersides, sucking away the plant's life-giving fluids. To the untrained eye, they are hard to spot. Most people notice the tell-tale yellowish-white spots (stippling) on the tops of the leaves first. More careful inspection will reveal tiny spider webs on the stems and under leaves. Webs may easily be seen when leaves are misted with water. The spider mites appear as tiny specks on leaf undersides. The naked eye has a hard time distinguishing the pests; nonetheless, they can be seen. A magnifying glass or low power microscope helps to identify the yellow, white, two-spotted, brown or red mites and their light-colored eggs.

Mite eggs above look like transluscent dots on the leaf underside. The bottom photo shows a close up of stippling caused by spider mites.

CONTROL: has a logical progression. First make sure all preventative measures have been taken. NOTE: The spider mite thrives in a dry - 70 to 80° F. It can reproduce in five days if the temperature is above 80° F. In order to create a hostile environment for mites, lower the temperature to 60° and spray the plants with a jet of water, making sure to spray under leaves. This will *blast* them off the leaves as well as increase humidity. Their reproductive cycle will be slowed and you will have a chance to kill them before they do much damage. If the leaves have been over 50 percent damaged, remove and throw away, making sure bugs and eggs do not re-enter the garden. If mites have attacked only one or two plants, isolate the infected plants and treat them separately. Now that there is a hostile environment and leaves over 50 percent infected have been removed, the horticulturist may select one or more of the following control methods:

Manual removal: Smash all mites in sight between the thumb and index finger or wash leaves individually with two sponges.

Homemade sprays work very well when there is not yet an infestation of mites. If these sprays have not eradicated the mites after four or five applications, switch to another, stronger spray.

Safer's Insecticidal Soap is a wonderful product and controls mites. Usually two or three *heavy* applications at intervals of five to 10 days will do the trick.

Pyrethrum (aerosol) is the best natural miticide! Apply two or three applications at intervals of five to 10 days.

Predatory spider mites work very well. There are many things to consider when using the predators. First and foremost, they only can eat about 20 eggs or five adults daily. This gives you an idea of how fast they can really control the spider mites, which are their only source of food. As soon as the predators' source of food is gone, they cannibalize one another or die of starvation. A general dosage of 20 predators per plant is a good place to start. You might even want to throw in a few more for good measure. Spider mites have a difficult time traveling from plant to plant, so setting them out on each plant is necessary. In maintaining the predators, the most important factors are temperature and humidity. Both must be at the proper level to give the predators the best possible chance. There are two kinds of predators that are commonly used indoors: *amblyseius californicus* and *phytoseiulus longipes*.

When spider mites have *infested* a garden, predatory mites can not eat them fast enough to solve the problem. Predatory mites work best when there are only a few spider mites. The predators are introduced as soon as spider mites are seen, and released every month thereafter. This gives predators a chance to keep up with mites. Getting started with predatory mites will cost about $30. Before releasing predators, rinse all plants thoroughly to ensure that all toxic spray residues from insecticides and fungicides are gone.

Kelthane is the best chemical for spider mite extermination. Kelthane, mixed with oil spray, is the most effective way to get rid of spider mite infestations. Spider mites should be gone after two or three applications, at intervals of five to 10 days, providing sanitary, preventative conditions are maintained.

Outdoors, Kelthane has a toxic life of two to three days. Indoors, The *toxic life* is usually much longer. Wait at least two weeks after spraying to pick flowers or vegetables. The entire plant has to be thoroughly washed before harvesting. Spray the plants with fresh water until the excess beads up and rolls off the leaves.

Malathion and *Diazinon* will also kill mites, however they do not work well. The percentage killed is very low. Many repeat applications are necessary, and mites build up a resistance to these chemicals easily.

Whiteflies

Whiteflies, like mites, may cause white speckles (stipples) on the tops of leaves and hide underneath. The easiest way to check for the little pests is to grab a limb and shake it. If there are any whiteflies, they will fly from under leaves. A whitefly looks like a white moth about one millimeter long. Most whiteflies have wings but some do not. They usually appear near the top of the weakest plant first. They will move downward on the plant or fly off to infest another plant.

CONTROL: Take all preventive measures. Whiteflies are very difficult to remove manually; they fly faster than the hand is able to squish them. Adults are attracted to the color yellow. To build a whitefly trap similar to flypaper, cover a bright yellow object with a sticky substance. Place the traps on the tops of the pots. The traps work very well, but are a mess to clean.

Whiteflies are easily eradicated with natural sprays. Before spraying, remove any leaves that have been over 50 percent damaged and cure with heat or burn infested foliage.

Homemade sprays applied at intervals of two to 10 days work well.

Safer's Insecticidal Soap applied at intervals of five to 10 days.

Pyrethrum (aerosol) applied at intervals of two to 10 days does it.

KXL applied at intervals of five to 10 days works well.

The parasitic wasps **encarisa formosa** are the most effective whitefly predator. The small wasps *attack only* whiteflies, they do *not* sting people! As with all predators, all toxic sprays must be washed completely off before their introduction. Since the *encarisa formosa* is a parasite, about an eighth-inch long, much smaller than the whitefly, it takes it much longer to eliminate or even control the whitefly population. Once the parasite affixes to the whitefly, death is slow. The parasite feeds for some time on the host insect, then hatches its eggs inside its victim's body cavity. If you use them, set them out at the rate of two or more parasites per plant as soon as the first whitefly is detected. Repeat every two to four weeks throughout the life of the plants.

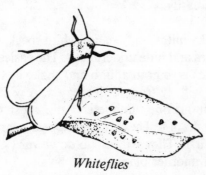

Whiteflies

Malathion and **Diazinon** are chemical sprays that kill whiteflies dead! Repeat applications every five to 10 days.

Aphids

Aphids are most common indoors when they are plentiful outdoors. About the size of a pinhead, aphids are easily spotted with the naked eye. This insect may be green, yellow, black or even pink, and with or without wings. Aphids excrete a sticky honeydew and prefer to attack weak plants. They attack growing tips or buds first, but love to hide on the leaves' undersides. An infestation of aphids can devastate a garden in a matter of days.

CONTROL: Even though aphids may have wings, manual removal is easy and works well to kill them. They do not fly as well as whiteflies. Aphids bite into the plant, sucking out life-giving juices. When affixed to foliage, aphids are unable to move and easy to squish.

Homemade and **Safer's sprays** are very effective. Apply two or three times at intervals of five to 10 days, after manually removing as many aphids as possible.

Pyrethrum (aerosol) applied two to three times at intervals of two to 10 days does it.

KXL applied at intervals of five to 10 days works well.

Lacewing are the most effective available predators for aphids. Release one to 20 lacewing per plant, depending on infestation level, as soon as aphids appear. Repeat every month. If possible, buy adult lacewing rather than larvae, which take several weeks

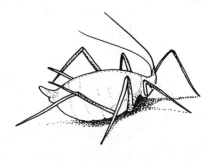

Aphids

to hatch and mature into adult aphid exterminators.

Ladybugs also work very well to exterminate aphids. Adults are easily obtained at many retail nurseries during the summer months. The only drawback to ladybugs is their attraction to the HID lamp. Release about 50 lady bugs per plant. About half of them will go directly for the HID, hit the hot bulb and buzzzz . .

Within a week or two all the ladybugs will fall victim to the lamp, requiring frequent replenishment.

Malathion and **Diazinon** applied at intervals of five to 10 days work well.

Thrips

Thrips are not very common indoors. These tiny, winged, fast-moving creatures rasp on the leaves and buds, then suck out the juices for food. They tend to feed inside flower buds or wrap up and distort leaves. Thrips are hard to see but not hard to spot. Upon careful inspection, thrips appear as a herd of specks thundering across foliage.

CONTROL: Preventive maintenance. Manual removal works if only a few thrips are present, but they are hard to catch.

Homemade sprays are very effective. Apply two to four times at intervals of five to 10 days.

Safer's Insecticidal Soap is very effective. Apply at intervals of two to 10 days.

Pyrethrum (aerosol) applied at intervals of two to 10 days does it.

KXL applied at day intervals of five to 10 days works acceptably.

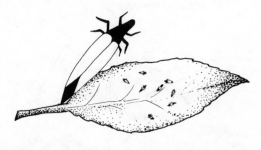

Thrips

Malathion or **Diazinon** applied at 10-day intervals will kill them for sure if the natural sprays fail.

Thrips have no readily available natural predators.

Mealy Bugs

Mealy bugs are somewhat common. These oblong, waxy white insects, 2 to 7 millimeters long, move very little, mature slowly and live in colonies that are usually located at stem joints. Like aphids, mealy bugs excrete a sticky honeydew. Mealy bugs are fairly easy to control, since they reproduce and move slowly.

CONTROL: Preventive maintenance. Manual removal works very well for small populations. Pry them off by getting a fingernail underneath or wet a *Q-Tip* with rubbing alcohol to wash them off.

Homemade sprays work well especially if they contain a lot of rubbing alcohol. Apply two or three times at intervals of five or 10 days.

Safer's Insecticidal Soap applied at 5-10 day intervals works well.

The **lady beetle** and the **green lacewing** are effective natural predators. Both work very efficiently and have no trouble eating mealy bugs faster than they can reproduce. If using these predators, manually remove all visible mealy bugs; release five to 10 predators per plant, depending on need, as soon as the mealy bugs are noticed. Repeat releases at two week intervals. Within a month, there should be a noticeable reduction in mealy bug population.

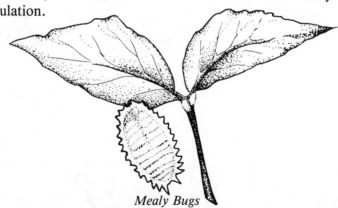

Mealy Bugs

Diazinon is the favorite of most nurserypeople for mealy bug control. Many professionals prefer nicotine sulfate mixed with Diazinon for complete, rapid extermination. Apply at intervals of five to 10 days.

Scale

Scale is uncommon on many plants indoors. Scale looks and acts similar to mealy bugs, but is usually more round than oblong. Scale may be white, yellow, brown, gray or black. Their hard protective shell is 2 to 4 millimeters across and they rarely move, if ever. Check for them around stem joints, where they live in colonies. Scale sometimes excretes a sticky honeydew.

CONTROL: Preventive maintenance. Manual removal may be tedious, but is very effective. Wet a *Q-Tip* in rubbing alcohol and wash scale away. A small knife, fingernails or tweezers may also be necessary to scrape and pluck the tightly affixed scale from the plants.

Homemade sprays work well if they contain a lot of rubbing alcohol.

Safer's Insecticidal Soap works well for scale control. Apply at 10-day intervals.

Pyrethrum (aerosol) applied two or three times at intervals of two to 10 days does it.

KXL applied at intervals of five to 10 days works acceptably.

Nature holds many natural scale predators, but to date there are no readily available commercial predators.

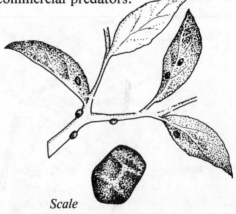

Scale

Malathion mixed with **Diazinon** applied intervals of five to 10 days is the most effective chemical spray. Oil spray mixed with nicotine sulfate works well also.

Bees, Flies etc.

Bees and *wasps* may become a nuisance. They are not harmful to plants but hurt when they sting. They sneak into the grow room through vents or cracks, in search of flowering plants, a valuable commodity to bees and wasps in midwinter. Manual removal is out of the question. *A circulation fan* in the room is the best form of preventive maintenance. The artificial wind will impair their flight, causing them to seek a more hospitable garden. There are many aerosol sprays that work well to kill bees and wasps. *Sevin,* found at the nursery, in either liquid or wettable powder, works as well as aerosol sprays and costs less. Wasp traps are also available and work well. *No-Pest strips* do a fair job of eradication. *Sweet flypaper* is also a good alternative. Bees and wasps are attracted to the HID lamp. Many will fall victim to its outer envelope....BUZZ...POP!

Fruit flies and *gnats* can become a problem. They do no harm to the indoor garden, but are a nuisance to be around. In a few days, they will fall victim to the lamp. If you are impatient and the chore of cleaning up bug bodies is not appealing, just about any indoor bug spray in the aerosol form will get rid of them. One friend used one cup of *Wisk* per gallon of water to kill all the larvae in the soil.

Fungus Control

Fungus is a very primitive plant. In fact, it is so primitive that it does not produce chlorophyll, the substance giving *higher plants* their green color. Fungi reproduce by spreading tiny microscopic spores rather than seeds. Many fungus spores are present in the air at all times. With proper conditions, these spores will settle, take hold and start growing. I know of several cases where entire gardens have been *wiped out* in a matter of days. One of these grow rooms was close to a swamp that is filled with fungus spores. Unsterilized, soggy soil and humid, stagnant air provide the environment most fungi need to thrive. Although there are many different types of fungi, they are usually treated by the same methods.

 Prevention

Prevention is the first step and the true key to fungus control. In "Setting Up the Grow Room," I recommended you remove anything that might attract fungus or harbor mold, such as cloth curtains or clothes. Make sure the advice is followed as part of a preventive program. If the room is carpeted, make sure to cover it with a white plastic (Visqueen). If mold should surface on the walls, spray it heavily with the fungicide used in the garden, wash down the wall with Pinesol (made from natural pine oil) or paint damp, fungus covered walls with whitewash (page 77). Get all of the mold off when it is washed down. Repeat applications if the mold persists. The basic ingredients of mold and fungi control are cleanliness and climate control. All the clean, well-ventilated grow rooms I have visited had little or no problem with fungi. All of the dingy, ill-kept gardens had fungus problems and yielded sickly flowers and vegetables. If the garden is in a basement, the use of a flat white paint with a fungus-inhibiting agent is essential. One garden basement was carpeted with fungi. The walls were whitewashed and lime was spread on the earth floor. The vent fan was cranked up and the room kept clean. There has been no trouble with mold in over a year.

LOGICAL PROGRESSION OF FUNGUS CONTROL

1. Prevention
    a. cleanliness
    b. low humidity
    c. ventilation
2. removal
3. KXL
4. Captan
5. Copper, lime, sulfur sprays

There are many ways to lower humidity. Ventilation is the least expensive, the easiest and most often used. Remember, one of the by-products of burning a fossil fuel in CO_2 generators is water vapor. Dehumidifiers work exceptionally well, offering exact humidity control. They are not very practical for the average gardener to buy, but many rental stores rent them for about $30 a month. Wood, coal, gas and electric heat all work well to dehumidify the air. Many grow rooms have a central heating vent. This vent may be opened to provide additional heat and lower humidity.

Control

Fungus is prevented by controlling all the factors contributing to its growth. If prevention fails and fungus appears, the horticulturist may elect to take preventive measures. Remove dead leaves and alter soil, moisture and air conditions to prevent fungus from spreading. These methods work well in gardens that have only a few signs of fungus. Another method of treating fungus is to isolate the infected plant and treat it separately. Fungus can spread like wildfire. If it gets a good start, take all preventive measures, as well as spraying the entire garden with a fungicide. Spraying will be necessary if the fungus gets a good start and appears to be spreading, even though preventive measures have been taken.

Fungicides come in two basic categories: (1) narrow-spectrum, specific against a few organisms and (2) broad spectrum, effective against numerous fungi.

Fungistats inhibit but do not destroy fungi. These chemicals are used by busy growers to keep fungi in check.

Growers must alternate broad- and narrow-spectrum fungicides to effectively fight Gray Mold, alternating or mixing combats resistance to the fungicide.

KXL is a combination insecticide/fungicide. The main fungicide is natural copper oleate. This fairly mild fungicide does a good job of arresting fungi. More complete information about KXL is available of page 174.

CAPTAN a wettable powder fungicide, is available in most nurseries and works very well on both **soil borne** and **foliar fungus**. The EPA classifies Captan as safe to use for edible vegetable crops. Other sources classify it as a toxic carcenogen.

MANEB is a fungicide that is similar to Captan and works well on just about any kind of fungus. If unable to find Captan or Maneb, ask the nurseryperson for a similar product.

Other fungicides can be used safely, including the bordeau mixture, copper and sulfur sprays, in light mixtures. Be careful when using these heavy metal and lime sprays: they can severely damage young tender growth.

When using a fungicide, spray the garden or plant at least twice, five to 10 days apart, even if you cannot see the fungus during the second or third sprayings. The fungus spores can be present on the recently infected foliage, but not visible.

Damping-off

Damping-off is a fungus condition in the soil that rots the newly sprouted seedlings and occasionally attacks rooting cuttings at the soil line. The stem will weaken, then grow dark at the soil line, and finally fluid circulation will be cut, killing the seedling or cutting. Damping-off is normally caused by: (1) fungus already present in an unsterile rooting medium, (2) over-watering, maintaining soggy soil, or (3) excessive humidity.

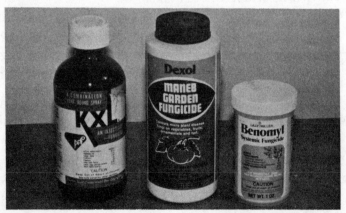

KXL, Maneb and Benomyl are three effective fungicides for various indoor fungi attacks.

Prevent all three conditions. Use *fresh,* sterile soil or soilless mix and clean pots. This will guard against harmful fungus in the soil. Careful daily scrutiny of soil will ensure that the proper amount of moisture is available to seeds or cuttings. Many gardeners prefer to start seeds and root cuttings in fast-draining, sterile, coarse sand, fine vermiculite or my favorite, root cubes. Using these mediums makes it almost impossible to over-water. Do not place a humidity tent over sprouted seedlings. A tent can lead to excessive humidity and damping-off. Cuttings are much less susceptible to damping-off and love a humidity tent to promote rooting. (See Chapter 4 for seed and cutting water requirements).

Control damping-off in its early stages by watering with a fungicide such as Captan or a mild bleach solution (two to five drops per gallon). Damping-off usually progresses rapidly and kills the young seedling in a matter of days. Over-watering is the biggest cause of damping-off and the key to prevention. An alternative to a tent is to mist cuttings with water several times daily to maintain leaf moisture and high humidity.

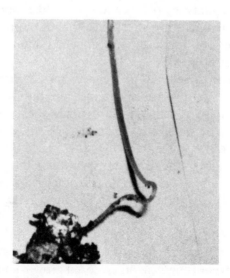

Damping off rots the stem at the soil line and is usually caused by soggy soil.

Soil-borne Fungus

Soil-borne fungus attacks the root system. It is usually seen on the soil surface first, then growing around the roots in the soil. Soil born fungus normally starts from using an unsterile planting medium and/or improper drainage. Poor drainage keeps roots too wet, making them susceptible to fungus and rot.

To **prevent** this type of fungus, a sterile planting medium and good drainage are essential. As explained in Chapter 3, good drainage is easily attained by having adequate drain holes and the proper soil texture.

Control soil-born fungus by applying Captan, Maneb or a biodegradable soap solution to the soil. Three or four applications are usually necessary. Mix the fungicides following directions, and apply in a water solution. Make sure the soil is not over-watered and there is adequate drainage.

Foliar Fungus

Leaf and *stem fungus*, including *leaf spot*, attack foliage. They appear as dark spots or splotches just about anywhere on the foliage. These types of fungus are usually caused by (1) using cold water when misting plants and fungus-like spots are formed as a result of temperature stress (See "About Spraying," pages 236-240). The spots could develop into a fungus. (2) excessive humidity (over 60 percent).

Prevention of these types of fungi attacks is easy. Spray with tepid water, have a hygrometer to measure humidity, and most important, employ a vent fan to dissipate the excess moisture. Vast quantities of water are applied to actively growing plants. They transpire the water back into the air. If this moist air is allowed to remain in the tiny grow room, it will stifle growth. A vent fan will remove it rapidly. A hygrometer may be purchased for less than $10 at some nurseries and most HID stores. When humidity goes over 60 percent, many fungi have a chance of getting started. The HID lamp and ballast emit a dry heat. This heat, along with a vent fan, usually provide enough humidity control to prevent fungus in an enclosed grow room. During the winter or cooler months, dry heat from the HID system may maintain low humidity and 72° temperatures while turned on.

At night, when the HID is off, the temperature will drop, causing moisture condensation and raising humidity. Check the humidity, both day and night, to see if there is a substantial variation in day and night humidity. If the humidity registers above 60 percent, and fungus is a problem, turn on the vent fan at night. This will vent off all the moist air. If the temperature is a problem, use dry heat to raise the night time temperature to 5° or 10° below the daytime temperature. This will keep humidity more constant.

Control foliar fungus by removing all seriously damaged foliage, take all preventive measures, then spray with one of the recommended fungicides three or four times at intervals of three to five days.

Gray Mold

Gray mold Botrytis cinerea - is a form of fungus that is familiar to all of us. It is grayish, whitish to bluish green in color, with a hair-like appearance. The mold can appear on just about anything in the garden, from the walls to the soil surface.

Mold is easily abated with fungicide sprays.

Gray mold spores are always in the air. The can be present even in the cleanest of rooms. But as long as the proper environment is maintained, they will not grow and reproduce. Gray mold occurs in two stages: non-germinated spores that live on foliage , and germinated spores that grow and penetrate foliage tissue where the spores remain in a latent, inactive form until conditions promote disease outbreak. Gray mold loves to enter plant wounds, natural openings and attach weak plants, but seldom invades healthy growing tissue.

Symptoms of gray mold attack: Plants can carry Botrytis and have no outward sign at all so it is difficult to tell where the disease came from if there are new plants continually being introduced into the garden. Yellowing of foliage; defoliation; brown, soft areas on dark-colored petals; or white, circular spots on white to tan flowers such as roses. Spots will soon develop into the characteristic fuzzy gray mold during the reproductive stage when spores are released into the air.

Prevent gray mold with low humidity (50 percent or less). Remove any standing water, allow ample air circulation and especially ventilation. Humid geographic areas with an outside humidity over 70 percent present the biggest problem to fungus abatement. Bud mold may be triggered when dead foliage rots. When removing yellow leaves between dense buds, pluck the entire leaf so no foliage is left to rot. See box in photo below.

Control *gray mold* on the soil or walls by removing it *manually*. Just use Pinesol in a heavy concentration and wash mold from walls or wherever it is growing. Do not use harsh Pinesol on plants. You must use a vegetable fungicide on plants. This kind of fungus - gray mold - does best when the grow room is dirty or stagnant water is present.

About Spraying

A large one- or two-gallon sprayer costs from $15 to $30 and works well for small and large gardens. All nurseries and many department stores carry these sprayers. Watch for spring and fall sales to get the best deal. The sprayers have an application wand and nozzle attached to a flexible hose, which makes it very easy to spray *under* leaves, the most important part! Garden sprayers are also made of heavy duty materials and can take frequent use. I like plastic rather than galvanized steel because it does not corrode or rust. Brass nozzle parts with rubber gaskets are easily cleaned with a paper clip. Just pump the sprayer up, and application is easy.

An electric fogger works well for large jobs. The fogger has an electric blower. The spray is metered out the nozzle under a good deal of pressure. The result is a fine, penetrating fog of spray. The fogger works best with Safer's Insecticidal Soap and various fungicides. Electric foggers are used to mist commercial greenhouse plants, and are usually available through greenhouse suppliers.

This small sprayer is easy to handle in the confines of a grow room and will hold enough liquid to spray the entire room.

One serious gardener uses a *jackrabbit* pump as a sprayer. The suction hose is placed in the nutrient solution, insecticide etc. and the spray is applied with a pumping motion. The *jackrabbit* pump is used mainly for foliar feeding. This horticulturist notes that with daily, early morning foliar feeding, little or no problem with fungus is realized. The pump works exceptionally well for heavy organic fertilizers.

Another favorite is a small, one- or two-quart spray bottle. A Windex bottle is acceptable, but will probably clog up or break in a couple of weeks. The best bottle is found at a nursery. It will have a removable nozzle that may easily be taken apart and thoroughly cleaned if it clogs up. These new pump-up spray bottles are very convenient, deliver an adjustable spray and are an excellent value. Homemade organic *teas* clog the most. A straight pin should be handy to punch out the nozzle hole. Get a heavy-duty spray bottle that can take a lot of use. It takes about ¾ quart of spray to cover a 10-by-10-foot garden. That is a lot of pumping for a very small plastic spray bottle!

Always wash bottle and pump thoroughly before and after each use. Using the same bottle for fertilizers and insecticides is OK. However, for best results: *Do not mix fertilizers and insecticides or fungicides* together when applying. Mixing chemicals will lessen their effectiveness. There could also be a chance the two chemicals are incompatible and one inhibits the other's effects.

Mix pesticides and fungicides just before using. Fertilizer solutions may be mixed and used for several months afterward. When finished spraying, empty the excess spray into the toilet. Spray residues have a tendency to build up in a partially clean bottle. Fresh water is the only liquid to leave in the spray bottle overnight.

Always spray early in the day. The moist spray needs a chance to be absorbed and dry out. If sprayed just a few hours before nightfall, moisture left overnight on foliage could cause fungus or *water spots*.

Always use tepid or room-temperature water. Water too hot or cold shocks the plants and will cause *water spots* on leaves.

Plants are able to absorb and process tepid water more rapidly.

Before spraying fungicides and pesticides, make sure the plants are well watered. With more water in the system, a plant suffers less *shock* from the killing spray. When foliar feeding the garden with a soluble fertilizer, just the opposite is true. Plants will absorb the soluble nutrients more rapidly when there is less moisture in the plant and soil. This is not a reason to dry plants out!

When mixing, follow directions to the letter, and read entire label before using. Mix wettable powders and soluble crystals in a little hot water to make sure they get dissolved before adding the balance of the tepid water.

Novice gardeners who have never sprayed before may want to talk it over with their nurseryperson before starting.

Always spray the *entire* plant, *both sides of the leaves,* stems, soil and pot. When spraying heavily, be careful with new tender growing shoots; they are easily burned by harsh sprays.

Have an accurate measuring cup and spoon that are used only for the garden. Keep them clean. If the spray is too heavy (easy to do when mixing small amounts) it will not kill any more bugs any deader; it will burn plants. Extreme precision should be exercised when mixing small quantities. A few drops could make the spray too potent and burn tender plants.

Spraying could promote mold once flower buds form and growth becomes dense. The moisture is trapped in the dense foliage of the flower cluster. If this water is allowed to remain in the flower top a day or longer, mold will find a new home.

Always rinse plants with tepid water one or two days after spraying. The water needs to actually drip from the leaves to have a cleansing effect. Misting plants heavily washes away all the stomata-clogging film and residue left from sprays. Fertilizer left on leaves is dissolved and absorbed by the rinse. Make sure both sides of the leaves are thoroughly rinsed.

Spray plants with fragile foliage with wettable powders rather than emulsions (liquids); inert diluents used in the liquid concentrate will wilt frail plants. A visible white residue results from the powder spray but not from the emulsions. A wetting or spreader-sticker is often required with wettable powders, and continuous agitation of the solution is necessary. This heavy, powdery film could require two or three rinsings to wash it off. More robust plants can be sponged off.

Always give vegetables several days of rinsing with a fresh-water spray a week before harvesting.

Every time a plant is sprayed with a fungicide, insecticide or soap, the stomata are clogged and growth slows. Rinsing off spray helps, but if sprays are used over and over, the garden will be slow-growing. Sprays are beneficial if not overdone.

In choosing an insecticide or fungicide, use only *contact sprays* that may be used on *edible* fruits and vegetables. Read the entire label to find the *toxic* or *active* life of the chemical. Wait a few more days than the label recommends and thoroughly wash all vegetables before eating. *Toxic life* is many times longer indoors because sunlight breaks down many chemicals.

Smart indoor gardeners use a respirator when spraying, especially if using an *aerosol/fogger*. In the enclosed grow room, the fumes and contents of a spray remain very concentrated. This makes it easy for even the safest spray to be irritating if inhaled for long.

CAUTION: Raise HID lamp out of the way, so mist from spray will not touch the bulb. Temperature stress, resulting from the relatively cold water hitting the hot bulb, may cause it to implode. This could not only startle you, but could burn eyes and skin. If the bulb breaks, **TURN OFF SYSTEM IMMEDIATELY - UNPLUG!**

SECTION II

Stages of Growth

Typically, an annual plant goes through three stages of growth. The *seedling* stage lasts about a month. During this stage, the seed germinates or sprouts, establishes a root system, and grows a stem and a few leaves. During *vegetative* growth, the plant produces much bushy green growth as well as a supporting root system. This stage may last from two months to over a year. The last stage of the life cycle comes when *flowers* form. If the flowers are pollinated, seeds will form.

CHAPTER EIGHT

The Seed and Seedling

The seed contains all the genetic characteristics of a plant. A seed is the result of sexual propagation, having genes from both male and female parents. An exception to this rule is found in hermaphrodite plants that bear both male and female flowers. The genes within a seed dictate the plant's size, disease and pest resistance, root, stem, leaf and flower production, yield, and many other variable growth traits. *The genetic makeup of a seed is the single most important factor dictating how well the plant will grow under HID lamps.*

A simple picture of a seed reveals an embryo, containing the genes and a supply of food, wrapped in a protective outer coating. Fresh, dry, mature seeds sprout quickly, while older (one year or more) seeds may take longer to sprout.

Plant seeds need only water, heat and air to germinate. They sprout without light in a wide range of temperatures. Seeds, properly watered, will normally germinate in two to 10 days, in temperatures from 70 to 90° F. The warmer it is, the faster germination, but watering with a mild mix of liquid fertilizer or Up-Start will hasten growth. In a humid climate, water with a mild bleach or fungicide solution (two to five drops per gallon) to prevent fungus. Once the seeds have sprouted and the white sprout is visible, plant them. Take care not to expose the tender rootlet to prolonged, intense light or wind. Plant the germinated seed in a quarter-inch to half-inch of fine planting medium with the white sprout tip (the root) pointing down.

The second popular planting and germination method is to sow the seed in a shallow planter, one-to five-gallon pot, peat pellet or rooting cube. The planting medium is then maintained evenly moist. If the seedling is to be transplanted from the shallow planter, use a spoon to contain the root ball. Peat pellets or root cubes may be transplanted in two to three weeks or when the roots show through the sides. Do not forget to fertilize them if they begin to yellow.

A meticulous gardener has labeled each seedling under this bank of four-foot fluorescent lights.

Some friends put the seeds in a couple of nursery flats and place them in the drawer of their heated waterbed. As soon as the seeds sprout, they are placed on top of the waterbed for a few more days to take advantage of the bottom heat. Then they are placed into the grow room.

A moisture tent may be constructed over the seedling container. Just put plastic or cellophane bag over the seeded soil. This will maintain high humidity and temperature. Usually, the seeds need only one initial watering when this method is used. Remove the bag as soon as the first sprout appears. Leaving it on will lead to damping-off or other fungi.

It is not necessary, but the planted seeds may be placed under the HID lamp while germinating. The lamp will add dry heat, but the soil will require more watering. Placing heat tape under or in soil will expedite germination without drying the soil out as fast.

The biggest problem most people have with germinating seeds is over-watering. The soil must be uniformly moist. A shallow flat or planter with a heat pad underneath may require daily watering, while a deep, one-gallon pot will need watering every two or three days. When the surface is dry (a quarter-inch deep) it is time to water. Remember there are *few* roots to absorb the water early in life, and they are very delicate.

It is a good idea to plant many times the number of seeds that are expected to mature to harvest. This is the best way to ensure success and a full grow room. When plants are small, they take up very little room. The HID lamp uses the same amount of electricity to grow 10 small plants as it does to grow 100. As the plants mature, the small and sick may easily be *weeded out*. The strong and healthy plants may be transplanted to larger containers, traded or given to friends.

When the seed sprouts, the first leaves that appear are called seed or seedling leaves. The seed leaves will then spread out as the stem elongates. Within a few days, the first true leaves will appear. The plant is now in the seedling stage, which will last about three more weeks. During this time, a root system grows rapidly and green growth is slow. Water is critical. The new root system is very small and requires a small but constant supply of water. Too much water will drown the roots and may cause root rot or damping-off. Lack of water will cause the infant root system to dry up. As the seedlings mature, some will grow faster, be stronger and appear generally more healthy. Others will sprout slowly, and be weak and leggy. If many seeds were planted, the sick and weak can be *thinned out* and the strong kept. This thinning process should take place around the third to fifth week of growth. Seedlings may also be transplanted easily without any damage.

CHAPTER NINE

Vegetative Growth

After the seedling is established, it enters the vegetative growth stage. When chlorophyll production is in full swing, the plant will produce as much vegetative or green, leafy growth as light CO_2, nutrients and water will permit. Properly maintained, many flowers and vegetables will grow from half an inch to two inches a day. If the plant is stunted now, it could take weeks to resume normal growth. A strong, unrestricted root system is essential to supply much-needed water and nutrients. UNRESTRICTED VEGETATIVE GROWTH IS THE KEY TO A HEALTHY HARVEST. During vegetative growth, the plant's nutrient and water intake changes. Transpiration is carried on at a more rapid rate, requiring more water. High levels of nitrogen are needed; phosphorus and potassium are used at much faster rates. The larger a plant gets, the faster the soil will dry out. A larger root system is able to take in more water and nutrients. Strong lateral branches are produced. They will soon be filled with flower buds. The more vegetative growth, the more flowers and weight at harvest.

Eighteen hours of halide light is conducive to vegetative growth; after that a point of diminishing returns is reached and the light loses effectiveness. Since most seed is of uncertain origin, the best way to promote maximum vegetative growth is to have the maximum amount of daylight! An annual plant will remain in the vegetative growth stage more than a year (theoretically forever) as long as the 18-hour photoperiod is maintained.

Cloning and the Mother Plant

Taking cuttings or clones[1] is one of the most efficient and productive means of plant propagation known today. Almost all flowers and vegetables may be reproduced or propagated sexually or asexually. Seeds are the product of sexual propagation; cuttings are the result of asexual or vegetative propagation. Taking cuttings is simply cutting some growing branch tips and rooting them. Many people have taken cuttings or slips from a houseplant such as a philodendron, ivy or coleus, and rooted them in water or sand. The rooted cutting is then placed in rich potting soil.

Identical cuttings will vary if they are grown in different climates. If the climate is poor for growth, the plant will develop poorly and be stunted. If the grow room is well cared for and has a perfect climate, strong, healthy flowers and vegetables can be harvested.

Vegetative propagation yields an exact genetic replica of the *mother plant*. These cuttings will all have the characteristics of the favorite *mother*. Fast, squat, bushy growth is at the same rate and lends itself to easy maintenance. Under HIDs, cuttings grow thick, heavy flower buds and huge vegetables.

Cuttings from the same plant grow into identical adults if grown in the exact same environment. The same cuttings grown in different grow rooms will look like different plants.

Light intensity is much greater, since the cuttings do not have a chance to get too tall. Remember, the closer the light is to the entire plant and garden, the faster they grow. Lower branches, heavily shaded by upper branches and leaves, will grow slow and spindly.

Because a cutting of any age is larger than a plant grown from seed, the root system is small and compact, making cuttings well suited for containers. By the time the root system is inhibited by the container, it is time for harvest. A five- or six-month old plant, grown from seed, is easily pot-bound and stunted. This compounds any bug or nutrient disorder and generally makes

[1] Technically, cloning is taking one cell of a plant and promoting its growth into a plant.

for unhealthy growth.

The stronger a plant and the faster it grows, the less chance it has of being affected by disease. A spider mite infestation, developed in the fifth or sixth month of a sexually propagated (seed) crop, may have to suffer through many sprayings until the infestation is arrested. The grow room cannot be totally cleaned out and fumigated until the plants have completed flowering or producing vegetables and been harvested. This could take several months.

All plants may be removed for a couple of days in order to fumigate the room or paint it with antiseptic whitewash. Moving a roomfull of six-month old plants in 50-pound containers of

This entire crop was propagated asexually.

soil is hard work. The plants are sick to begin with, and moving injures them. When returned to the grow room, they will take a long time to resume normal growth. On the other hand, cuttings are not in the grow room as long; the infestations have less time to launch an all-out attack or build an immunity to sprays.

Healthy cuttings taken from a proven, disease-resistant *Mother* are the route to a bountiful harvest. A bug infestation that gets out of hand among small cuttings is easily dealt with. The small cuttings are easily removed with little or no damage; then fumigate the grow room.

Experiments are more easily controlled with cuttings. Since cuttings are all the same, different stimuli (fertilizer, light, bending etc.) may be introduced on selected groups of cuttings and a true comparative analysis may be made.

A single branch of the mother plant can be cut into several pieces. Each one of them can be rooted and will turn into a plant just like the female.

Cuttings have some negative points. The *mother* plant will produce cuttings just like her, if she is not disease-resistant, cuttings also share this weakness. A bug or fungus infestation, left unchecked, could *wipe out* an entire cutting crop.

Taking cuttings from three or four different *mothers* will help ensure a healthy garden. The *wipe-out* effect is very uncommon in clean grow rooms. Infestations are also promoted by continued use of an ineffective spray used to kill bugs or fungus.

Taking cuttings is simple and easy. A consistent 100 percent survival rate may be achieved by following the simple procedures outlined in this book. The *mother* plant can be grown from seed or propagated by cutting. She should be at least two months old and possess all the characteristics you find desirable.

Cuttings can be taken from just about any plant, regardless of age or growth stage. Cuttings taken in the vegetative stage root quickly and grow fast. Cuttings taken from flowering plants may root a little slower.

Taking cuttings is the most traumatic experience plants ever go through. Cuttings go through an incredible change when growing branch tips are cut from the *mother* plant. Their entire chemistry changes. The stem that once grew leaves must now grow roots in order to survive. Sprays should be avoided now, as they compound cutting stress.

Research has found that plants tend to root much better when the stems have a high carbohydrate and low nitrogen concentration. In leaching the soil with copious quantities of water, nutrients including N, are washed out. Heavy leaching could keep soil too soggy. An alternative to soil leaching would be to leach the leaves themselves by *reverse foliar feeding*. Just fill the sprayer with clean, tepid water, and mist heavily every morning for a week. This gets the N out of foliage rapidly. The *mother* plant's growth slows as the N is used up, and carbohydrates have a chance to accumulate. Carbohydrate content is usually highest in lower, older more mature branches. A rigid branch that will *fold* over quickly when bent, rather than bend, is a good sign of high carbohydrate content. Older branches low on the plant give the best results. While rooting, cuttings require a minimum of nitrogen and increased levels of phosphorus to promote root growth.

There are several products available that stimulate root growth. They are available in a liquid or powder form. Professionals prefer the liquid type (root-inducing hormones) for penetration and consistency. The powder types are avoided because they adhere inconsistently to the stem and yield a lower survival rate.

In order for a cutting to grow roots from the stem, it must change from producing *stem* cells to producing *undifferentiated* cells to producing *root* cells. The rooting hormone promotes the rooting process by stimulating *undifferentiated* growth. Substances that are known to stimulate this type of growth are: napthalenacetic acid (NAA), indolebutyric acid (IBA) and 2,4-dichlorophenoxyacetic acid (2,3 DPA). The following products have been used as rooting hormones with successful results. Many of these commercial rooting hormones have one or all of the above synthetic ingredients and a fungicide to help prevent damping-off and mold.

Cuttings root faster if the soil is a few degrees warmer than normal. The soil heat promotes faster chemical activity, spurring growth. For best results, the rooting cuttings' soil should be kept at 70 to 80° F. The cuttings will transpire less if the air is about 5° cooler than the soil. Misting cuttings with water is a good way to cool foliage and lower transpiration. This helps the traumatized cuttings retain moisture that the roots do not yet supply.

1) Dip-N-Grow   5) Rootone - F

2) Woods Rooting Compound   6) Up-Start

3) Hormodin   7) Willow water

4) Hormex

NOTE: Some of these products are not recommended for use with edible plants, so read the label carefully before deciding to use a product.

Cloning: Step By Step

STEP ONE: Choose a *mother* at least two months old and 24 inches tall. Leach the soil daily with at least one gallon of water per five gallons of soil (make sure drainage is good), or wash down leaves (reverse foliar feeding) heavily every morning. Start seven days before taking cuttings, and leach every morning. This will wash out N.

STEP TWO: Choose some of the older lower branch tips. With a sharp blade, make a 45-degree cut across firm, healthy branches about an eighth- to a quarter-inch in diameter and two to eight inches in length. It is very important to keep from

 Clone five to 10 practice clones before making a serious cloning.

A cutting of a geranium is being taken.

smashing the end of the stem when making the cut. Trim off two or three sets of leaves and buds so the stem can fit in soil. *There should be at least two sets of leaves above the soil line and one or two sets of trimmed nodes below ground.* When cutting, make the slice halfway between the sets of nodes. Getting too close to nodes could cause one of the remaining nodes to have mutated growth. *Immediately* place the cut end in fresh, tepid water. This is a must to keep an air bubble from lodging in the tiny hole in the center of the stem, blocking the transpiration stream. If this hole is blocked, the new cutting will die within 24 hours. Leave the cuttings in the water overnight in subdued or no light.

The cutting is then dipped into diluted Hormex, a liquid root hormone, and then placed in a small slab of rockwool. Roots will emerge in about two weeks.

STEP THREE: If possible, use peat pots or root cubes, because they make maintenance easier and facilitate transplanting. Fill small containers or nursery flats with coarse, washed sand, fine vermiculite, soilless mix or, if nothing else is available, potting soil. Line them up and saturate with tepid water. Use a pencil or chopstick to make a hole in the rooting medium a little larger than the stem. The hole should bottom out at least half an inch from the bottom of the container to allow for root growth.

STEP FOUR: Use a root hormone. Professional nurserypeople prefer a liquid root hormone. Mix it just before using. There will be dilutions for hardwood and softwood cuttings in the mixing instructions. Use the formula for the softwood cuttings. Swirl each cutting in the hormone solution for 10 to 20 seconds. Place the cutting in the hole. Pack rooting medium gently around the stem. Powder root hormones require no mixing. Just roll the stem in the powder. When planting, take special care to keep a solid layer of hormone powder around the stem while gently packing soil into place.

STEP FIVE: Lightly water with a mild solution of B_1 or Up-Start, until the surface is evenly moist. Water as needed.

STEP SIX: Cuttings root best with 18 hours (some gardeners swear by 24 hours) of fluorescent light. If no fluorescent lamp is available, place the traumatized cuttings three to four feet under the halide and shade them with a cloth or screen. The shade will cut light intensity and prevent excessive shock.

STEP SEVEN: Place a tent over rooting cuttings to keep humidity near 80 percent. Construct the tent out of plastic bags, plastic film or glass. Remember to leave a breeze way so the little cuttings can breathe. An alternative to the humidity tent is to mist the rooting cuttings with tepid water several times daily. Either method helps retain moisture, since there are no roots to supply the leaves with water.

STEP EIGHT: The humidity tent will maintain the temperature at about 70 to 80° F. However some plants may fall victim to damping-off if there is not an ample supply of fresh circulating air. If more heat is needed, just moving the flat up off the floor will raise the temperature a few degrees. If this does not raise it enough, place a heat pad, heat tape or incandescent light bulb below rooting cuttings.

The photograph above shows small root nubs emerging from the stem of a minerature rose that has been rooting for only ten days. Below, is a bed of carnation clones rooting under fluorescents.

STEP NINE: Some cuttings may wilt for a few days or the leaves may rot if touching moist soil. Remove rotten leaves. Cuttings should look normal by the end of the week. If cuttings are badly wilted at the end of a week, they probably won't make it or will be so stunted they will never catch up to the others.

STEP TEN: In one to four weeks, the cuttings should be rooted. The tips of leaves will turn yellow, and roots may be seen growing out drain holes, and cuttings will start vertical growth. To check for root growth in flats or pots, carefully remove a cutting to see if it has good root development. Roots will show through the bottom and sides of peat pots and root cubes.

Transplanting

When a plant has outgrown its container, it must be transplanted into a larger pot to ensure that the roots have room for continued rapid outward growth. Inhibiting the root system will stunt plants. Some of the signs are slow, sickly growth and legginess. Branches develop with more distance between them on the main stem. In fact, the closest thing I have ever seen to *bolting* is root-bound plants. The plant will grow straight up. It will take a long time for the plant to resume normal growth. This costs the horticulturist money and patience. Transplant into the same type of soil, so there is no *new* soil for the roots to get used to. For cuttings rooted in vermiculite or sand, just shake away as much of the medium as possible (without damaging roots) before setting the root ball into the new soil. Novice and lazy gardeners, myself included, may want to start seeds or cuttings in root cubes or peat pots. They are very easy to transplant: Just set the cube or peat pot in the soil.

Next to taking cuttings, transplanting is the most traumatic experience a plant can live through. It requires special attention and manual dexterity. Tiny root hairs are very delicate and may easily be destroyed by light, air or clumsy hands. Roots grow in darkness, where their environment is rigid and secure. When roots are taken out of contact with the soil for long, they dry up and die.

Transplanting should disturb the root system as little as possible. Ortho **Up-Start** or **Vitamin B$_1$** is recommended to help ease transplant shock. Plants need time to get settled-in and re-establish a solid flow of fluids from the roots through the plant. They will require low levels of N and K, but use large quantities of P. When Up-Start is applied properly and roots are disturbed little, there will be no signs of transplant shock or wilt.

After transplanting, give new transplants filtered or less intense light for a couple of days. If there is a fluorescent lamp handy, place transplants under it for a couple of days before moving them under the HID.

Transplant late in the day so transplants will have all night to recover. The secret to successful transplanting is: manual dexterity, Up-Start and lots of water. Water helps the soil pack around roots and keeps them from drying out. Roots need to be

To transplant the four-inch rockwool cube simply place it on top of the larger slab.

in constant contact with the soil so they can supply water and food to the plant. Transplants will be a little shocked no matter what is done. Think about the plant; it has changed soil and will need to settle in. During this time of settling in, photosynthesis and chlorophyll production are at a low, as is water and nutrient absorption through the roots. It needs subdued light to keep foliage growing at the same rate as roots are able to supply water and nutrients. BE GENTLE!

Plants should be as healthy as possible before being traumatized by transplanting. Nonetheless, transplanting a sick, root-bound plant to a large container has cured more than one ailing plant.

Transplanting: Step By Step

In this example, we will use a one-month-old cutting started in a four-inch container of vermiculite and transplant it to a six gallon pot.

STEP ONE: Water four-inch cutting with half strength Up-Start or Vitamin B_1, one or two days before transplanting.

This pothos root ball is ready to be carefully placed in a larger container.

STEP TWO: Fill the six-gallon container with rich potting soil or soilless mix to within two inches of the top.

STEP THREE: Water soil until saturated.

STEP FOUR: Roll the four-inch pot between hands to break sand away from the sides of pot. Place hand over top of container with stem between fingers; turn it upside down and let root ball slip out of pot into hand. Take special care at this point to keep the root ball in one integral piece.

STEP FIVE: Carefully place root ball in a prepared hole in the six-gallon container. Make sure all roots are growing down.

STEP SIX: Backfill around the root ball. Gently but firmly place soil into contact with root ball.

This pothos will have much more room to grow in its new container.

STEP SEVEN: Water with half strength Up-Start or Vitamin B_1, making sure soil is completely saturated, but not soggy.

STEP EIGHT: Place new transplants on the perimeter of the garden or under a screen, so light remains subdued for a couple of days. The transplants should be able to take full light within a day or two.

STEP NINE: The new, rich potting soil will supply enough nutrients for about a month. Then supplemental fertilization will probably be necessary. Soilless mixes require balanced N-P-K fertilization a week or less after transplanting.

STEP TEN: See: Chart On "Minimum Container Size" in Chapter 3, page 125.

Pruning

Bending and pruning alter the basic growth pattern of a plant. The alteration affects physical shape, liquid flow and growth hormones. Pruning *strongly* affects the plant, while bending has more *subdued* affects. When a branch is pruned off, two branches will grow from the nodes just below the cut. This does not mean the plant will grow twice as much; a plant can grow only so fast. A quick branch amputation is not going to make it grow faster or add any more foliage. In fact, an indoor garden is already being pushed to the limit, and trimming or cutting it will slow growth for a few days. Think about it before hacking away! Any time a plant is pruned, valuable foliage is being removed that could be covered with flowers in less than two months.

PRUNING will make a plant grow bushier. The lower branches will develop more rapidly when the terminal bud is removed. Removing the terminal bud alters the concentration of growth-inhibiting hormones. These hormones (auxins) prevent the lateral buds from growing very fast. The further a branch is from hormones at the plant tip, the less effect the auxins have.

Always use clean instruments when pruning. A single-edged razor blade, a sharp pair of pruners or a pair of scissors - all work well. Do not use indoor pruners on anything but the indoor garden. If using pruners outdoors, they will have everything from aphids to dog dung on them. If outdoor clippers must be used, use rubbing alcohol to sterilize them before use.

Pinching back branches will diffuse floral hormones, making the plant bushier. Pruning the plant when it is one or two months old and again a month later will make it bushier. Continual pruning will keep it in a solid hedge-like shape. Some gardeners even prune plants into ornamental shape.

Pinching back the growing tip of this coleus will force growth on lower branches and make it more bushy.

Another pruning technique removes all but four main branches. This method is commonly used with tomatoes. The central growing tip is removed but the four branches are left intact. This concentrates the floral hormones in the four main branches. Note: Only complete branches are pruned; leaves are left alone! The idea behind this principle is that if there are fewer branches, they will be stronger, bearing more and heavier flowers and vegetables. The seedling or cutting is generally one month old when the four main branches are selected. The branches selected are usually the first four that grew, or the strongest.

Pruning all the branches is not advised. It shocks the plant too much. Just pruning the tall branches that get in the way and rob light from the rest of the garden works well. However, if taking cuttings from a *mother*, you may want to sacrifice her well-being for more cuttings. Remember, if she is pruned down to stubby branches, it could take her a month to resume normal growth.

Pruning too much over a period of time may alter the hormonal balance so much that the plant produces spindly growth. If a plant must be pruned heavily for cuttings it is usually best to prune it right down to a few leafy growing tips on the trunk or main stem and let it grow back from there.

ALL LEAVES ARE TO BE LEFT ALONE! Unless you are growing tomatoes, which benefit from leaf pruning after fruit has set. Removing large shade leaves will not supply more light to smaller growing tips, making them grow faster. This is bad gardening! A plant needs all the leaves it can get to produce the maximum amount of chlorophyll. Removing the leaves slows chlorophyll production and stunts growth. Removing the leaves stresses the plant. Stress inhibits growth, especially during vegetative growth. Only leaves that are clearly dead bug- or fungus-infected should be removed. Leaf removal is not pruning, it is hacking up a normally healthy plant.

Pruning or trimming off lower branches that have spindly, sickly growth, is acceptable. When pruning, cut off the entire branch. Pruning the lower branches has a minimal effect on floral hormone concentration.

CHAPTER TEN

Flowering

In order for a plant to complete its annual life cycle successfully, it must first flower. Dioecious plants are either male (pollen producing) or female (ovule producing). Most plants are hermaphrodite (bisexual), with both male and female flowers on the same plant. These plants are self pollinating.

One of the many tiny grains of pollen from the male (staminate) flower pod lands on a pistil of the female (pistilate) flower. Each calyx harbors an ovule and a protruding set of pistils. Actual fertilization takes place when the grain of male pollen slides down the pistil and unites with the female ovule, deep within the calyx. Once fertilization takes place, pistils turn brown and a seed will form within the calyx or seed bract. Seeds are the result of this sexual propagation and contain genetic characteristics of both parents.

Long-day is the category most all annual plants fall into. Marigolds, alessiums, zinnias, petunias and lobelia are all long-day annuals. They are not effected by the photoperiod and bloom after they are just a few inches tall. Most vegetables fall into the long-day classification as well. Tomatoes, egg plants, squash and beans all flower and fruit for several months if they receive 18 hours of light per day. In gardens with 18 hours of light, a true *Garden of Eden* is possible.

Short-day plants bloom when there is an even 12-hour day and 12-hour night. The photoperiod must be 12 hours of *uninterrupted darkness* for the short-day plants to bloom properly. Poinsettias and chrysanthemums are two of the most popular flowers that fall into this short-day category. For more information about short- and long-day plants see pages 24-29.

In nature, flowers' lives come to an end in the fall, after the long, hot, days of summer. The long nights and short days of autumn signal short-day plants to start the flowering stage. Growth patterns and chemistry change: Stems elongate, flower formation is rapid at first, then slows. All this causes new nutrient needs. Attention is now focused on flower production, rather than on vegetative growth. Production of chlorophyll, re-

Chrisanthemums are short-day plants that bloom under 12 hours of light and 12 hours of total darkness.

quiring much nitrogen, slows. Phosphorus uptake increases to promote floral formation. Light needs change as well. During autumn, in most climates, the sun takes on a slightly reddish appearance, emitting a light that is a more *red* than a balanced *white* light. The sun produces this reddish glow by shining at a greater angle through more particles in the atmosphere. Growth and floral hormones are stimulated by this *red* or *harvest sun*.

The *harvest sun* phenomenon is not fully understood. However, experiments have proved that by increasing the amount of red light during flowering, floral hormones are stimulated and flower yield increases substantially.

Indoors, flowering may be induced in short-day plants just as it is in nature, by shortening the photoperiod from 18 to 12 hours. Once the days are changed to 12 hours, flowers should be clearly visible within one to three weeks. In fact, many gardeners have two grow rooms: a vegetative grow room with one metal halide *on* for 18 hours, the other room for flowering having both a halide and HP sodium *on* 12 hours a day. Using this combination of rooms and lamps, the electricity bill remains relatively low and the horticulturist has the luxury of having both summer and fall every day of the year.

The additional stimulation of a *red* or *harvest sun* may be simulated by an HP sodium lamp (the phosphor-coated halide also emits a little more red than the clear halide). The HP sodium may increase flower production 20 to 50 percent.

The *harvest sun* is simulated one of three ways: (1) Adding an HP sodium lamp to a grow room already containing a metal halide. This more than doubles the available light, especially in the red end of the spectrum. The halide maintains blues in the spectrum necessary for continued chlorophyll production. (2) Replacing the halide with an HP sodium. This increases the reds, but cuts the blues. A result of this practice has been more yellowing of vegetative leaves, due to lack of chlorophyll production and more elongation (two to six inches) than if the halide were present. (3) Adding or changing to a phosphor-coated halide. Not only are these halides easier on the eyes, their coating makes them produce a little bit more red in their spectrum, thus promoting flowering.

Water needs of a flowering plant are somewhat less than in the vegetative stage. Adequate water during flowering is important to carry on the plant's chemistry and resin production. Withholding water to *stress* a plant will actually stunt growth, and the yield will be less.

 Removing large fan leaves to create more intense light to small flower buds or to stress plants is unacceptable. Large leaves are necessary to keep the plant healthy. Remove *only* dead or dying leaves.

All these blooming flowers have strong healthy foliage.

Hermaphrodites

A hermaphrodite is a plant that has both male and female flowers on the same plant. The majority of plants fall into this category.

Indoors, the outdoor environment is manufactured and the *normal* life cycle of any plant can be altered. Creating summer in December, cloning, prolonging the life cycle and leaching the soil: All the wonderful things we are able to do indoors mix up even the strongest plant somewhat. When this necessary stress is coupled with freaky seeds, the outcome is uncertain. High humidity, over-pruning and old age seem to promote hermaphrodites more than other environmental factors. In short, if a plant starts to go sour and you do not know the reason why, it could be because it was stressed too much.

Seed Crops

Seed crops are harvested when the seeds are mature. Often seeds may actually split open their containing calyx or seed pod. The flowering female grows many ready, receptive calyxes until pollination occurs. Seeds are mature within six to eight weeks. Watch out for fungus that might attack the weakening female and her cache of ripe seeds.

When seeds are mature, remove them from the pods and store them in a cool, DRY place. The seeds are viable and ready for planting as soon as they are harvested, but they may grow sickly plants. Let the seeds dry out a few months before planting. Dry seeds will produce much healthier plants and the germination rate will be much higher.

A single 400 watt HP sodium lamp illuminates this beautiful greenhouse full of orchids.

CHAPTER TWELVE

Breeding

The purpose of this chapter is to give a basic outline of the selective, sexual propagation (breeding) of annual plants. For a more complete, detailed discussion on breeding, refer to specific plants in books about breeding.

Seeds that are the product of several generations of selective indoor breeding are highly prized for their *acclimatization* to the indoor environment.

Breeding is fun and easy. It will let you be the "Gene Master" of the garden. With the possibilities of indoor growing, a person could breed many more times per year.

Selective breeding is simply assuming and controlling the role of Mother Nature once again. In nature, pollen is shed into the wind to randomly fertilize *any* receptive female. The breeder adds precision and control to this process, catching pollen from a desirable male and putting it in contact with chosen female pistils.

There are two basic kinds of breeding: (1) *inbred* or *true bred*: plants of the same plant varieties or ancestry that are crossed with one another. (2) *outbred* or *hybrid*: plants of different strains that are crossed or cross-pollinated.

Inbreeding is necessary for a *pure breed* to be established. This *true or pure breed* is necessary so common growth characteristics may be established. If the plants are not a pure breed, it will be impossible to predict the outcome of the *hybrid* plant. After the fifth to sixth generation, negative characteristics, such as legginess and lack of vigor tend to dominate. Inbreeding is necessary to establish a true breed, but should be avoided after the strain has been established.

Inbreeding is used to establish a stable reference point or plant to start from. The chosen females are bred back with males of the same strain. This will establish a *true breed* or plants with the same growth characteristics. These plants, of *known* ancestry and growth characteristics, will be used to breed *hybrid* plants.

This variety of false aralia breeds true.

History students will remember the inherited physical and mental problems that plagued European royal families who inbred for generations. The more generations that practiced inbreeding, the more physical deformities and mental deficiencies surfaced. Seeds from self-pollinated hermaphrodite plants are inbred.

OUTBREEDING or producing **hybrid** seed has been the norm in horticulture for many years. Horticulturists have found choosing parents of different strains, exhibiting exceptional, positive, dominant characteristics, will result in a super plant, referred to as having *hybrid vigor*.

This hybrid vigor is also responsible for plants able to survive a wider latitude of temperatures and overall growth inducing factors. A plant from one variety that is bred with another variety will pick up some of the more favorable characteristics from each.

Breeding: Step-By-Step

STEP ONE: Choose male breeding stock exhibiting desirable characteristics.

STEP TWO: One branch of male flowers is all that will be needed, unless a large crop of seeds is desired. Other branches may be stripped of flowers to help contain pollen and guard against accidental, random pollination. The male can be isolated from the females once flowers have developed but not yet opened, by placing him in a sunny window or in a vegetative grow room. This will slow flower development and not hurt the male in any way.

A branch of ripe male flowers may be cut and placed in water. It will remain healthy for several weeks. When the pollen sacs open, proceed with step three. The remaining male plant may then be cut back or harvested.

STEP THREE: When the pollen pods start to open, place a clean bread sack or other plastic bag over the branch to collect pollen. Secure the bag at the bottom with a piece of string or wire tie. Keep the bag over the branch for several days to collect pollen.

STEP FOUR: When enough pollen has been collected, shake remaining pollen off into the bag. Remove spent branch.

STEP FIVE: Ideally, pistils should be ready for fertilization three to four weeks after the first calyx has appeared. Receptive pistils are white and fuzzy, not starting to turn brown. Cover the selected female branch that has many ripe, receptive pistils with the pollen filled bag. Shake the bag.

Self pollination of this jade plant is helped along with an artists paint brush.

STEP SIX: Use a small paintbrush to apply the pollen from the bag to the pistils if just a few seeds are from many different females are desired. Be very careful. Just use a little pollen on each calyx and keep it from spreading to other plants that you do not want to pollinate.

STEP SEVEN: Leave the bag for two or three days, to ensure fertilization. Be careful not to scatter pollen on adjacent plants that you do not want fertilized.

STEP EIGHT: After fertilization, seeds will be ripe in three to six weeks. Harvest seeds when they split open the containing calyx or *rattle in the pod.*

STEP NINE: Let seeds dry for two or three months in a cool, dry place before planting.

Jerusalem cherry fruit contains seeds that will be viable when they are removed from the fruit and dried.

Growth Regulators

The world of growth regulators will make the indoor grower a true Dr. Frankenstein. With these chemicals, growth can be slowed or speeded up, stems can elongate, internodes shorten, male turn female and vice versa!

Growth regulators have been the rage in commercial nurseries for several years. They make plant growth more predictable and easy to control. Now they are starting to filter down into the retail hobby greenhouse and grow rooms. Growth-regulating chemicals control or alter the hormonal balance of a plant. Hormones are responsible for the way a plant grows; whether it is short, tall, bushy, male, female etc. is determined by hormones.

Many of you have probably used one of these growth-regulating hormones and not realized it. If you have used any kind of a rooting formula (Rootone-F, Hormodin, Hormex) you have used one of these growth regulators.

These growth regulators can be divided into four classes:

     (1) Growth-retarding

     (2) Growth-promoting

     (3) Anti-ethylene - ethylene-producing

     (4) Root-inducing

Growth retardants reduce internode length and thus the overall height of susceptible plants. Their most common use is in flower production. All other growth, flowering and foliage, except for internode shortening, is normal. These growth retardants are fundamental in the production of smaller sizes of chrysanthemums, poinsettias, hydrangeas, many varieties of bedding plants and other crops.

Another effect of growth retardants is to promote earlier flowering, more flowers or both in some plants. The most common plants are azaleas, fuchsias, gardenias and Chinese hibiscus.

Growth regulators are applied by foliar spray, root absorption or seed soak, depending on the regulator you choose. They are measured in parts per million and a specific ppm dosage is given to each plant. The regulators are also proportioned in percent of solution. For example a 2 percent solution would have 2 percent chemical and 98 percent water.

Many chemicals are capable of dwarfing and inducing branching, but many of them will also induce abnormal or mutated growth. Atrinal is the only chemical on the market that is approved for ornamentals.

Ethylene-producing compounds are numerous. FLOREL (3.9 percent ethephon) is labeled for use on bromeliads to induce flowering, it is also used worldwide on rubber trees and peanuts. Ethylene is the most universal dwarfing compound, but sparse or no leaves and flowers may be a possible side effect. There are many times when dwarfing and no flowering is desirable, such as during rooting of geraniums or rooting other perennial flowers.

Growth-promoting chemicals are auxins, gibberilins and cytokenins. Auxins promote rooting and leaf and fruit retention. Gibberillins promote internode extension and also release buds form dormancy and promote flowering in some plants. Cytokenins promote strong, dark green leaves and branching types of growth and delay old age (senescence).

Gibberillins are generally used in low concentrations. Some of the uses of gibberillins are to break perennial plants out of dormancy forcing growth and promoting a bigger plant.

Roses treated with gibberillins will have beautiful long stems and slightly larger flowers.

Anti-ethylene compounds are produced within a plant, particularly in flowers and fruits.

Plant Selection Guide

The following plants do extremely well under lights: African violets, impatiens, episcias, gloxinias, columneas etc. African violets, begonias and impatiens flower constantly under lights. Begonias of all types, ferns, oxalis, geraniums, annuals, small shrubs and trees such as jasmine, gardenia, crape myrtle, dwarf lantana and dwarf pomegranate, citrus and figs.

Succulents (jade, miniature crassulas, Christmas, Easter and Thanksgiving cactus, etc.) and members of the cactus family are probably the easiest to care for. They require a minimum of care and infrequent watering, but lots of light.

African Violets, both mother plants and cuttings of this short-day plant are given 18 hours of light a day at a level of 6,000 mW/m2. Flowering is induced with a short 12 to 14-hour photoperiod.

Azalea cuttings propagated under a light level of 6,000 mW/m2, 18 hours a day grow fast and uniform. Flowers are effectively forced by supplying 3,000 mW/m2 for 16 hours a day.

For *begonias*, supplemental lighting promotes cuttings to form on the varieties Rieger, Elatior and Lorraine when natural light is lacking. Light level of 6,000 mW/m2 is the norm. Anything goes with the semperflorens begonia. Use 6,000 mW/m2 18 hours a day to nurture young seedlings and to speed flowering. All begonia cuttings rooting is stimulated by artificial light.

Bromeliads: A light level of 6,000 mW/m2 18 hours a day is used to promote stronger growth and the development of seedlings and young plants. On larger bromeliads, supplemental lighting is normally used to help stimulate floral formation.

A light level of 4,500 mW/m2 for 24 hours a day is used to stimulate flowering. Many times other flower-inducing means are combined with lighting to hasten blooming.

Cacti: In winter when the days are short, cacti greatly benefit from intense supplemental light. A lighting level of 9,000 mW/m2 for 18 hours a day will produce phenomenal results in seedlings, clones and adult cacti. Some varieties of cactus respond more favorably to 24 hours of light.

Calceolaria Early flowering is achieved by applying supplemental lighting (3,000 mW/m2) for 24 hours a day from bud induction until flowering. Maintain the temperature between 60 and 65 degrees for maximum productivity.

Carnations, like chrysanthemums, are propagated very successfully by using a mother plant and supplemental light. In fact, side shoots from cut flowers make excellent cuttings. Cuttings are taken and given 16 hours of light (6,000 mW/m2). Excessive flowering may occur if more than 16 hours of light per day is permitted. The carnation is a long-day plant, it is possible to light it 24 hours a day to grow more and more profuse flowers. However after 18 hours of light a day, the extra light produces a minimum of growth.

A large indoor garden full of flowers and vegetables. The trellis on the right will hold a large crop of tomatoes.

HP sodium lamp keeps this garden blooming.

Chrysanthemums are one of the most common and most responsive flowers to supplemental light in all stages of life. In winter mother plants are given 9,000 mW/m2, 20 hours a day. Given lighting during the first month of vegetative growth increases bud count and foliage production. Being a short-day plant, the chrysanthemum requires 20 hours of light a day during the first month of vegetative growth and 12 hours of light (4,500 mW/m2 and 12 hours of uninterrupted darkness to flower properly.

Cucumber seedlings grow exceptionally well under HID lights. Give young seedlings a light level of 4500 mW/m^2 for the first 10 days of growth for 24 hours a day. After this, shorten the photoperiod to 16 to 16 hours per day, and increase the light level to 6000 mW/m^2.

Young Bearss limes are forming on the tips of branches. Lime trees grow quite well under HID's and produce fruit all year round.

Cyclamen Seedlings given supplemental lighting (6,000 mW/m2) have more uniform growth and less damping off. The young plants are given 18 hours of light a day.

This Cyclamen has been blooming for over three months and continues to bloom.

Geraniums and pelargoniums propagated by seed or from cuttings greatly benefit from supplemental light. Mother plants are given 18 hours of light at a level of 6,000 mW/m2 to increase cutting production. The cuttings are given less light but for the same 18 hours a day. Geraniums are a short-day plant and flower with shorter days or colder temperatures.

F1 hybrid seed-propagated geraniums can be given 24 hours of light a day at a level of 6,000 mW/m2 from the beginning of life. These F1 hybrids do not need short days for flower induction.

Gloxinas are given a light level of 6000 mW/m^2 18 hours a day to enhance growth and development of seedlings and young plants. Give potted gloxinas a light level of 4500 mW/m^2 to promote large healthy flowers.

Planted on the same day, the small stone plant on the left was in a dim corner of the grow room and the large stone plant received intense halide light.

Kalanchoe mother plants are given 18 hours of light a day to prevent flowering of this long-day plant. Normally propagated vegetatively, cuttings are given 18 to 24 hours of light at a level of 6,000 mW/m2. Flowering is induced by giving the plants an equal 12 hours of light and 12 hours of darkness.

Lettuce is lighted at a level of 6000 mW/m^2 during their entire life. If given a higher level of light, lettuce might bolt.

Orchids: The blooms and overall growth of many varieties of orchids are greatly enhanced by supplemental lighting during the winter. See: special section below on light requirements of orchids.

Roses love light. Miniature roses grow incredibly well under HID light. Levels of 6,000 mW/m2, 24 hours per day will greatly increase flower yield, size and quality. CO2 is very important to these super-productive roses.

The *snapdragon* is a favorite fall and early spring flower. There are two genetically different types of snapdragons; short-day, referred to as Group I or II, or "winter flowering" and long-day, referred to as Group III or IV, or "summer flowering." When setting this plant out for early spring blooms, give seedlings supplementary lighting at a level of 9,000 mW/m2 so that a daylength of 16 hours is reached. This will speed flowering about four weeks. In fact even better results can be achieved by giving long-day plants 24 hours of light (4,500 mW/m2) all their life. Short day snapdragons should receive short 12 hour days after they are about two months old for maximum blooming potential.

Tomatoes, peppers and eggplants flourish under HID light. In short the more light these plants are given the bigger they grow and the more fruit they produce. Give these plants 9000 mW/m^2 as soon the first true leaves appear and maintain the light level throughout their entire life.

Weight Measurement Equivalents

1 kg. or 1,000 g.	= 2.2 lbs.
1 g. or 1,000 mg.	= .035 oz. or (¼ tsp.)
1 lb.	= 453.6 g.
1 oz.	= 28.35 g.

Tables & Measures

1 part per million (p.p.m.):	1% solution:
1 mg. per liter	10.00 p.p.m.
1 mg. per kilogram	10 grams per liter
1 mg. per %₁₀ qt. (approx.) .0001%	1.28 oz. per gallon

.1%	= 1.000 p.p.m.	= 1.000 mg. per liter
.01%	= 100 p.p.m.	= 100 mg. per liter
.001%	= 10 p.p.m.	= 10 mg. per liter
.0001%	= 1 p.p.m.	= 1 mg. per liter

One Cup Measurement Equivalents

236.5 ml. or c.c.	= 8 fl. oz.
	.5 pt.
	.25 qt.
	16 tbs.
	48 tsp.

Conversions to Smaller Quantity from 100 Gallons

100 Gallons	50 Gallons	10 Gallons	5 Gallons	1 Gallon
2 gal.	1 gal.	1.6 pt.	12.8 oz.	2.56 oz.
1 gal.	2 qt.	12.8 oz.	6.4 oz.	1.28 oz
2 qt.	1 qt.	6.4 oz.	3.2 oz.	3 ⅓
1 qt.	1 pt.	3.2 oz.	1.6 oz.	2 tsp.
1 pt.	1 c.	1.6 oz.	.8 oz.	1 tsp.
4 oz.	2 oz.	.4 oz.	.2 oz.	¼ tsp.

Power Data

1 BTU = 0.293 watthour
1 kw.hr = 3,413 BTU's
Wattage = Amps × Voltage
Amps   = Wattage/Voltage
Voltage = Wattage/Amps

Liquid Volume Equivalents

Gallons	Quarts	Pints	Fluid Oz.	Cups	Tbs.	Milliliters.
1	4	8	128	16		
	1	2	32	4		
		1	16	2	32	473
			1	⅛	2	30
				1	16	240
					1	15
						5

Temperature Conversion

$$°C × \tfrac{9}{5} + 32 = °F$$
$$(°F - 32) × \tfrac{5}{9} = °C$$

GLOSSARY

This GLOSSARY contains many very simple and some not so simple words in the context of their usage in this book. Many examples are given to promote good indoor horticultural practices.

Absorb — draw or take in: Rootlets **absorb** water and nutrients.

AC (alternating current) — an electric current that reverses its direction at regularly occurring intervals. Homes have AC.

Acid — a sour substance: An **acid** or *sour* soil has a low pH.

Active — a hydroponic system that **actively** moves the nutrient solution

Adobe — heavy clay soil, not suitable for container gardening

Aeration — supplying soil and roots with air or oxygen

Aeroponics — growing plants by misting roots suspended in air

Aggregate — medium, usually gravel, that is all nearly the same size, and used for the inert hydroponic medium.

Alkaline — refers to soil with a high pH: Any pH over 7 is considered **alkaline**.

All-purpose (General-purpose) fertilizer — A balanced blend of N-P-K: **all purpose fertilizer** is used by most growers in the vegetative growth stage.

Amendment — changing soil texture by adding organic or mineral substances

Ampere (amp) — the unit used to measure the strength of an electric current: A 20-amp circuit is overloaded when drawing more than 17 amps.

Annual — a plant that normally completes its entire life cycle in one year or less: Marigolds and tomatoes are examples of **annual** plants.

Aphid — small insect of various colors: **Aphids** suck the juices from plants.

Arc — luminous discharge of electricity (light) between two electrodes.

Arc tube — container for luminous gases; also houses the arc.

Auxin — classification of plant hormones: **Auxins** are responsible for foliage and root elongation.

Bacteria — very small, one-celled organisms that have no chlorophyll.

Ballast — a stabilizing unit that regulates the flow of electricity and starts a HID lamp.

Bat guano — bat feces: the organic *super-bloom* fertilizer.

Bed — Plants grow in containers or **beds**.

Beneficial insect — a good insect that eats bad flower and vegetable-munching insects.

Biodegradable — able to decompose or break down through natural bacterial action: Substances made of organic matter are **biodegradable**.

Biology — the study of physical life and living matter: Botany is a branch of **biology**.

Biosynthesis — production of a chemical compound by a plant.

Bleach — Ordinary laundry **bleach** is used in a mild water solution as a soil fungicide.

Blood meal — high-N organic fertilizer, made from dried blood: Dogs love **blood meal!**

Bloom — yield flowers.

Blossom booster — fertilizer high in phosphorus (P) that increases flower yield.

Bolt — term used to describe a plant that is severely root-bound and starved for light. The plant will grow straight up or **bolt.**

Bone meal — organic fertilizer high in P: **Bone meal** is mixed in soil to stimulate root growth of clones and seedlings.

Bonsai — a very short or dwarfed plant.

Branch — a secondary or lateral stem growing.

Breaker box — electrical circuit box having on/off switches rather than fuses.

Breathe — Roots draw in or **breathe** oxygen, stomata draw in or **breathe** CO_2.

Break down — to **Biodegrade**

Breed — sexually propagate plants under controlled circumstances

Bud — a small stem on a branch containing thick rows of calyxes.

Bud blight — a withering condition that attacks flower buds.

Buffer — a substance that reduces shock and cushions against fluctuations. Many fertilizers contain **buffer** agents.

Bulb — 1. the outer glass envelope or jacket that protects the arc tube of an HID lamp 2. clove or **bulb** of garlic.

Burn — 1. Leaf tips that turn dark from excess fertilizer and/or salt **burn** 2. Foliage that gets to close to a hot HID will **burn**

Calyx — the pod harboring female ovule and two protruding pistils, seed pod.

Captan — commercial wettable powder fungicide. **Captan** stops soil and foliage fungus.

Carbon dioxide (CO_2) — a colorless, odorless, tasteless gas in the air necessary for plant life.

Carbohydrate — neutral compound of carbon, hydrogen and oxygen: Sugar, starch and cellulose are **carbohydrates.**

Caustic — capable of destroying, killing or eating away by chemical activity

Cell — the base structural unit that plants are made of: **Cells** contain a nucleus, membrane, and chloroplasts.

Cellulose — a complex carbohydrate that stiffens a plant: Tough stems contain stiff **cellulose.**

Centigrade — a scale for measuring temperature in which 100° is the boiling point of water and 0° is the freezing point of water.

CFM — Cubic feet per minute.

Chelate — combining nutrients in an atomic ring that is easy for plants to absorb.

Chemical — substance of or relating to chemistry: **Chemical** fertilizers are loosely *synthetic.*

Chlorophyll — the green photosynthetic matter of plants: **Chlorophyll** is found in the chloroplasts of a cell.

Chlorine — chemical used to purify water in water systems.

Chlorosis — the condition of a sick plant with yellowing leaves due to inadequate formation of chlorophyll: **Chlorosis** is caused by a nutrient deficiency, usually iron or imbalanced pH.

Circuit — a circular route traveled by electricity.

Clay — soil made of very fine organic and mineral particles: **Clay** is not suitable for container gardening.

Climate — the average condition of the weather in a grow room or outdoors.

Clone — 1. a rooted cutting of a plant 2. asexual propagation.

CO_2 enrichment — adding CO_2 to the atmosphere of a grow room to speed growth.

Cold — temperatures below 50° F.

Color spectrum — the band of colors (measured in nm) emitted by a light source.

Color tracer — a coloring agent that is added to many commercial fertilizers so the horticulturist knows there is fertilizer in the solution. Peters has a blue **color tracer**.

Compaction — soil condition that results from tightly packed soil: **Compacted** soil allows for only marginal aeration and root penetration.

Companion planting — planting garlic, marigolds, etc. along with other plants to discourage insect infestations.

Compost — a mixture of decayed organic matter, high in nutrients: **Compost** must be at least one year old. When too young, decomposition uses N; after sufficient decomposition, **compost** releases N.

Container — pot or planter having drainage holes: A **container** contains a growing medium.

Control — regulate and influence all factors contributing to healthy flowers and vegetable growth.

Copper — one of the trace elements necessary for plant life.

Core — Many times the transformer in the ballast is referred to as a **core**.

Cotyledon — seed leaves, first leaves that appear on a plant.

Cottonseed meal — acidic organic fertilizer and soil amendment high in nitrogen.

Cross-pollinate — pollinate two plants having different ancestry.

Cubic foot — volume measurement in feet: Width times length times height equals **cubic feet**.

Cultivate — encourage plant growth by controlling growth-inducing factors.

Cutting — 1. growing tip cut from a parent plant for asexual propagation 2. clone 3. slip.

Damping — off — fungus disease that attacks young seedlings and clones causing stem to rot at base: Over-watering is the main cause of **damping — off**.

DC (direct current) — an electric current that flows in only *one* direction

Decompose — rot or decay etc., through organic chemical change.

Dehydrate — remove water from foliage.

Deplete — exhaust soil of nutrients, making in infertile: Once a soil is *used* it is **depleted**

Desiccate — cause to dry up. Safer's Insecticidal Soap **desiccates** its victims.

Detergent — liquid soap concentrate used as a: 1. wetting agent for sprays and water 2. pesticide. NOTE: **Detergent** must be totally organic to be safe for plants.

Diazinon — commercial insecticide that kills aphids, mealy bugs and white flies.

Dioecious — having distinct male and female flowers.

Dip-N-Grow — liquid root hormone: **Dip-N-Grow** is one of the best on the market.

Directions — guidance or supervision of an act: Always read **directions** before acting.

Dirt — 1. filthy or soiling substance 2. soil from back yard, generally not suited for container gardening.

Disease — sickness of any kind.

Disease resistant — able to fight off disease.

Dissolve — make or become liquid: Fertilizer crystals **dissolve** in water.

Dolomite — a limestone high in calcium and magnesium, pulverized and used to raise and balance soil pH: **Dolomite lime** is slow release and maintains a constant soil pH.

Dome — the part of the HID outer bulb opposite the neck and threads.

Dome support — the spring-like brackets that mount the arc tube within the outer envelope.

Dose — amount of fertilizer, insecticide etc. given to a plant, usually in a water solution.

Drainage — way to empty soil of excess water: with good **drainage**, water passes through soil evenly, promoting plant growth; with **bad drainage** water stands in soil, drowning roots.

Dripline — a line around a plant directly under its outermost branch tips: Roots seldom grow beyond the **drip line**.

Drip system — a very efficient watering system that employs a main hose with small water emitters. Water is metered out of the emitters, one drop at a time.

Dry ice — a cold, white substance formed when CO_2 is compressed and cooled: **Dry ice** changes into CO_2 gas at room temperatures.

Dry soil pocket — a small portion of soil that remains dry after watering: **Dry soil pockets** may be remedied by adding a wetting agent (soap) to water and/or waiting 15 minutes between waterings.

Dry well — drain hole, filled with rocks.

Ecogrow — all natural organic commercial fertilizer.

Electricity — flow of electrons: **Electricity** is the energy source used to produce HID light.

Electrode — a conductor used to establish electrical arc or contact with non-metallic part of circuit.

Elongate — grow in length.

Encarisa formosa — a parasitic wasp that preys on whiteflies.

Envelope — outer protective bulb or jacket of a lamp.

Environment — everything that surrounds and governs a plant's life.

Epsom salts — hydrated magnesium sulfate in the form of white crystalline salt: **Epsom salts** add magnesium to soil.

Equinox — the point at which the sun crosses the equator and day and night are each 12 hours long: The **equinox** happens twice a year.

Evaporate — convert liquid into vapor: Much water **evaporates** into the atmosphere of a grow room.

Exhaust fan — a fan that PULLS air OUT of the grow room: An **exhaust fan** is very efficient.

Extension cord — extra electrical cord that must be 14-gauge or larger (i.e. 12- or 10-gauge).

Fan, oscillating — a fan that swings back and forth in an arc.

Feed — fertilize.

Female — pistilate, ovule, seed-producing.

Fertilize — 1. apply fertilizer (nutrients) to roots and foliage 2. impregnate (unite) female ovule with male pollen.

Fertilizer burn — over-fertilization: First leaf tips burn (turn brown) then leaves curl.

Fish emulsion — fish particles suspended in a liquid: **Fish emulsion** is high in organic nitrogen.

Fish fertilizer — organic fertilizer made from fish, high in N: **Fish fertilizer** stinks like year-old fish.

Fixture — electrical fitting used to hold electric components.

Flat — shallow (three-inch) deep container, often 18 by 24 inches with good drainage, used to start seedlings or clones.

Flat white — very reflective, whitest white paint available.

Fluorescent lamp — electric lamp using a tube coated with fluorescent material, which has low lumen and heat output: A **fluorescent lamp** is excellent for rooting cuttings.

Foliage — the leaves, or more generally, the green part of a plant

Foliar feeding — misting fertilizer solution which is absorbed by the foliage.

Food — 1. nutrients: Fertilizer is plant food. 2. Carbohydrates, sugar and starches are **foods** produced by plants.

Foot-candle — f.c. One f.c. is equal to the amount of light that falls on one square foot of surface located one foot away from one candle.

Fresh soil — potting soil that has not been *used*.

Fritted — fused or embedded in glass. **Fritted** trace elements (FTE) are long-lasting and do not leach out easily.

Fungicide — a product that destroys or inhibits fungus.

Fungistat — a product that inhibits fungus keeping it in check.

Fungus — a *lower* plant lacking chlorophyll which may attack green plants: Mold, rust, mildew, mushrooms and bacteria are **fungi**.

Fuse — electrical safety device consisting of a metal that MELTS and interrupts the circuit when circuit is overloaded.

Fuse box — box containing fuses that control electric circuits.

GPM — Gallons per minute

General purpose fertilizer — See: ALL-PURPOSE FERTILIZER.

Gene — part of a chromosome that influences the development and potency of a plant: **Genes** are inherited through sexual propagation.

Genetic make — up — the genes inherited from parent plants: **Genetic make — up** is the most important factor dictating vigor and potency.

Gravel — soilless medium used in many *active recovery* hydroponic systems.

Green lacewing — an insect that preys on mealy bugs.

Guano — dung from birds, high in organic nutrients: Sea bird **guano** is noted for being high in nitrogen (N).

Halide — binary compound of a halogen(s) with an electropositive element(s).

Halogen — any of the elements fluorine, chlorine, bromine, iodine and astatine existing in a free state: **Halogens** are in the arc tube of a halide lamp.

Hermaphrodite — one plant having both male and female flowers: The breeding of **hermaphrodites** is hard to control.

Hertz (Hz) — a unit of a frequency that cycles one time each second: A home with a 60 **hertz** AC current cycles 60 times per second.

HID — High Intensity Discharge.

Honeydew — a sticky, honey-like substance secreted onto foliage by aphids, scale and mealy bugs.

Hood — reflective cover of a HID lamp: A large, white **HOOD is very reflective.**

HOR — The abbreviation stamped on some HID bulbs meaning they may be burned in a **horizontal** position.

Horizontal — parallel to the horizon, ground or floor.

Hormone — chemical substance that controls the growth and development of a plant. Root-inducing **hormones** help clones root.

Horticulture — the science and art of growing plants.

Hose bib — water outlet containing an on/off valve.

Hostile environment — environment that is unfriendly and inhospitable to disease and conducive to plant growth.

Hot — temperature over 90° F.

Humidity (relative) — ratio between the amount of moisture in the air and the greatest amount of moisture the air could hold at the same temperature.

Humus — dark, fertile, partially decomposed plant or animal matter: **Humus** forms the organic portion of the soil.

Hybrid — an offspring from two plants of different breeds, variety or genetic make-up.

Hydrated lime — instantly soluble lime, used to raise or lower pH.

Hydrogen — light, colorless, odorless gas: **Hydrogen** combines with OXYGEN to form water.

Hydroponics — method of growing plants in nutrient solutions without soil.

Hygrometer — instrument for measuring relative humidity in the atmosphere: A **hygrometer** will save time, frustration and money.

I-line — metal halide HID lamp manufactured by Sylvania: Made for use in some mercury vapor ballasts.

Inbred — (true breed) offspring of plants of the same breed or ancestry.

Incandescent lamp — electric lamp having a filament that gives off light and heat: An **Incandescent** is best used as a heat source.

Induce — effect, cause or influence via stimulation: Flowering is **induced** via a 12-hour photoperiod.

Inert — chemically non-reactive: **Inert** growing mediums make it easy to control the chemistry of the nutrient solution.

Infestation — condition resulting from many bugs or fungus attacking plants.

Inhibit — restrain, stunt or hold back from free and spontaneous growth.

Insect — small invertebrate animal: Aphids, mealy bugs and spider mites are **insects**.

Insecticide — a product that kills or inhibits insects.

Intensity — the magnitude of light energy per unit: **Intensity** diminishes the farther away from the source.

Iron — one of the trace elements essential to plant life.

Jacket — protective outer bulb or envelope of lamp.

Jiffy 7 pellet — compressed peat moss wrapped in an expandable plastic casing: When moistened, a **Jiffy 7 pellet** expands into a small pot that is used to start seeds or clones.

Kelthane — the best commercial chemical miticide on the market: **Kelthane** kills mites dead!

Kill — to put a plant to death via negligence or harvest

Kilowatt-hour — measure of electricity used per hour: A 1000-watt HID uses one kilowatt per hour.

Lacewing — insect that preys on

Ladybug — orange spotted beetle that preys on aphids and other insects (not MITES): **Ladybugs** are attracted to bright light . . . BUZZZZZZZ . . . POP!

Lamp — a device that produces light (and heat).

Leach — dissolve or wash out soluble components of soil by heavy watering.

Leaf — thin, broad outgrowth from stem that manufactures food.

Leaf curl — leaf malformation due to over-watering, over fertilization, lack of Mg, insect or fungus damage or negative tropism.

Leaflet — small immature leaf.

Leggy — abnormally tall, with sparse foliage: **Legginess** of a plant is usually caused by lack of light.

Life cycle — a series of growth stages through which plant must pass in its natural lifetime: The stages for an annual plant are seed, seedling, vegetative and floral.

Light balancer — a device that moves a lamp back and forth across the ceiling of a grow room to provide more *balanced* light.

Lime — used in the form of DOLOMITE or HYDRATED LIME to raise and/or stabilize soil pH.

Limp leaves — Leaves that are lacking in vitality, strength and firmness: Lack of ventilation or poor growing conditions usually cause **limp leaves**.

Litmus paper — chemically sensitive paper used for testing pH.

Loam — organic soil mixture of crumbly clay, silt and sand.

Lucalox — High-Pressure Sodium lamp produced by General Electric.

Lumalux — High-Pressure Sodium lamp produced by Sylvania.

Lumen — measurement of light output: One **lumen** is equal to the amount of light emitted by one candle that falls on one square foot of surface located one foot away from one candle.

Macro-nutrient — one or all of the *primary nutrients* N-P-k or the *secondary nutrients* Mg and Ca.

Malathion — commercial insecticide, kills about all insects, except for spider mites.

Male — staminate, pollen-producing.

Manual removal (of insects) — is with a quick squish of the fingers or set of sponges (more civilized).

Manure — cow dung, rabbit dung, chicken dung, etc. used as an organic fertilizer and soil amendment: **Manure** must be thoroughly composted and free of acid salts to be a good fertilizer.

Mealy bug — a small, round, whitish, shell-like insect that lives in colonies, infesting gardens.

Mean — average throughout life: HID's are rated in **mean** lumens.

Mercury vapor lamp — outdated and oldest member of the HID family.

Meristem — tip of plant growth, branch tip.

Micro-nutrients — also referred to as TRACE ELEMENTS, including S, Fe, Mn, B, Mb, An and Cu.

Millimeter — thousandth of a meter; approximately .04 inch.

Milorganite — processed sewage sludge: **Milorganite** not acceptable for indoor vegetable cultivation, yuck!

Miracle — Gro — commercial soluble fertilizer.

Mite, spider — the indoor horticulturists most hated enemy! A microscopic spider (in a broader sense INSECT) that may be white, red, or two-spotted. **Mites** live on leaf undersides and suck the tender leaves dry of life-giving fluids.

Moisture meter — a fantastic electronic device that measures the exact moisture content of soil at any given point.

Monochromatic — producing only one color: LP sodium lamps are **monochromatic**.

Mother Nature — the vast outdoors and all she holds: The indoor horticulturist assumes the role of **Mother Nature**.

Mother plant — a plant that is used for cutting (cloning) stock: A **mother plant** may be grown from seed or be a clone.

Mulch — a protective covering of organic compost, old leaves, etc.: Indoors, **mulch** keeps soil too moist, and possible fungus could result.

Nanometer — .000001 meter, nm is used as a scale to measure electromagnetic wave lengths of light: Color and light spectrums are expressed in **namometers (nm)**.

Necrosis — localized death of a plant part.

Neck — tubular glass end of the HID bulb, attached to the threads.

Nitrogen (N) — element essential to plant growth. One of the three major nutrients.

Non — recovery — describes a hydroponic system that does not recover nutrient solution once applied.

Nursery — gardening store that sells many of the things indoor horticulturists need: A **nursery** is a great place to gather information.

Nurseryperson — person who, if knowledgeable, can be a wealth of information: Every indoor horticulturist should have a **nursery-person** *buddy*.

Nutrient — plant food, essential elements N-P-K, secondary and trace elements fundamental to plant life.

Ohm's Power Law — a law that expresses the strength of an electric current: Volts times Amperes equals watts.

Oil spray — petroleum **oil spray** mixed (one drop per pint) with KELTHANE to kill mites, larvae and eggs by suffocation.

Organic — made of, derived from or related to living organisms.

Outbred — see hybrid.

Overload — load to excess: A 20-amp circuit drawing 17 amps is **overloaded**.

Ovule — a plant's egg; found within the calyx, it contains all the female genes: When fertilized, an **ovule** will grow into a seed.

Oxygen — tasteless, colorless element, necessary in soil to sustain plant life.

Parasite — organism that lives on or in another *host* organism: Fungus is a **parasite**.

Passive — describes a hydroponic system that moves the nutrient solution **passively** through absorption or capillary action.

Peat — partially decomposed vegetation (usually moss) with slow decay due to extreme moisture and cold.

Perennial — a plant, such as a tree or shrub, that completes its life cycle over several years.

Perlite — 1. sand or volcanic glass, expanded by heat, holds water and nutrients on its many irregular surfaces. 2. mineral soil amendment.

Peters fertilizer — high-quality soluble fertilizer used by many professional nurseries and horticulturists: Available in many N — P — K, secondary and trace element formulas.

pH — a scale from 1 to 14 that measures the acid-to-alkaline balance a growing medium (or anything): In general plants grow best in a range of 6 to 6.8 pH.

pH tester — electronic instrument or chemical used to find where soil or water is on the pH scale.

Phosphor coating — internal bulb coating that diffuses light and is responsible for various color outputs.

Phosphorus (P) — one of the three macro-nutrients that promote root and flower growth.

Photoperiod — the relationship between the length of light and dark in a 24-hour period.

Photosynthesis — the building of chemical compounds (carbohydrates) from light energy, water and CO_2.

Phototropism — the specific movement of a plant part toward a light source.

Pigment — The substance in paint or anything that absorbs light, producing (reflecting) the same color as the **pigment**.

Pistils — small pair of fuzzy white hairs extending from top of calyx: **Pistils** catch pollen and channel it into contact with the ovule for fertilization.

Plug (IN) — establish an electrical circuit by inserting **plug**: There are two types of 110 volt **plugs**, two-prong and GROUNDED three-prong. Safety requires use of the three-prong **plug**.

Pollen — fine, yellow, dust-like microspores containing male genes.

Pod seed — a dry calyx containing a mature or maturing seed.

Potassium (K) — one of the three macro-nutrients necessary for plant life.

Pot-bound — bound, stifled or inhibited from normal growth, by the confines of a container: Root system become pot-bound.

Potting soil — sterile soil, usually purchased in bags. Most **potting soils** have the proper texture, pH and nutrient content for indoor horticulture.

Power surge — interruption or change in flow of electricity.

Predator — beneficial bug or parasite that hunts down and devours harmful insects.

Prevent — keep bugs and fungus from attacking garden by creating a hostile environment.

Primary nutrients — N-P-K.

Propagate — 1. Sexual - produce a seed by breeding a male and a female plant 2. Asexual - to produce a plant by cloning.

Prune — alter the shape and growth pattern of a plant by cutting stems and shoots.

Pumice — lightweight volcanic rock, full of air and water-holding cavities: **Pumice** is a mineral soil amendment.

PVC pipe — plastic (polyvinyl chloride) pipe that is easy to work with, readily available and used to pipe water into a grow room or make a watering wand.

Pyrethrum — natural insecticide made from the blossoms of various chrysanthemums: Raids' **Pyrethrum** is the most effective natural spider mite exterminator.

Ra-Pid-Gro — commercial soluble fertilizer, available in MULTI-USE 23-19-17 formula.

Razor blade — used to make fine, precision cut, when taking cuttings.

Recovery — a **recovery** hydroponic system **recovers** the nutrient solution and recycles it.

Reflect — throw back light. Flat white **reflects** the optimum amount of light, about 30 percent.

Rejuvenate — Restore youth: A mature plant, having completed its life cycle (flowering), may be stimulated by a new 18 hour photoperiod, to **rejuvenate** or produce *new* vegetative growth.

Rinse — wash thoroughly with tepid water; mist.

Rockwool — fibrous growing medium manufactured from molten rock known for its ability to retain water and air.

Root — 1. the tender light- and air-sensitive underground part of a plant: **Roots** function to absorb water and nutrients as well as anchor a plant in the ground. 2. to **root** a cutting or clone.

Root-bound — see POT BOUND.

Root hormone — root-inducing substance.

Rootone F — powder, root-inducing hormone with fungicide.

Safer's Insecticidal Soap — Insecticidal soap: Controls just about all bad bugs including the hated and feared SPIDER MITE.

Salt — crystalline compound that results from improper pH or toxic buildup of fertilizer. **Salt** will burn plants, preventing them from absorbing nutrients.

Sand — heavy soil amendment: Coarse **sand** is excellent for rooting cuttings.

Scale — 1. tiny, round, shell — like insects that affix themselves to plants, live in colonies and infest crops. 2. instrument of measurement.

Secondary nutrients — calcium (Ca) and magnesium (Mg).

Seed — the mature, fertilized, ovule of a pistilate plant, containing a protective shell, embryo and supply of food: A **seed** will germinate and grow, given heat and moisture.

Short circuit — condition that results when wires cross and form a circuit. A **short circuit** will blow fuses.

Soap — 1. cleaning agent 2. wetting agent 3. insecticide. All **soap** used in horticulture, should be biodegradable.

Socket — threaded, wired holder for a bulb.

Sodium Vapor (HP) — High-Pressure (HP) **Sodium Vapor** lamp.

Soilless mix — a growing medium, made up of mineral particles such as vermiculite, perlite, sand, pumice etc. NOTE: Organic moss is often a component of **soilless mix**.

Soluble — able to be dissolved in water.

Sphagnum moss — moss grown in Canada, used for soil amendment: **Sphagnum moss** is normally decomposed into moss peat.

Spore — seed — like offspring of a fungus.

Spray — to mist plants with water or solutions.

Sprout — 1. a recently germinated seed 2. small new growth of leaf or stem.

Sponge rock — light, mineral soil amendment.

Square feet (sq. ft.) — length (in feet) times width equals **square feet**.

Staminate — male, pollen-producing.

Starch — complex carbohydrate: **Starch** is manufactured and stored food.

Stem — the main supporting trunk of the plant: The terminal bud is attached to the tip of the **stem**.

Sterilize — make sterile (super-clean) by removing dirt, germs and bacteria.

Stroboscopic effect — a quick pulsating or flashing of a lamp.

Stress — a physical or chemical factor that causes extra exertion by plants: A **stressed** plant will not grow as well as a non — stressed plant.

Stunt — dwarf; slow or inhibit growth: A **stunted** plant will take a long time (if ever) to resume normal growth.

Stomata — small mouth-like or nose-like openings (pores) on leaf underside, responsible for transpiration and many other life functions: The millions of **stomata**, must be kept very clean to function properly.

Sudburry Soil Test Kit — commercial pH, N-P-K soil test kit: Test by mixing soil sample with chemical.

Sulfur — one of the trace elements essential to plant life.

Sugar — food product of a plant.

Super-bloom — a common name for fertilizer high in phosphorus (P) that promotes flower formation and growth

Swingle — Metalarc **Swingle** by Sylvania is designed to work in SOME mercury vapor ballasts. A **Swingle** lamp produces substantially fewer lumens than the standard metal halide.

Synthesis — production of a substance, such as chlorophyll, by uniting light energy and elements or chemical compounds.

Sump — reservoir or receptacle that serves as a drain or holder for hydroponic nutrient solutions.

Tap root — the main or primary root that grows from the seed: Lateral roots will branch off the **tap root**.

Teflon tape — tape that is extremely useful to help seal all kinds of pipe joints. I like **Teflon tape** better than putty.

Tepid — warm 70 to 80° F. Always use **tepid water** around plants to facilitate chemical processes and ease shock.

Terminal bud — bud at the growing end of the main stem.

Thermostat — a device for regulating temperature: A **thermostat** may control a heater, furnace or vent fan.

Thin — cull or weed out weak, slow growing seedlings.

Thrips — a small sucking insect detrimental to flowers and vegetables

Timer — an electrical device for regulating photoperiod, fan etc.: A **timer is a must for all grow rooms.**

Toxic life — the amount of time a pesticide or fungicide remains *active* or *live*.

Transformer — a devise in the ballast that transforms electric current from one voltage to another.

Transpire — give off water vapor and by products via the stomata.

Trauma — injury suffered during cloning, transplanting or abuse.

Trellis — frame of small boards (lattice) that trains or supports plants.

True breed — see INBRED.

Tungsten — a heavy, hard metal with a high melting point which conducts electricity well: **Tungsten** is used for a filament in **tungsten** halogen lamps.

Ultraviolet — light with very short wave lengths, out of the visible spectrum.

Unalux — High-Pressure Sodium lamp manufactured by Sylvania for use in SOME mercury vapor ballasts.

Up-Start — Ortho product that contains 3-10-3, Vitamin B_1, and root-inducing hormones **Up-Start** is excellent for use with seedlings, clones and transplants to ease *shock*.

Variety — strain, phenotype (see strain).

Vegetative — growth stage in which annual plants rapidly produce new growth and green chlorophyll.

Vent — opening such as a window or door that allows the circulation of fresh air.

Ventilation — circulation of fresh air, fundamental to healthy indoor garden. An exhaust fan creates excellent **ventilation**.

Vermiculite — mica processed and expanded by heat. **Vermiculite** is a good soil amendment and medium for rooting cuttings.

Vertical — up and down; perpendicular to the horizontal.

Vitamin B_1 — **Vitamin** that is absorbed by tender root hairs, easing transplant wilt and shock.

Wetting agent — compound that reduces the droplet size and lowers the surface tension of the water, making it wetter. Liquid concentrate dish soap is a good **wetting agent** if it is biodegradable.

White fly — a small, white, moth-like plant muncher.

Wick — part of a *passive* hydroponic system using a **wick** suspended in the nutrient solution, the nutrients pass up the **wick** and are absorbed by the medium and roots.

Wire ties — Paper-coated **wire ties** are excellent for tying down or training plants.

Yield — the product or harvest of a garden.

Zap — the sound a bug makes when it flies into a hot HID bulb.

Zinc — an essential trace element.

INDEX

DIRECTORY OF INDOOR GARDEN SUPPLIERS

A-1 Hamilton Technology Corp.
14902 S. Figureoa St.
Gardena, CA 90248
(800) 458-7474 Nationwide
(800) 635-3344 California
Expanded Business
Manufacturers of complete indoor growing equipment (M.H. lights, H.P. sodiums, light movings systems, CO2, hydroponics and accessories.
Free Catalog

Alternative
599 Williams St.
Thornton, Il 60476
(800) 423-0876 Nationwide
(312) 877-1616 in Illinois
Two years in business
Preditor mites, ROCKWOOL, Applied Hydroponics authorized dealer
Free Catalog

Applied Hydroponics
3135 Kerner Blvd.
San Rafael, CA 94901
(800) 634-9999 Nationwide
(415) 459-7898 in California
10 years in business
Manufacturer of Hydrofarm,TM hydroponics, Hydrolite,TM metal halides, HP & LP sodiums, Vita-Lite, Power-Twists, Geolite,TM growing medium, CO2 regulators & timers
Free Catalog

Applied Hydroponics
4527 San Fernando
Glendale, CA 91204
(818) 243-0068
1 year in business
Manufacturer of Hydrofarm,TM hydroponics, Hydrolite,TM metal halides, HP & LP sodiums, Vita-Lite, Power-Twists, Geolite,TM growing medium, CO2 regulators & timers
Free Catalog

Aqua Culture Inc.
P.O. Box 26467
Tempe, AZ 85282
(800) 633-2137 Nationwide
(602) 966-6429 In Arizona
5 years in business
Manufacturers of the Solar ShuttleTM light balancer, automated hydroponics system AquaGrow TM hydroponic plant food and CO2 systems.
Free Catalog

Canadian Hydroponics Ltd.
8318 120th St.
Surrey, B.C. CANADA V3W 3N4
(604) 591-8820
5 years in business
Largest selection and best prices in Canada, featuring "Powerplant" modular garden systems.
Catalog $2.00

DANSCO Valley Halide
14109 E. Sprague #5
Spokane, WA 99216
(800) 527-7012 Ext. 294 Nationwide
(509) 924-8333 in Washington
3 years in business
HID lighting, hydroponics, CO2 equipment, nutrients and much much more.
Catalog

Diamond Lights
713 Mission Avenue
San Rafael, CA 94901
(800) 331-3994 Nationwide
(415) 459-3994 in California
7 years in business
Manufacturers of halides, HP sodiums, CO2 systems and the AquafarmTM modular hydro system. Products with features you won't find anywhere
Free Catalog

East Coast Hydroponics Inc.
432 Castleton Ave.
Staten Island, NY 10301
(800) 255-0121 U.S.A.
(718) 727-9300 New York
Store and mail order - Distributors
of ROCKWOOL, Bat and Seabird guano. Most
complete East Coast supplier.
Free Catalog

Eco Enterprises
2821 N.E. 55th
Seattle, WA 98105
(800)-426-6937 Nationwide
(206) 523-9300 in Washington
15 years in business
Eco Grow hydroponic plant nutrients,
metal halides, hydroponic supplies,
CO2 systems, ROCKWOOL, and hormones
Free Catalog

Energy Savers Unlimited
22138 Vermont Ave. #C
Torrance, CA 90502
(800) 421-2994 Nationwide
(800) 538-3400 in California
8 years in business
Metal halide and HP sodium grow
lamps and hydroponic systems
Catalog

Full Circle Garden Supply
P.O. Box 6-HC
Redway, CA 95560
(707) 923-3988
16 Years in Business
Hard to find items - indoors and
outdoors.
Free Brochure

Full Moon
217 S.W. 2nd
Corvallis, OR 97339
(503)-757-2532
6 years in business
Everything for the indoor
horticulturist and homesteader, 6
grow rooms in operation, call today!
FREE Catalog

Geotechnology
303 Arden Ave.
(800) 346-2321 Nationwide
(408) 336-2321 California
Ben Lomond, (by Sta.Cruz)CA95005
12 years in business
HID lamps with horizontal reflectors,
low noise ballast boxes.
Catalog

Green Air Products
P.O. Box 1318
Gresham, OR 97030
(503) 663-2000
4 years in business
Manufacturer of CO2 equipment,
specializing in atmospheric
enrichment & controls, Propagation & water
control systems.
Free Catalog - Dealer Inquirys

Halide of Oregon
9220 S.E. Stark St.
Portland, OR 97216
(503) 256-2400
5 years in business
Customer service, halide and HP
sodium lighting, hydroponics, full
line of indoor growing supplies.

High Tech Hobbies
Light Manufacturing Co.
1634 SE Brooklyn
Portland, OR 97217
(503) 231-1582
3 years in business
Living System integrated hydroponic
components, HID's, light balancers,
CO2 systems, nutrients and
experienced professional consultation
Free Catalog

High-Tech Indoor Garden Supply
2164 Washington Rd.
Washington, IL 61571
(309) 745-5813
1 year in business
Applied Hydroponics Authorized dealer garden supplies, hydroponics, metal halides, HP sodiums, CO2 emitters and growing mediums.

Home Hydroponics Ltd.
Unit "D" 2960 Olafson Ave.
Richmond, B.C., CANADA V6K 2R3
(604) 270-6788
5 years in business
Gardens, halides, HP sodium lamps, nutrients, pumps, timers, CO2 enrichment and years of growing system experience.

Homegrown Inc.
12605 Pacific Avenue
Tacoma, WA 98444
(800) 237-6672 Nationwide
(206) 531-9641 California
7 years in business
Complete line of super halide and HP sodium lights, CO2 equipment, and state of the art hydroponics.
Catalog

Hydro-Tech
10929 N.E. Sandy Blvd.
Portland, OR 97220
(503) 254-7466
2 years in business
Plant lights, CO2 hydroponics, ROCKWOOL, organic soil, timers, fans pumps, and advice.
Catalog $1.00

Hydro-Tech
3929 Aurora Ave. N.
Seattle, WA 98103
(206) 632-8538
6 years in business
Plant lights, CO2 hydroponics, ROCKWOOL, organic soil, timers, fans pumps, and advice.
Catalog $1.00

The Indoor Gardener
1311 S. Pacific Hwy.
P.O. Box 210
Talent, OR 97540
(800) 344-9344 Nationwide
(503) 535-5313 Oregon
7 years in business
Halide lighting systems, hydroponic equipment, greenhouses, Hortiwool, CO2 systems, oorganic fertilizers.
Free Catalog

The Indoor Gardening Center
8539 Lilley Rd.
Canton, MI 48187
(313) 451-0797
New Location!
Specializing in High Intensity Lighting systems, hydroponics and nutrients also helpful garden tips

The Indoor Gardening Center - Madison Heights
26105 John Road
Madison Heights, MI 48071
(313) 451-0797
New Location!
Specializing in High Intensity Lighting systems, hydroponics and nutrients also helpful gardening tips.

Indoor Sun Systems
61 Allwood Ave.
Central Islip, NY 11722
(516) 234-2260
1 year in business
East Coast distributor for halides, HP sodiums, mylar & ROCKWOOL.
Catalog

I.G. Supply - Indoor Sun Shoppe
911 N.E. 45th
Seattle, WA 98105
(800) 426-6941 Nationwide
(206) 634-3727 in Washington
17 years in business
Everything you need! Fast service -
good advice - experience.
Free catalog

Jorge Cervantes' Indoor Garden Store
P.O. Box #02009
Portland, OR 97202
(800) 233-5729 Nationwide
(503) 771-6804 in Oregon
2 years in business
Hydrolite,TM halides, HP sodiums
(horizontal & vertical), Vita-Lite,
Geolite,TM growing medium, CO2
regulators, timers, & ROCKWOOL.
Free Catalog

Northwest Indoor Garden Store
9915 S.E. Foster Road
Portland, OR 97266
(800) 233-5729 Nationwide
(503) 771-6804 in Oregon
2 years in business
Hydrolite,TM halides, HP sodiums
(horizontal & vertical), Vita-Lite,
Geolite,TM growing medium, CO2
regulators, timers, ROCKWOOL & soil.
Free Catalog

M.A.H. Nursery
151 Alkier St.
Brentwood, NY 11717
(516) 231-9472
Established 1983
East Coast supplier of halides,
hydroponics and other growing aids.
Full service store. Hours: 12 noon to
8 pm EST
Free Catalog

Nature's Control
P.O. Box 35
Medford, OR 97501
(503) 773-5927
6 years in business
Pest controls Mother Nature would use -
Predator Mites, Ladybugs, White Fly parasite:
etc. Fast service - COD's
Free Brochure

Northern Lights & Hydroponics
4 Mahoning Ave.
New Castle, PA 16102
(412) 654-8383
Hydroponic systems, HID lighting and more.
Grow right with halide lights.

Paradise Hydroponics
306 W. Harris St.
Eureka, CA 95501
(800) 332-GROW Nationwide
(707) 445-5720 California
1 year in business
Complete indoor supplier,
manufacturer of the Black Maxx
hydroponic systems, High quality
lights, CO2 systems, nutrients and
all accessories.
Free Catalog

Plantastic Plant Products
1442A Walnut St.
Berkeley, CA 94709
(800) 227-1617 Ext. 453 Nationwide
(800) 772-3445 Ext. 453 California
5 years in business
Field-tested specialty plant hormones
designed to produce more females.
Free Catalog

Simeon's Organic Plant Food
2528 Albee St.
Eureka, CA 95501
(707) 443-4929
10 years in business
Guano "tea: Mixes. Mail order sea
bird and bat guano.
Free Catalog

Sun Circle Inc.
824 "L" Street #3
Arcata, CA 95521
(707) 822-5777
4 years in business
Manufacturers of Highly efficient industrial quality 360 degree HID lamp rotator - The Sun Circle. One two and three lamp rotators available.
Free Catalog

Superior Growers Supply, Inc.
4870 Dawn Ave.
East Lansing, MI 48823
(800) 227-0027 Nationwide
(517) 332-2663 in Michigan
4 years in business
Horticultural lamps, hydroponic systems, "the Gasser" CO_2 system. New store opening in Chicago - June 1987
Free Catalog

Worm's Way Organic
Indoor/Outdoor Garden Supply
4620 S. State Road 446
Bloomington, IN 47401
(812) 837-9901
2 years in business
Metal halide and HP sodium systems, hydroponics, CO_2 kits and more. The Midwests' most complete line of gardening supplies.
Free Catalog

HYDROPONIC SOCIETY
OF AMERICA

P.O. BOX 6067
CONCORD, CALIFORNIA 94524

Hobby

Science

Agriculture

Join the Hydroponic Society of America today!

With your membership in The Hydroponic Society of America you will receive our bi-monthly newsletter packed full of state-of-the-art information on the newest and best hydroponic systems available. And numerous articles and book lists about your favorite subject by the leading researchers in the hydroponic field. Plus a directory of hydroponic suppliers and numerous advertisements for the newest high tech equipment.

As a member of the Society, you will also receive 10% discount on all of the books in our bookstore and a FREE copy of the Proceedings to the Annual Hydroponic Conference (this 120-page book is easily worth the price of the membership).

Free and nominally priced tours are scheduled several times a year, check your Hydroponic Society of America newsletter for details.

Membership Information

Annual Membership (U.S., Canada & Mexico) $25 U.S.
Annual Membership (All other countries) $35 U.S.

Name_____   Send to:
Address_____   Hydroponic Society of
City_____State_____Zip_____   America
Tel._____   P.O. Box 6067-G
                                         Concord, CA 94524
                                         (415) 682-4193